P9-DFS-805

Southern Living

BIG BOOK OF

Flower gardening

Oxmoor House®

©2003 by Oxmoor House, Inc.
Book Division of Southern Progress Corporation
P.O. Box 2463, Birmingham, Alabama 35201

Southern Living® is a federally registered trademark of Southern Living, Inc.

All rights reserved. No part of this book may be reproduced in any form or by any means without the prior written permission of the publisher, excepting brief quotations in connection with reviews written specifically for inclusion in magazines or newspapers.

Hardcover ISBN: 0-8487-2789-4
Softcover ISBN: 0-8487-2721-5
Printed in the United States of America
Second Printing 2003

SOUTHERN LIVING®

Editor: John Alex Floyd, Jr.
Executive Editor, Homes and Gardens: Derick Belden
Garden Editor: Gene B. Bussell
Senior Writer: Stephen P. Bender
Associate Garden Editors: Ellen Ruoff Riley, Charles Thigpen
Associate Garden Design Editor: Glenn R. DiNella
Assistant Garden Design Editor: Troy H. Black
Senior Photographers: Jean M. Allsopp, Van Chaplin, Allen Rokach
Photographers: Tina Cornett, William Dickey, Laurey W. Glenn, Meg McKinney Simle
Production Manager: Katie Terrell Morrow
Editorial Assistant: Lynne Long
Production Coordinator: Jamie Barnhart

OXMOOR HOUSE, INC.

Editor-in-Chief: Nancy Fitzpatrick Wyatt
Executive Editor: Susan Carlisle Payne
Art Director: Cynthia R. Cooper
Copy Chief: Catherine Ritter Scholl

SOUTHERN LIVING® BIG BOOK OF FLOWER GARDENING

Editor: Susan Hernandez Ray
Senior Designer: Melissa M. Clark
Contributing Copy Editor: Adrienne Short Davis
Intern: Sarah Miller
Contributing Proofreader: Mary Ann Laurens
Contributing Indexer: Katharine R. Wiencke
Director, Production and Distribution: Phillip Lee
Books Production Manager: Larry Hunter
Production Assistant: Faye Porter Bonner

To order additional publications, call 1-800-765-6400.

For more books to enrich your life, visit
oxmoorhouse.com

page 21 page 34 page 73

contents

seasonal color

smart plant choices

flower garden solutions

small garden projects

page 105   page 95   page 153

plants at a glance

southern classics

beautiful gardens

contained gardens

rooms in bloom

flower garden checklist

page 205

page 154

foreword

Flowers are one of the defining elements of gardens and homes across the American South. This book contains the essence of how to use their beauty at home. From reviewing the region's favorite flowers, to helping you create a garden with colorful flowering plants, to showing simple arrangements to adorn the inside of your home, this big book of flowers represents the heart of the garden ideas *Southern Living*® gives its readers every month. An additional bonus in the book is the flower garden checklist on page 264, a monthly to-do list for gorgeous blooms.

Because I am a gardener who loves to be outside puttering around and making my garden beautiful, I think these pages offer proven advice; excellent design technique; and good, old-fashioned helpful hints about cultivating the most colorful garden in your community, and then bringing the flowers indoors to grace your interiors. It's a book I know I will surely use and enjoy.

John Alex Floyd, Jr.
Editor, Southern Living

seasonal
color

in the Southern garden

make an impact with color

Take advantage of the many ways color can be used to enhance the beauty of a garden by following a few simple guidelines.

Think back to elementary school art classes, and memories of the color wheel come rolling back. Primary colors red, yellow, and blue cannot be mixed or created from any other colors. Secondary colors orange, green, and purple are made by blending equal amounts of their primary parents.

In theory, this is child's play. In the garden, however, there is a fine line between color monotony and chaos. "Colors are families," says Sara Goves, a landscape designer in Oxford, Georgia. "It's like the Hatfields and the McCoys. Sometimes they can fight."

To simplify and understand how color works in the landscape, the color wheel is divided into two sections—warm and cool colors. Each has its own characteristics and special place in the garden.

WARM COLORS

Red, orange, and yellow (and their variations) make up the warm colors in the spectrum. They are also close to each other on the color wheel.

- In bright sunlight warm colors illuminate the landscape. They remain vivid and true.
- Red reaches the eye quickly and will dominate other colors. Use it to draw the eye and bring objects closer.
- To make a small garden feel larger, place warm colors in the front of the space and cool colors in the back.
- A large space will appear smaller when warm colors are placed at the back of a bed.
- Paired with yellow, red becomes warmer. When partnered with blue, it becomes a cool color.
- "Keep orange in the warm color family. After all, it's a child of primary red and yellow," Sara says.
- Warm colors are effective accents. Use them in small amounts to brighten up a cool color scheme.

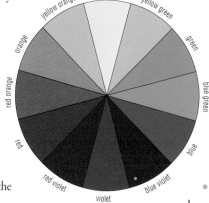

COOL COLORS

Blue, green, and purple are the cool colors. They are positioned together on the color wheel.

- Bright light washes out cool colors. Use them in shaded areas for maximum impact, or pair them with warm colors in sun.
- A space appears larger when cool colors are used.
- Blue and purple can pull opposing colors together. They work as a modifier in a color scheme.
- "Blue is serene, like my colonel husband. You use it to stabilize all those other colorful soldiers marching through the garden," Sara says.
- Yellow and white are effective in a night garden.
- Green is restful to the eye. "It's the dependable color," Sara says. "It's the one color that every other one can cozy up with, and it's the one color for all seasons," she says.
- Blue recedes and makes objects appear farther away.
- To balance a warm color planting, plant four to five times more cool colors than warm.

COMPLEMENTARY COMBINATIONS

A sure-fire way to plan a scheme that works together is using complementary or contrasting colors. On the color wheel, these are the shades that appear opposite each other. One is a warm color, the other cool. The colors make no attempt to blend, but the contrast is pleasing to the eye.

Opposite: The combination of red poppies and larkspur is a beautiful example of how contrasting colors can work together.

Above: Zinnias come in every color of the rainbow, from the hottest red to the coolest white.

Left: The cool greens, grays, and blues of artemisia, iris, forget-me-nots, and white roses bring a calming effect to the garden. Cool colors visually recede from the eye and can make a small garden appear more spacious.

Opposite: The sizzling blooms of melampodium, daylilies, and black-eyed Susans can really heat things up in the garden. Warm colors such as these command attention and visually draw the plantings closer to you.

color you can count on all year

Go with an experienced game plan and you'll have beautiful blooms in spring, summer, and fall.

Each season, gardeners learn—through trial and error—which plantings are successful and which ones should be abandoned for more suitable choices. All gardeners strive to grow a collection of flowers that offers continuous bloom, with one selection taking the place of another that has just passed its peak. You will find the exact bloom time of many plants difficult to predict until you have grown them to maturity in your garden. Once you have seen them through the year's blooming cycle, you can start rearranging plants to produce winning combinations.

Although learning exactly when flowers bloom in your garden takes experience, a few plants are so closely tied to seasonal changes that you can count on them to bloom at very specific times. For example, daffodils and tulips always bloom in early- to mid-spring, and asters and chrysanthemums are signature flowers of late summer and fall.

In the summer, annual flowers tend to have the longest bloom times and are the best plants for continuous color, whereas perennials come and go. To make the most of their long color display, tuck annuals in among your perennials. Try leaving a pocket of space in the foreground of a large clump or drift of perennials; then plant it with a small annual that blooms white or a soft pastel color. For example, you might use pansies for foreground planting in winter and replace the pansies with wax begonias or marigolds in summer.

COLOR FOR SPRING

Throughout the South, azaleas and dogwoods announce the arrival of spring. Many gardeners like to plan beds and borders so that color appears before or after the azaleas and dogwoods. Pansies and early tulips and daffodils often bloom before azaleas. For late-spring color, consider irises and the hardy annuals and biennials

SPRING

Above: Siberian and bearded irises shine in a spring border in the company of petunias, dianthus, daisies, and chives. After the irises are gone, the lilies will take center stage.

usually planted in fall, including foxgloves, hollyhocks, larkspur, poppies, snapdragons, and sweet Williams. Perennials that bloom early include blue phlox, candytuft, some daisies, and wallflowers (*Cheiranthus cheiri*).

SUMMER

Left: In the same border, a festival of lilies dances above coleus and Madagascar periwinkle in summer.
Below: In the fall, this border changes again, with warm tones of autumn reflected in chrysanthemums, goldenrod, narrow-leaf zinnias, and marigolds.

FALL

Most of the preparation for spring beds is done in the fall because plants need time to grow roots before they can put on a good flower show. And in the case of biennials, exposure to cold is necessary for future blooming. However, if you have no place to plant foxgloves, snapdragons, or sweet Williams in the fall, transplant the seedlings to 6-inch-wide plastic nursery pots, and grow them as container plants in a cold frame or cool greenhouse through the winter. In February or March, shift the plants to outdoor beds (try not to disturb their roots).

Tulip bulbs should be planted individually in 4-inch-wide nursery pots in November and left out in a cold place until February. Around the first of March, plant the bulbs in your garden. If you don't plan to keep the tulips for the next year, you can simply sink the plastic nursery pots into the ground, making it easy to pull them out after they bloom.

SLIPPING INTO SUMMER

In early May, the arrival of long warm days creates major changes in the garden. Hardy annuals finally show signs of fading, and evergreen shrubs may need pruning and shaping. This is an ideal time to deadhead spring-blooming perennials and to renovate beds. Many gardeners finish spring cleanup of foundation beds by planting a bed of low annuals or perennials such as ageratum, begonias, ferns, hostas, impatiens, or marigolds along the outside edge of foundation shrubs. If extensive tree and shrub roots make digging almost impossible, try digging out individual holes and sinking 12-inch-wide plastic nursery pots into the ground up to their rims. Then plant your annuals in these pots.

During the hot summer months, flowers and foliage in cool colors can make outdoor living areas seem cooler. Consider using pastel-colored begonias, hibiscus, impatiens, Madagascar periwinkle, and petunias in pots or flowerbeds to "cool down" your garden. Then, for an even cooler effect, mix in some ferns or the silvery foliage of dusty miller.

When planning a large bed or border, select a variety of plants so that something is always on the verge of flowering. Coneflowers, daylilies, and several other perennials have foliage that gracefully covers bare ground. However, many perennials look best with small annuals planted in front of them to cover the bare soil. This job also can be performed by low-growing perennials, such as hostas, lamb's ears, or moss verbena, or by short ornamental grasses or clumps of ground cover.

FIXING UP FOR FALL

In August, despite the heat and the appearance of your garden, the season is far from over. This is the time to compost dying plants, rejuvenate tired plants, and consider new plantings, such as mums and asters, for your fall garden. With a few simple changes, your garden can easily recover from summer and produce a new crop of flowers in fall.

Clearing spent annuals will reveal gaps in your garden along with a few surprises. Look for young seedlings of cleome, marigolds, melampodium, and zinnias that may have sprung up beneath ragged older plants. You can either nurture them into bloom where they are or carefully transplant them to a new location. You should also take stock of plants that have spent the hot summer months in pots on your terrace or deck. They may respond favorably if they are set out in freshly turned earth.

You should be able to find a few replacement plants by shopping around at local garden centers. Marigolds, for example, bloom for several months before winter nips their buds. Late summer is also the best time to set out asters and chrysanthemums. If you plant them while their buds are tightly closed, they will start blooming in a few weeks and will last for many weeks.

the perfect *color scheme*

Once you find the perfect color scheme for your landscape, stick with it. It's possible to stay focused on a particular palette from one planting to the next, even if you have to fudge a bit on specific shades. Refer to the lists here for seasonal options. All plants mentioned bloom for a month or more.

Above: Vibrant orange pansies and mums make a knockout fall combination.

ORANGE

Spring: English wallflower, nasturtium, pansy, poppy, pot marigold (*Calendula officinalis*), snapdragon, sweet pea
Summer: canna, cosmos, daylily, gerbera daisy, impatiens, lantana, marigold, Mexican sunflower, zinnia
Fall: chrysanthemum, cosmos, dahlia, marigold, pansy
Winter: nasturtium*, pansy*, pot marigold*, snapdragon*

YELLOW

Spring: daffodil, English wallflower, pansy, pot marigold (*Calendula officinalis*), snapdragon, sweet pea, viola
Summer: allamanda, black-eyed Susan, canna, common sunflower, daylily, gerbera daisy, hibiscus, lantana, marigold, melampodium, yellow shrimp plant, zinnia
Fall: chrysanthemum, cosmos, dahlia, pansy, viola
Winter: nasturtium*, pansy*, pot marigold*, snapdragon*, viola*

snapdragon

RED

Spring: pansy, poppy, snapdragon, stock, sweet pea, sweet William
Summer: caladium, canna, coleus, geranium, gerbera daisy, globe amaranth, hibiscus, impatiens, pentas, petunia, scarlet sage, verbena, wax begonia, zinnia
Fall: chrysanthemum, coleus, dahlia, petunia, pineapple sage, viola, wax begonia
Winter: pansy*, petunia*, snapdragon*

Above: Shades of pink, red, and white sweet William brighten the landscape.

PINK

Spring: English daisy, foxglove, larkspur, pansy, peony, poppy, snapdragon, stock, sweet pea, sweet William, viola

Summer: caladium, cosmos, geranium, gerbera daisy, globe amaranth, impatiens, mandevilla, pentas, petunia, purple cone-flower, spider flower *(Cleome hasslerana)*, verbena, wax begonia, zinnia

Fall: aster, chrysanthemum, cosmos, dahlia, hardy begonia, Japanese anemone, pansy, petunia, wax begonia

Winter: Lenten rose**, ornamental cabbage and kale+, pansy*, petunia*, snapdragon*, viola*

PURPLE, BLUE, AND LAVENDER

Spring: blue phlox, forget-me-not, larkspur, money plant, pansy, stock, sweet pea, sweet rocket *(Hesperis matronalis)*

Summer: ageratum, bachelor's-button, balloon flower, browallia, cape plumbago, impatiens, lily-of-the-Nile *(Agapanthus africanus)*, petunia, verbena, Victoria Blue salvia, wishbone flower *(Torenia fournieri)*

Fall: aster, dahlia, hardy ageratum, Mexican sage, chrysanthemum, pansy, petunia, viola

Winter: pansy*, petunia*, snapdragon*, viola*, 'Bowles Mauve' wallflower

Above: White pansies are a great addition to the winter garden.

WHITE

Spring: English daisy, larkspur, money plant, pansy, snapdragon, stock, sweet pea, sweet rocket *(Hesperis matronalis)*

Summer: caladium, geranium, gerbera daisy, impatiens, lantana, moonflower, morning glory, petunia, phlox, salvia, spider flower *(Cleome hasslerana)*, verbena, wax begonia, zinnia

Fall: cosmos, dahlia, ginger lily, Japanese anemone, pansy, petunia, wax begonia, viola

Winter: Lenten rose**, ornamental cabbage and kale+, petunia*

Salvia

* Blooms in winter only in the Coastal and Tropical South
** Blooms in winter in the Middle and Lower South
+ Blooms in winter in the Lower, Coastal, and Tropical South

the most treasured flower color

Perhaps the most versatile color in Southern gardens, blue seems the most elusive and difficult to use. Planted alone it disappears, but without it, the garden lacks sparkle. Two gardeners share their secrets for planting blue flowers in combination with other hues.

"Blue blends with anything else. You can put it with orange, you can put it with fiery red, and it's a good blend," says garden designer and retired horticulture professor Fred Thode of Clemson, South Carolina. "But if it gets a little bit dark, the color won't carry. Royal blue is rich looking, but it is ineffective. You have to go lighter and lighter until it gets to the point where you can see it. And you've got to get up near sky blue to do that."

Sunny yellow daffodils are pretty, but plant them with the light-colored blossoms of blue phlox, and the combination has far more impact than either color used alone. Blue is like that. It adds zip to any plant around it.

On the other hand, a solid bed of blue flowers needs other colors to perk it up. Texas gardeners see vivid demonstrations of this each spring on the roadsides. A pure stand of Texas bluebonnets is beautiful, but it comes to life when a few orange blooms of Indian paintbrush pop up here and there.

Early spring when the blue phlox blooms in frothy bouquets is a good time

to see what blue can do for the garden. Likewise, Spanish bluebells, Greek anemones, grape hyacinths, netted iris, and dwarf crested iris are all bulbs that offer blue in spring.

In the shaded garden, one of the most luscious colors of the season comes from the flowers of Virginia bluebells. Buds swell pink, but when they open they turn a clear, penetrating blue. The harmony of the two hues in the cluster is captivating. Lungwort, also known as pulmonaria, has a similar effect.

Among bedding plants, pansies and violas are outstanding sources of blue. When planting a color blend, be sure to include a few blue blossoms. Good choices include

---

Opposite: The aptly named baby-blue-eyes seems only a background for the daffodils. However, the sky blue makes the other colors more exciting. **Above:** The combination of blue phlox with a deeper shade pansy is a winner. The pansies give the border depth; the light blue phlox keeps the darker color from disappearing.

'Sorbet Blue Heaven' viola and 'Universal True Blue' pansy.

As spring progresses you'll enjoy the blue flowers of larkspur, wild blue flax, ajuga, Siberian and bearded iris, veronica, baptisia, and stokesia. Summer blues are fewer, but mealy-cup sage and Russian sage are two of the best for spikes. Blue daze evolvulus is excellent for a mat of dazzling color.

Fortunately, the sources of blue through the season are numerous. Some suggestions are listed on the opposite page. Remember, it is not enough to have blue; the key is to use it effectively. For this Fred offers his testimonial: "I've always used blue, but not so much for the sake of blue, but for what it can do for other things."

A GARDEN OF NATIVE BLUES

Blue phlox tumbles down the hillside at Weesie Smith's former home like a mountain stream each spring. She first discovered and purchased this plant at the farmer's market in Montgomery, Alabama, in the 1950s.

Weesie knew little about plants when she got that first blue flower, but now she is an accomplished gardener and self-trained native plant expert. She rescued many wildflowers from construction sites and relocated them to her wooded Mountain Brook, Alabama, home. She also has ordered plants through numerous catalogs and scrounged around countless nurseries searching for unusual garden treats. She looks after her plants like a trained schoolteacher, grading each one to see if it will pass or fail.

The thousands of plants that grace Weesie's garden are special, but none has prospered like the blue phlox. In spring, flowers carpet almost her entire 3 acres. Many of the numerous native azaleas that Weesie planted bloom at the same time as the phlox. The long, graceful branches of the native azaleas seem to rise from puffy blue clouds. Early spring is always filled with yellow daffodils and forsythia, so it sure is nice to see blue in the garden. It's an impressive show.

Several flowers cluster atop each phlox stem in March and April. Together they form loose balls of fragrant blooms. The show can last three to four weeks provided the temperatures stay cool and there is sufficient rainfall. They grow in clumps about 12 to 18 inches in height.

Weesie sometimes calls the phlox "weeds" and is constantly pulling them out of areas they don't belong. She doesn't really dislike the plant, but it tends to invade other spaces. Rather than throw out the weeded phlox, she gives it away to friends and fellow gardeners and then relocates a few plants to other areas of her yard.

After the blooms fade, little seedpods form where the flowers once were. These tiny pods eventually pop open, dispersing seeds throughout the garden. The tiny seeds will sprout in almost any soil and are native across much of the South. They like well-drained soil but can sometimes be found growing in boggy areas. They will thrive in partial sun or live in deep, deciduous shade. Don't mulch around them, so the seeds can make contact with the ground. Seedlings will begin to emerge in late spring and early summer but won't flower until the second year.

Once the small, brown seedpods open, the stems should be cut back to the ground. The remaining plant is not much to look at. That is why the phlox works well when mixed with ferns, hostas, and other late-rising perennials. Blue phlox provides strong color early; then it steps aside and lets other plants take over.

This plant sometimes can be found at nurseries or can be ordered from many mail-order catalogs. You should never dig it from the woods and disrupt native stands.

If you need a touch of blue in your garden, plant this wonderful woodland phlox. Like many native plants, it's pretty self-reliant. Although its ability to reseed in the garden is a problem for Weesie, most gardeners will enjoy the invasion of the blues.

Below: Normally considered a ground cover, ajuga can also be a showy spring bloomer.

Crested Iris

Spanish Bluebell

Morning Glory

Scorpion Weed

Lungwort *(Pulmonaria)*

Grape Hyacinth

Blue Daze

Greek anemone

Clematis

Netted Iris

BLUE OPPORTUNITY

annuals

baby-blue-eyes
bachelor's-button
blue daze
forget-me-not
larkspur
lobelia
love-in-a-mist
pansy
salvia
scorpion weed

perennials

baptisia
campanula
columbine
dayflower
lungwort
Southern stars
Russian sage
stokesia
veronica
wild blue flax

bulbs

dwarf crested iris
grape hyacinth
Greek anemone
netted iris
Spanish bluebell

vines

clematis
morning glory
sky vine

easy spring flowers

How easy? Only seven flats of annuals and a few choice perennials went into this bursting flower border. Given the span of just a few months, the front yard looked like a cottage garden. The plants added appeal and charm. It hardly resembled the barren earth that surrounded the house not long ago. If you want a colorful spring garden like this one, you have to realize that the real work starts in the fall.

This curved flowerbed, which runs along the edge of a gravel parking area, is 4½ feet wide and 66 feet long. A small bed of Zoysia grass sweeps across the front edge of the border,

making the flowerbed accessible from both sides of the border. Weeding and planting can be done without having to step all over plants or compacting the loose, freshly tilled, and amended soil.

The area receives lots of direct light, so it required sun-loving plants. A few die-hard perennials, such as maiden grass *(Miscanthus* sp.), butterfly bush *(Buddleia* sp.), Rose-of-Sharon *(Hibiscus syriacus),*

and some 'Homestead Purple' verbena (*Verbena canadensis* 'Homestead Purple') did the trick. The plan is to install a few perennials each year and keep the open spaces covered with seasonal flowers.

To fill in the open areas, foxgloves, pansies, violas, snapdragons, and sweet Williams were used. Lots of pink, yellow, purple, and white bloomers were placed in the border because these colors blend well together. On a cool autumn day, seven flats were planted to produce a colorful April and May border. Each flat contained 36 little plants. When setting them out, a little timed-release fertilizer was worked into each hole.

After the fall planting, little maintenance was needed. A blanket of pine straw mulch covered the ground, keeping most weeds out and helping to protect the new plants. The border was checked once a week and any weeds were quickly pulled. Little watering is needed in winter, unless you're experiencing extended dry spells. The pansies were groomed occasionally by removing spent blooms. The snapdragons needed to be cut back after a few subfreezing nights turned their foliage brown, but cutting them back actually made them fuller in the spring. The tall foxgloves were supported using twine and a bamboo stake for each plant.

Why plant in the fall? The plants actually grew little in the fall and winter months, but underground roots began to spread, creating good anchorage and a strong growing base. The spring sun warmed the soil, and the tops of the plants began to flush with new growth. The foxgloves that were about 6 inches in March quickly grew to 4- and 5-foot-tall, multicolored spikes by May. Don't forget to set out plants in the fall for lots of spring blooms.

Opposite: In the foreground, white violas, purple verbena, and sweet Williams mingle for a carefree look. Tall foxgloves give the border height and dimension.

Plants to make your yard *sparkle* in the spring

Foxglove *(Digitalis purpurea)*—This is the most common foxglove. It's a biennial and sometimes a short-lived perennial in most of the region; in the Lower and Coastal South, treat it as an annual. The flowers are 2 to 3 inches long and look like clusters of bells dangling from the sturdy stalks. Blooms vary in color from creamy white to dark pink and purple with spotted throats. Common foxglove grows 3 to 5 feet tall. It may need to be staked to withstand the beating of heavy rains. Plant foxgloves in protected areas next to walls or fences and away from windy locations. You get a lot of bang for your buck with foxgloves. They're easy to grow, and they add height and charm to any garden.

Foxglove

Snapdragon *(Antirrhinum majus)*—These are great flowers for sunny borders. They grow 6 to 36 inches tall, and come in many colors, including white, pink, red, yellow, and orange. Medium and tall snapdragons work well in the middle or back of a border underplanted with pansies. When planted in fall, they bloom on and off in winter and heavily in spring, except in the Upper South where they may be planted in spring for summer blooms. Or they can be grown as short-lived perennials in the Upper South. Elsewhere, snapdragons are discarded after spring and replanted in fall.

Sweet William *(Dianthus barbatus)*—These vigorous, old-fashioned biennials are often grown as annuals. Small plants set out in the fall garden quickly spread to form a mass of foliage. The plentiful leaves keep the garden green throughout winter. In spring, dense clusters of white, pink, rose, purple, or bicolored flowers appear. The blooms look like small clouds on top of tall stems.

Snapdragon and pink geranium

Pansy and viola *(Viola sp.)*—These compact annuals provide sporadic color in winter and then a carpet of blooms in the spring. Their cheery-cheeked flowers look like children's faces. Violas, also known as Johnny-jump-ups, are a compact version of pansies. Many violas will reseed freely in the garden.

Both pansies and violas come in a variety of colors ranging from white to blue, red, orange, yellow, and purple. Petals are often striped or blotched, but 'Crystal Bowl' pansies are a selection without the blotch. 'Crystal Bowl True Blue' and 'Crystal Bowl Yellow' are two reliable performers, and the yellow is also extremely fragrant. In the Upper South, plant them in the early spring; elsewhere, plant in the fall. To prolong bloom time, remove faded flowers regularly before they go to seed.

Sweet William

summer blooms
to beat the heat

Spring blooms are easy for us all. The temperatures are nice, and there's usually adequate rainfall to keep flowers healthy and happy. Then summer rolls in like a sauna, the heat can be suffocating, and watering becomes a daily affair. Nobody wants to spend hours in the baking sun slaving over a garden. Let us show you which plants need little attention through the warm weather.

Most people have a hard time pulling up flowering plants. In late May, spring bloomers, such as pansies, still provide a little color in the garden; however, they begin to grow leggy and their bloom size decreases. Don't wait for your cool-weather plants to completely decline; pull them out, and start planting for summer.

Most summer-blooming bedding plants do best when they're put out in May and June before summer becomes unbearable. This gives them a chance to root in, get established, and endure late-summer droughts.

Take a look at some of the plants that performed well for us in this landscape. Texas sage *(Salvia coccinea)*, purple heart, lantana, and narrow-leaf zinnia *(Zinnia angustifolia)* are favorite summer beauties that beat the heat. It's a good thing we used these tough plants, because part of the summer we were unable to water due to drought-imposed watering restrictions.

Above: Narrow-leaf zinnia *(Zinnia angustifolia)* frame the front door; lantana mixes with ivy geraniums. **Left:** Purple heart, variegated ivy, and ferns add color, interest, and texture to the border.

'Coral Nymph' Texas Sage | Lantana

Tips for your **summer** *garden*

When adding color to your garden, don't forget about foliage plants. Purple heart, sweet potato vine, ornamental grasses, elephant's ears, ferns, coleus, and caladiums add bold colors and wonderful textures to the garden. And don't limit yourself—try colorful, tropical plants that thrive in the heat.

When your plants do need a drink, water them well. Try to soak the first couple of inches of soil, watering as little as possible and letting your soil dry a bit between waterings. Twice a week waterings are usually sufficient. Don't water daily, and remember frequent overhead waterings can cause plants to become infected with fungus or other disease. When possible, use drip irrigation systems and soaker hoses to minimize runoff. Make sure plants have a thick mat of mulch around them to help retain moisture, keep out weeds, and dress up beds.

Every few years you should add some organic matter, such as finely shredded pine bark, sphagnum peat moss, mushroom compost, or leaf mold to beds. Use a tiller or turning fork to mix the organic material thoroughly, loosening the soil and making it easy to dig and plant.

TIMING IS CRITICAL

• In late spring, pansies grow leggy and begin to melt in the heat. As they decline, pull them out, and weed and mulch beds. Then replace them with summer-blooming annuals.
• Mulch beds before you plant. We put out a couple of inches of pine straw, and then planted through the mulch.
• Space plants according to planting directions. These narrow-leaf zinnias (opposite page) spaced about a foot apart looked sparse at first, but quickly grew together for a full-flowered look.

'Profusion' zinnia | Ivy geraniums

no-fail fall color
The secrets behind beautiful fall blooms.

Autumn is a season of brilliance, but usually it is in the clarity of the blue sky and the vivid hues of the treetops. In this garden, however, the flower border plays host to a dynamic display that starts small in spring with drifts of bulbs and grows ever taller, fuller, and more robust until annuals and perennials proudly stand shoulder to shoulder in a season when many gardens are simply tired. They spill their colors onto the path and present fresh flowers at eye level.

Flowers and foliage of strong, saturated reds, purples, and bronzes mingle with other hues to make a sweep of color that easily endures the strong Southern sun. This garden was planted in the fall and spring, allowing time for plants to fill out and add height to the border. Although this is a large, mature garden, you can enjoy a smaller version by selecting some of the combinations shown here. For a plan to help you plant, see the chart below.

COLOR SELECTION
"The colors in this garden were dictated by the light," says garden designer Mary Zahl of Birmingham. "We tried pale pink in the first planting, and it was horrible. The reds, purples, the black-eyed Susan yellow, and the burgundy foliage look great because these deeper, stronger colors absorb the light."

Color choices are personal, just as when choosing your clothing. But the clothes you wear can be influenced by your hair, skin, and even your destination. Naturally, a garden's colors have different influences and results.

"People think they like certain colors, usually the colors they wear," says Mary.

"You may think you hate orange, but it may look great in a border. Just because you are a person who doesn't like strong colors doesn't mean that they may not be the best ones to use in your garden."

PROPER PRUNING
Salvias play a major role in this planting, and essential to their success is pruning. Left on its own, fall-flowering forsythia sage may reach 8 feet in height. By cutting back the plant by half in midsummer, Mary keeps it 4 to 5 feet tall with numerous spikes of flowers. Other plants in the border are also managed this way, including Mexican bush sage (*Salvia leucantha*) and Tatarian aster (*Aster tataricus*). Salvias in the border that do not require pruning are 'Lady in Red,' 'Indigo Spires,' and pineapple sage (*S. elegans*).

SUPPORTS FOR GROWTH
Another technique for a full fall bloom is to support these tall-growing plants so they stand upright. Plastic-coated metal grids are placed over the young plants in late spring and early summer. Rather than trying to stake plants after it is too late and risk breaking stems, Mary supports them as they grow. These grids are available at many garden centers and through mail-order companies. Plants that benefit from this care include the salvias, garden phlox, pink boltonia (*Boltonia asteroides* 'Pink Beauty'), switch grass (*Panicum virgatum* 'Heavy Metal'), and yellow shining coneflower (*Rudbeckia nitida* 'Herbstsonne').

TRICKS OF THE TRADE
At 120 feet long, this border is relatively narrow—only 4 feet. Mary compensates by taking space from behind the fence. 'Callaway' crabapple trees with their bounty of red fruit echo the colors of the border and give the illusion of depth.

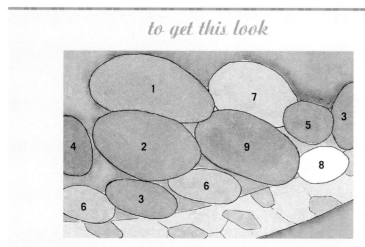

to get this look

1. Tatarian aster
2. pineapple sage
3. 'Lady in Red' salvia
4. *Salvia leucantha*
5. 'Indigo Spires' salvia
6. 'Margarita' sweet potato vine
7. forsythia sage
8. narrow-leaf zinnia
9. coleus

Above: 'Lady in Red' salvia, chartreuse 'Margarita' sweet potato, and white narrow-leaf zinnia fill this garden. The flower spikes of the red-leaved coleus echo the form of the spikes on the forsythia sage.

Gardens with a long blooming season have foliage from perennials that have already finished flowering—daylilies, iris, and such. Mary sees the leaves as assets. They are full, green, and offer vertical form and interest. There are also plants grown strictly for their ornamental foliage—grasses, sweet potatoes, Caribbean copper plant *(Euphorbia cotinifolia),* and coleus.

The stone walk that separates the border from the lawn becomes less of a path as the garden spills onto it. Still, it is probably best to step back and view the border from the lawn. It's almost more than you can absorb at a single glance.

With the help of Mary's tips and favorite plant combinations, you can savor a lush fall border in your garden, too.

winter bright

When it comes to winter gardens, folks in the Tropical South must wonder what's the big deal. After all, their plants are still green, and many trees and shrubs continue to bloom the same as before. And if people want extra color, they plant winter annuals.

But for everyone else, having winter color is a big deal. Southerners hate their gardens to look "dead," even briefly. So we make liberal use of evergreen trees and shrubs to counter the barren look of deciduous plants. This demonstrates the most important rule of winter design—use evergreens to establish the garden's form. Then work seasonal interest, provided by flowers, berries, and bark around this green framework.

FLOWER SELECTION

Bulbs are a great option this time of year. Crocuses and snowdrops that bloom from fall throughout the winter months are a nice option. Cyclamen also bloom through the cold season, beginning with *Cyclamen hederifolium,* which offers fall flowers and winter foliage.

One of the showiest small trees is Japanese flowering apricot *(Prunus mume).* Another showy tree this time of year is *Prunus subhirtella 'Autumnalis,'* which blooms from late October through winter.

The most dominant plants this time of year are the masses of Lenten roses *(Helleborus* x *hubridus).* The Christmas rose is another favorite, but it can be challenging. It is important for it to be planted from a well-established, container-grown plant, never bare-root. And it needs protection. Once you get it growing, it will do well.

PROPER CARE

There's more to the winter garden than just picking the right plants and growing them correctly. Plants protected from drying wind or morning sun are less prone to winter damage, as are those planted near a wall or foundation.

In addition, excellent soil preparation yields deep-rooted, vigorous plants that are very hardy. Basically, you build the soil up by adding organic matter. In this part of the country, you have to irrigate, and with summer's high temperatures and humidity, the organic matter is constantly breaking down. You've got to get that initial good drainage.

BLOOMING BERRIES

For months of winter color, count on berries. Hollies are tops in this regard, from evergreen types to deciduous species, such as possumhaw *(Ilex decidua)* and winterberry *(Ilex verticillata).* Other "berry-nice" plants include crabapple, viburnum, nandina, and hawthorn. And don't overlook beautiful bark. The winter bark of crepe myrtle, Chinese elm *(Ulmus parvifolia),* eastern red cedar, beech, and birch can be stunning in late afternoon sun.

Paperbush

PLANTS FOR WINTER FLOWERS

trees
Japanese flowering apricot
Rosemary Clarke
Winter flowering cherry

shrubs
Japanese pieris
Paperbush
Primavera witch hazel
Winter daphne
Winter Sun mahonia

perennials and bulbs
Algerian iris
Arisaema sikokianum
Bearsfoot hellebore
Christmas rose
Clematis cirrhosa
Cyclamen
Daffodils
   February Gold
   Green Castle
   Prefix
Lenten rose
Snowdrops

Snowdrops

Opposite: Winter blossoms in this North Carolina border, which features the blooms of Lenten rose, mahonia, flowering quince, and heath.

smart plant choices

the secrets behind beautiful blooms

timing secrets revealed:
when to buy, when to plant

Probably the greatest advantage Southern gardeners enjoy is the potential to have something blooming outdoors nearly every month of the year. However, realizing this potential means planting ahead.

Depending on where you live, spring can come early in the South. Once spring finally does arrive, there's not much you can do to embellish, beyond sticking in some potted pansies and snapdragons at the last minute. But you can start planning for future seasons. This seasonal timetable will help you.

LATE SPRING

• Set out annual transplants for summer color before the weather gets hot. They'll become established quicker and give you a better, long-lasting show. This means replacing cool-weather annuals while they're still blooming, but the results are worth it.

• For an informal, cottage-style garden, sow seeds of quick-germinating annuals, such as cosmos, zinnias, spider flower *(Cleome hasslerana)*, marigolds, common sunflower, and Mexican sunflower *(Tithonia* sp.*)*, directly into the garden. Barely cover with soil. They'll bloom throughout summer and into fall.

• Plant summer- and fall-blooming bulbs, such as glads, cannas, callas, dahlias, spider lilies *(Lycoris* sp.*)*, and ginger lilies. And don't forget caladiums for spectacular summer foliage.

• Set out shrubs and perennials that add blooms to either the fall (roses, sasanqua camellias, Mexican bush sage, ornamental grasses, asters, mums) or winter (winter honeysuckle, winter daphne, common camellia, Lenten rose).

PEG'S PICKS

Peg Moore, owner of one of Charleston, South Carolina's most beautiful gardens, says, "Thinking ahead is important. I like to have color going constantly." To that end, she employs a couple of uncommon plants for flower-challenged months. The first is Tatarian aster *(Aster tataricus)*, which grows 6 to 7 feet tall with showy blue flowers. "It blooms nonstop for two months beginning in late August," she notes. The other is 'Bowles Mauve' wallflower *(Erysimum* 'Bowles Mauve')*, a short-lived perennial with gray-green leaves and abundant lavender flowers. It blooms all winter and through the spring.

SUMMER

• Midsummer isn't too late to add fall-blooming plants to your perennial border. Good choices include asters, joe-pye weed, Mexican bush sage, pineapple sage, ironweed, mums, and goldenrod (no, it doesn't cause hayfever). Look for plants with healthy roots growing in 1-gallon pots. After planting, be sure to water daily for two to three weeks until the plants are established.

• In late summer, sow seeds of cosmos and large-flowered zinnias for an easy color display throughout the fall.

FALL

• Get out to your garden center early for the best selection of winter- or spring-flowering bulbs, such as daffodils, tulips, hyacinths, snowdrops, and crocus. Plant by early December. If you live in an area with short, mild winters, chill bulbs in the refrigerator for 8 to 10 weeks before planting.

• Set out transplants of cool-weather flowers that will bloom next spring. Good choices include foxgloves, pansies, violas, snapdragons, stock, and sweet Williams.

• Sow seeds of spring-blooming annuals, such as poppies and larkspur, directly onto bare soil, and barely cover.

• For winter flowers in Florida and the Tropical South, plant petunias, pot marigold *(Calendula officinalis)*, pansies, Drummond phlox *(Phlox drummondii)*, snapdragons, nasturtiums, and violas.

• Fall is a great time for planting hardy trees, shrubs, vines, and perennials to supply colorful flowers and foliage next year.

SECRETS OF FALL PREP

Occasionally pansies are cut down by a cold snap or hungry deer. These are the calamities no gardener can prevent. But in the end, nature is our friend. Most bulbs (such as daffodils) and biennials (such as foxgloves) require months of cold to enable them to bloom. Many annuals also benefit from fall planting in most areas of the South. As long as the soil is not frozen, their roots are growing, getting a head start on spring. If the weather is mild, they'll bloom all winter. So year after year, we plant for spring and hope for the best. The key to a spring garden is fall planting.

SPRING BEGINS IN FALL

First, choose a sunny place for a spring flower garden. Then prepare the soil by adding plenty of organic matter. Cover your bed several inches deep with compost, soil conditioner (composted pine bark), or leaf mold. Add a slow-release fertilizer such as Holland Bulb Booster (9-9-6) or Osmocote (18-6-12) at the rate recommended on the label. Then turn it all into the soil.

When you decide what to plant (see lists on opposite page), try to create a parade of flowers from early to late spring. During the cool days of early spring, it only takes a few blooms to make a gardener glad. By planting pansies in the same bed where you have already set out bulbs, you will have something to enjoy this winter until the early bulbs push through the soil. When the first daffodil raises its sunny head, you'll know that the fullness of spring is not far behind.

After you return from the garden center and unload the plants, bulbs, and seeds that you have purchased, spread them out in front of the freshly worked soil. Take transplants out of their containers, and lay them on top of the soil where you think they will look nice. As tempting as it might be, don't plant them yet. Then spread your bulbs around, remembering that they can come up between other plants.

Arrange the bed so that the taller flowers of mid- to late-spring will be at the back. For example, if you are growing sweet Williams and foxgloves, put the foxgloves in back. Early bulbs can go anywhere, even in the middle or background where taller, later-flowering plants will grow to hide their foliage.

Use your imagination to visualize the sweeps of color, the blooming sequence, and the plant heights. Make adjustments as needed. Then work your way across the bed with trowel in hand, planting as you go. Sow any annual seeds, such as larkspur or poppies, after setting out transplants.

COUNT ON SURPRISES

Because so much is dependent upon the weather, you could plant the same garden every year and get different results each spring.

Our garden plan worked well, particularly in early season. The daffodils and pansies were spectacular, but the peak of spring was very warm and the pansies grew smaller and their stems drooped. Closer examination revealed that they were developing seedpods. Cutting these off, as well as pinching and fertilizing, sustained them a while, but not as long as we had hoped.

The snapdragons and larkspur filled the back of the bed with color. Parsley grew full and lush.

Meanwhile, our foxgloves just sat there, as if they were determined not to be in any pictures with those trashy pansies. The bloom spikes appeared erratically, if at all, probably due to insufficient cold weather.

While not everything went as planned, the garden was very pretty. We pulled out the pansies in late spring and set out 'Homestead Purple' verbena to fill the front gaps and to carry us into summer.

GARDENING ON THE EDGE

The South is a diverse region with great variation in gardening climates. Those who live in the coldest areas of the Upper South will

Gardeners are optimists, always willing to try. Some ideas work and some don't. That is the fascination of a garden.

Above: Due to a warm winter, the pansies went to seed early, and the foxgloves were sporadic in their blooming. So we pulled the pansies early and replaced them with 'Homestead Purple' verbena, which will provide color into summer.

Right: Fill out the beds with flowers and greenery. Pansies are a nice choice for fall because they'll thrive all winter and early spring when there's little color.

Opposite: Plant daffodil bulbs in fall for early spring blooms.

probably do better to plant bulbs and biennials this fall and then set out annuals and seeds in early spring.

However, climates in the Coastal and Tropical South are the other extreme. There isn't enough cold weather to grow daffodils in many areas. But you can grow many cool-season annuals such as petunias and geraniums throughout the winter months.

how to make
WISE
plant purchases

Nurseries are filled with temptation. Go with a list and ask for advice if you're overwhelmed.

Beautiful flowers are available everywhere you turn. It's easy to pick up one of this and one of that on every outing from grocery stores to discount chains to garden shops. Suddenly, you are faced with a hodgepodge of mismatched colors and plants—all impulse purchases. "Before you head out to shop, have a plan," says Jimmy Collier, owner of Collier's Nursery in Vestavia Hills, Alabama. "Keep in mind the colors you want to work with, and then stick with them."

Color isn't the only consideration. "Do your homework before you shop. Know the areas you want to plant and how much sun each spot gets. Know the size of your beds and containers," Jimmy advises. When deciding where to shop, consider good information and healthy plants in addition to price.

FLOWER SHOPPING TIPS

For the time and dollars invested in planting, you want to begin with the best materials. Follow Jimmy's suggestions for an educated purchase.

• When purchasing annuals, visit the garden center early so you'll get a good selection. Don't buy the tallest plants. Plants more than 3 inches tall are probably root bound and destined for stunted growth.

• Choose plants that are compact and have few blooms. Also look for dark green foliage with no yellow leaves. Your annuals should look as if they've just come off the truck.

• If the foliage appears mottled, look at the underside of the leaves for aphids, whiteflies, or spider mites.

Left: Choose plants that are compact and show no signs of yellowing foliage. **Middle:** Don't be afraid to slide the plants out of their containers to check the roots. **Right:** Look for bulbs that are fat and fleshy (top). Avoid ones that are moldy or dried (bottom).

• Slide a plant out of its container. Roots should be white, thin, and fibrous. The root ball should not crumble when the plant is gently handled. This indicates that a small plant has just been placed in a larger container. Don't pay extra for a large container unless the plant has grown to a proportional size. Avoid plants with brown roots. Plants held in place by a snarl of roots have been in their pots too long. (If the roots have wrapped around themselves, it's harder for the plant to become established in your yard.)

• Check soil moisture. A dry plant is stressed.

• Purchase only labeled plants. Without a label, there's no sure way to identify what you're bringing home.

• Annuals come in packages that hold three or four small plants, permitting you to purchase small quantities. For convenience, packs are sold in larger containers, called flats. Each flat will usually hold 36 small plants, and the price is slightly discounted. "Choose flats that are complete," Jimmy says. "If there are partial flats, they've been raided by other shoppers and picked through. If flats are full, employees have been restocking and giving the plants the attention that they need."

FLOWER PLANTING TIPS

Jimmy offers this advice for planting seasonal color.

• Pinch back most of the flowers at planting time to encourage new growth and healthy roots.

• Amend the soil seasonally with combinations of topsoil, peat moss, manure, and soil conditioner.

• Plant annuals with a balanced timed-release fertilizer such as Osmocote (14-14-14), and follow up with a liquid food such as 15-30-15 every two weeks.

Questions to ask when selecting plants

To combine plants that will complement each other, you should know as much about each plant as possible. Here are some questions to ask that will help you pair plants with compatible growth habits, bloom times, form, and horticultural requirements.

How tall and wide will it grow?

What shape and color are the flowers?

How long does it bloom?

When does it bloom?

Does the foliage stay green through the winter?

Does it spread?

Does it form clumps?

Does it like sun or shade?

Will it tolerate poor soil or bad drainage?

• Soak the soil after planting; then let the garden dry out slightly between waterings. Containers require water more consistently than flowerbeds.

BUYING BETTER BULBS

• Make sure that the bulbs are firm and solid. If they seem spongy when you gently squeeze them, they may be old and dehydrated or even rotting inside.

• Avoid bulbs with nicks and cuts, which could make them susceptible to decay, or with bits of blue or gray mold at the bottom.

• Some bulbs are sold only at specific times of the year, so it pays to shop early for the best selection even if it is not time to plant. In the South, Dutch bulbs, such as tulips, are sold in September but the best time to plant them is after the first frost. The bulblike tubers for caladiums and other summer plants arrive at the nursery in March. However, they prefer warm soil, so you should plant them in April or May—or at least two weeks after the last frost.

SEED SHOPPING SECRETS

• Some plants, such as cosmos and spider flower, are rarely found as transplants because they grow unwieldy very quickly. To grow them, you must purchase seed from either a garden center or a mail-order seed company and start your own transplants indoors or sow seed directly in the garden.

• Always buy seed dated for the current year and only purchase packets that have been properly stored in a cool, dry environment.

• Packets that are wrinkled with moisture or left sitting in the sun may contain seed that has lost its viability.

pick the right plants for the South

Alien beings have moved in next door. Steve Bender's family is justifiably concerned. They know the neighbors are not from around here because of all the weird plants they've brought with them—lilac, paper birch, blue spruce, delphinium. Word has it their new neighbors come from a planet named Wisconsin.

Alien plants from the North look nice when first set out. But they usually can't hack the South's hot, humid summers and short, mild winters. So they either fail to bloom, fail to thrive, or simply croak. Why, then, do aliens keep trying?

For an answer, I consulted several admitted aliens. Kathy Foster, who grew up in wintry Northern Kentucky and Ohio before moving south to Fort Walton Beach, Florida, told me, "We try because we have pass-along plants from grandparents, family, friends, and deceased loved ones that we don't want to lose. These plants evoke pleasant memories." Other aliens said they just like to buck advice and plant something people living here say won't do. And if they do succeed, native Southerners will often copy them.

Of course, the ultimate fate of such plants depends largely on where in the South you live. Many of them do okay in the Upper South but struggle elsewhere. You could make them feel more at home by refrigerating the soil or dressing your kids in stripes and plaids, but this is a lot of trouble. It's easier to simply substitute plants better adapted to the South that possess similar qualities.

For example, you love lilac, the favorite plant of the planet Wisconsin, but you now live in New Orleans. Lilacs won't bloom in the Big Easy, due to the lack of winter chill. So, instead, plant

BETTER PLANTS, BETTER CHOICES

If You Can't Grow This:	Try This:
lilac	chaste tree, crepe myrtle
rhododendron	French hydrangea, camellia
English holly	lusterleaf holly
delphinium	larkspur
tuberous begonia	angel-wing begonia
bearded iris	Louisiana iris
lupine	foxglove
tulip	amaryllis
Colorado blue spruce	'Carolina Sapphire' Arizona cypress
paper birch or European white birch	'Heritage' river birch

chaste tree *(Vitex agnus-castus)*. It has beautiful blue flowers like lilac, grows 15 to 20 feet tall, tolerates heat and drought, and resists pests. Or plant a crepe myrtle. Its flowers are just as striking as a lilac's. Crepe myrtle also features colorful autumn foliage and handsome winter bark, where lilac is ornamental only when blooming.

Want a few more examples? Okay. Rather than planting the paper birch *(Betula papyrifera)* or European white birch *(B. pendula)* you remember from your home world, try 'Heritage' river birch *(B. nigra* 'Heritage'). Its bark is just as lovely, but it doesn't get the borers that plague the other two down here. Do rhododendrons wilt and die before your eyes? Substitute French hydrangea *(Hydrangea macrophylla)*. It loves our climate and flaunts gorgeous flowers of blue, purple, pink, rose, or white for many more weeks than a rhodie does.

Can't grow delphinium? Try larkspur. This reseeding annual gives you the same shape and flower colors, but it's much easier to grow. And instead of maintaining tuberous begonias on life support throughout the hot summer, grow the lovely and carefree angel-wing begonias. Lots of blooms, little fuss.

My new neighbors from Wisconsin desperately need this advice, but we don't know how to approach them. We saw them having brats and beer for breakfast, and we're very much afraid.

Above: 'Heritage' river birch features beautiful bark; thrives in hot, humid climates; and isn't plagued by borers. **Left:** Northerners grieving for lilacs should try crepe myrtle.
Below: Angel-wing begonias combine showy flowers with striking foliage.

choose annuals
for nonstop color

Unlike perennials, annuals may not come back year after year, but they have a number of distinct advantages. First, they bring instant showy color to a garden. Second, on average, they bloom much longer than perennials. Indeed, many bloom nonstop for months on end. Third, there's a fantastic array of annuals from which to choose in almost every color. Finally, the fact that annuals die at the end of a growing season means you get the chance to try something new.

Depending on the type of weather they prefer, annuals are classified as either warm-season or cool-season. Warm-season annuals are planted in spring and include such favorites as impatiens, zinnias, marigolds, wax begonias, ageratum, and salvia. Cool-season annuals are planted in fall and among their ranks are pansies, violas, Shirley poppies, larkspur, sweet Williams, and flowering cabbage and kale. Petunias can be either warm- or cool-season bloomers, according to where they're grown—summer flowers in most places, but winter flowers in Florida.

Some cool-weather annuals are really perennials that die when our hot weather begins. Delphiniums, snapdragons, and lupines are good examples. And tropical perennials, such as pentas, Mexican heather, and coleus, become annuals as soon as freezing weather strikes.

There is hardly any limit to the ways you can use annuals. They're ideal for massing in large, prominent beds for blazing impact or planting in graceful, curving sweeps that tie the garden together. You can spot them throughout the garden in pots, hanging baskets, and window boxes. They're also superb for filling the gaps in mixed borders or providing temporary or seasonal color to perennial and rose gardens.

For maximum impact, don't be stingy when setting out annuals. Plant in masses of six or more. Annuals come in inexpensive market packs, making this easy to do. It's also a good idea to plant in blocks of single colors, rather than creating a mishmash. Exceptions always exist, of course. Mixed colors of Shirley poppies, bachelor's-buttons, pastel cosmos, and large-flowered zinnias look just great.

Below: A foreground of pansies is perfect for shorter selections of foxglove.

ANNUAL JOURNAL

Annuals in a landscape need to be replaced at the end of the season, lest you have a bed of dying plants. Keep a journal or notebook to jot down selections of plants that pleased you so that you will be sure to buy them again. Record those that did not work well to avoid future disappointment. Your notebook may be as detailed as you wish. Entries could include planting dates, disease or insect problems and solutions, length of bloom, cold hardiness, tolerance to rainy weather, and anything else that will help you next time around.

stage a show with perennials

No garden is more dependable than one that's liberally stocked with perennials. These plants are available in crayon colors and boast season-long flowering times—from spring's first warm breath to fall's lingering frost. And best of all, a well-tended perennial bed fills the garden with colorful blossoms that grow fuller and more beautiful through the years.

Creating your own perennial paradise is no mystery. It doesn't require a large growing area or a degree in horticulture. By carefully selecting your plants you can easily stage a show in your garden that's guaranteed to steal the neighborhood spotlight. Our tips will help you get started and keep your garden looking its best, year after year.

Perennials prefer rich and well-drained soil. You can improve on Mother Nature's soil recipe by adding organic material in the form of composted manure, leaf compost, or peat moss. If your soil isn't sandy to start with, adding sand can enhance drainage. Organic fertilizers such as cottonseed meal or bonemeal will create a nutrient-packed soil perfect for hungry roots.

Soon after the first crocuses poke through the ground to brighten winter's drab palette, clean your perennial patch. Remove last year's stalks, leaves, or other material that has collected around overwintering plants. Take care to cut perennial stalks—instead of pulling them—so you don't damage young, growing roots or emerging shoots. Late winter is a great time to tackle weeds. Remove seedlings as they emerge, before they have a chance to become established in the garden.

Although fall is the best time to plant perennials, you can add them to your garden in early spring, too. For a quicker show of flowers, plant gallon-size perennials or large divisions from mature plants.

Divide summer and fall-blooming perennials, such as black-eyed Susan, Autumn Joy sedum, or aster before the growing season starts. Divide crowded clumps of spring bloomers when flowering is finished. Feed established plants every spring by working well-aged compost or manure into the soil around plants with a weeding claw.

Once flowers begin to unfold, extend the blooming season by faithfully removing spent blossoms. Perennials such as coralbells, veronica, and coreopsis will continue to flower well into the growing season as long as they aren't allowed to set seed.

Give your perennial garden pizzazz by borrowing design tips from the professionals. Plant in groups of three or five for visual impact, stair-step plants (tall ones in back, low-growing ones in front), and combine spiky flowers with rounded or flattened ones.

Below: Pair the towering spires of false indigo with bearded iris and peonies to transform your perennial bed into a work of art.

adding bulbs to the mix

Some of our best-loved garden flowers, such as daffodils and tulips, arise from bulbs—or similar forms, tubers, rhizomes, or tuberous roots. Although most familiar in dazzling spring displays, many bulbs bloom in late winter, summer, or fall.

You can use bulbs in either informal or formal designs. Bulbs that multiply freely, such as jonquils, grape hyacinths, Spanish bluebells, and spider lilies can be "naturalized" in woodland gardens, lawns, and grassy meadows. They'll gradually form loose drifts. New bulbs will pop up to surprise you each year. However, bulbs with long, sturdy stems and big flowers, including tulips, Dutch hyacinths, and true lilies, look better in more ordered circumstances, such as patterns, mass displays, and mixed borders.

Bulb blossoms may be spectacular, but they're also fleeting; many bloom for only a week each year. There are several tricks to extend the bulb season. First, plant early-, midseason-, and late-flowering selections of the same type of bulb. Or you can plant some summer-flowering bulbs, such as glads and calla lilies, at two-week intervals in spring. Finally, you can combine spring-, summer-, and fall-flowering bulbs within a mixed border.

Using bulbs in design is a bit like using annuals. For big impact, you need to plant them by the dozens. To make sure they all bloom at the same height, be sure to plant all the bulbs at the same depth. Don't mix up lots of colors or your bed will end up looking like a clown's pants. Instead, plant drifts of single colors.

One common problem with spring-flowering bulbs is that their foliage becomes unsightly after the flowers fade. This isn't a concern with tulips, which are treated as annuals in most of the South. After they finish blooming, you simply yank them up.

Above: Plant tulips with pansies for a nice spring show. A small handheld mattock is useful when planting bulbs.

But the foliage of perennial bulbs, including crocus, daffodil, and Spanish bluebells must be left in place until it yellows. Fortunately, a little advance planning effectively disguises this. After you plant these bulbs in the fall, plant pansies, violas, forget-me-nots, pot marigolds, and other cool-weather annuals on top of them. These long-blooming flowers will camouflage the withering bulb foliage. Or plant bulbs amid an evergreen ground cover, such as English ivy, mondo grass, or common periwinkle.

flowering trees

Flowers are the most popular ornamental contribution that a tree makes to the garden. While fall color occurs all at once, flowers bloom at different times during the growing season.

To vary the display of blooms in your garden, plant trees that flower at different times during the growing season, from the very early flowers of red maple to the late summer flowers of sourwood and crepe myrtle. Early-blooming saucer magnolia may be followed by Bradford pear, redbud, Yoshino cherry, flowering dogwood, and Kousa dogwood for a continuous array of blooms throughout the year.

Choosing different species of flowering trees adds variety in both color and form and brings different moods to the garden. Saucer magnolias have huge, tulip-shaped flowers that look like candelabra while Yoshino cherry has delicate pink-white flowers.

Both flowering dogwood and crepe myrtle are excellent specimen trees that can convey vastly different moods. Dogwood blossoms float like great snowflakes and impart serenity to the garden while crepe myrtle is more festive, bursting against the hot sky like a midsummer firecracker. Crabapple and Kwanzan cherry are very showy specimens, but Yoshino cherry, alone or in a group, seems delicate, refined, and reflective. Keep the tone in mind when selecting trees for your garden.

Do not put all of your flowering trees in one place; position them throughout the garden to highlight different areas. Early-flowering trees, such as red maple or star magnolia, placed in a favorite view can help chase away winter's blues. Use summer-flowering plants next to an outdoor sitting area so that you can enjoy using them throughout the warm season.

Above: Flowering dogwoods announce that spring has arrived in the South.

Trees that have a single flower on each twig, such as dogwood, saucer lily, and Loebner magnolia, appear more graceful when seen against a dark backdrop. Plant these trees in front of an evergreen screen or a dark wall.

Trees with aggregate flowers, those that are clustered together, do not need a contrasting backdrop to have vivid impact. Those that flower after their leaves emerge work well as specimen plants.

These are just a few things to keep in mind when you are selecting trees for the garden.

shrubs in bloom

All shrubs have a certain appeal throughout the year, but the flowering shrubs will dominate when they are in bloom. However, you should also remember that this is the shortest period of show in the year-round life of a landscape plant, often lasting only two to four weeks.

Select several different flowering shrubs for each season to increase the variety in your garden and the effectiveness of blooms spread throughout the garden year. Always choose a few shrubs for their fragrance, too. Elaeagnus blooms are barely visible, but you can smell their sweetness from yards away.

Choose shrubs that bloom at different times during the year, not just in spring. While the exact time of bloom will vary according to your location, you can count on shrubs to bloom in a predictable sequence.

The order of bloom does not vary dramatically from North to South, but the calendar dates will be different between higher and lower latitudes. It is common for bloom times to vary four to eight weeks between warm and cold climates. For example, in the lower South, the flower season begins as early as January with shrubs like flowering quince, usually one of the earliest blooming shrubs, and leatherleaf mahonia, which rivals it for eagerness to bloom. March typically brings forsythia, native azaleas, and some hybrid azaleas in the deep South while April holds the greatest azalea show. In the upper South and farther north, quince may not bloom until March or April.

PRUNING POINTERS

Nearly all shrubs need some pruning to maintain their form and vigor. So consider the shrub's growth rate and your own energy level before selecting a plant at the garden center.

- Be especially mindful of the shrub's eventual size when placing it near the house. If you have to take loppers to the plant every other week to keep it from devouring a doorway or harpooning an overhang, you've obviously chosen the wrong plant. Fast-growing shrubs that cause frequent problems near the house or other structures include pyracantha (firethorn), Hetz Chinese juniper, thorny elaeagnus, Burford holly, and photinia.
- The best time to prune spring-flowering shrubs is immediately after their blossoms fade. Prune summer-flowering shrubs in late winter or early spring. You can prune non-blooming evergreens at almost any time.

azalea, opens its scarlet trumpets in summer's heat and sometimes spills over into early August. In October, sasanqua camellia opens the camellia season, which can last into November and sometimes December.

If you plant shrubs with different blooming times, combine them in such a way that the peak of interest moves around the garden. Highlight one garden corner with early native azaleas (early spring) underplanted with Gumpo azaleas (early summer), and plant another corner with later-blooming sasanqua camellias (fall) and leatherleaf mahonia (late winter).

Many shrubs have ornamental berries or other fruit that follow the show of flowers at a time when there is little flower color in the landscape. For example, cranberry viburnum flares with fall color and then begins the leafless months clad with abundant fruit. Cotoneasters sparkle back to life as their fruit ripens through fall; the berries are bright and showy in winter. The same is true of wax myrtle, which picks up a classy look with the addition of bright blue fruits on the female plants.

Nandina has profuse red berries that make it an even more indispensable shrub by rounding out a year of sustained ornamental interest. The bright berries of Burford holly are well-known mainstays of the winter landscape; their bright orange-red spots of color lighten the garden and hold the

Look for May as the month of rhododendron and mountain laurel; Gumpo azaleas bloom in May and June. June and July bring out the hydrangeas. One last native azalea, the plumleaf

Above: The delicate-looking blooms of andromeda last for weeks.

Above left: Plumleaf azalea is a rare native azalea.

Left: Pyracantha produces beautiful orange to red berries in the fall.

promise of visiting birds, such as cedar waxwings, swooping into the plantings to eat the fruit.

Although most shrubs present their berry show in fall and winter, the display of brightly colored fruit can begin earlier, such as the grape blue fruit of leatherleaf mahonia.

A few shrubs are worth having for the fruit alone. Plant beautyberry along paths or wooded driveways; you are not likely to notice it until fall, when it is covered with purple fruit. The fruit of pyracantha is so spectacular that this ornamental quality alone is the shrub's hallmark. Espalier pyracantha to a brick wall or a wooden structure, or plant it as a free-standing specimen.

classic vines

Cascading in gardens throughout the South, these blooming beauties enhance fences, walls, and gates.

When the stakes are high, don't let your plants down. Stakes don't have to be poles stuck in the ground. We found morning glories gobbling up a brick wall, moonflowers stretching on a viny arch, and 'Margarita' sweet potato vine forming a lime-green tunnel over a garden gate. Plants can be trained to grow almost anywhere.

With a little assistance, some plants will twist and twine their way above the garden, creating a cloudlike effect. A vine's free-flowing form adds a loose element to an otherwise stuffy garden. It can also be used to disguise or hide an unattractive structure.

In most landscapes, you look down at the flowers, but with vines you can have flowers at eye level and even overhead. Find a place in your garden where vertical climbers can rise. Here are a few easy vines that drape the Southern landscape and are just waiting to take your garden up a notch.

Morning glory (*Ipomoea purpurea*) is a fast-growing annual vine that can be a nuisance. It grows like kudzu and reseeds with abandon. But because of its self-sufficient nature, it's also a favorite of gardeners. This vine comes in many colors, is simple to grow from seed, and can cover an arbor in the blink of an eye. Each morning, pointed, swollen buds twist open, turning into saucerlike blooms. On cloudy days the flowers can be tricked into staying open all day, but sunny, warm days will cause the blooms to close by noon.

Moonflower (*Ipomoea alba*) has large, perfumed, dishlike flowers that open late in the afternoon. The white blossoms will also ap-

Above: Rebar, bent with a pipe bender and set into holes drilled into the stone columns, forms this arch. 'Margarita' sweet potato vine trained on the arch makes a glowing entryway. **Opposite:** These morning glories flourish on a support of fishing line that runs from nail to nail.

pear on cloudy days. It is in the same family as the morning glory and has the same growth habit. Like morning glory, it's easy to grow from seed. Moonflowers and morning glories work well when they are planted together. One opens in the morning, while the other blooms at night.

'Margarita' sweet potato vine (*Ipomoea batatas 'Margarita'*) has no flowers, but its large, heart-shaped, lime-green leaves can really put on a show. 'Margarita' is usually found growing on the ground or creeping over the edge of a wall or a container. Though not known as a climber, it can be trained easily to get off the ground. Just tie it to a support. Under ideal conditions—good soil, hot sun, and ample water—it may grow 20 feet or more in a season. The 'Margarita' sweet potato vine actually produces potatoes. They should not be eaten, but they can be dug in the fall and stored in a cool, dark, dry place and replanted the following spring.

Red trumpet honeysuckle (*Lonicera sempervirens*) is an evergreen vine found in the Middle South. In the Upper South it's hardy but will defoliate in winter. The flowers resemble red trumpets that sound off in the spring and summer calling hungry hummingbirds. It produces an orange-to-scarlet fruit that many birds enjoy. Trumpet honeysuckle is vigorous but can be maintained easily. It will grow in sun to shade, but needs sun to bloom heavily.

This spring would be a great time to plant a climber and be innovative in the way you support it. You may just take your garden to new heights.

Left: Trumpet vine hugs a tree with a little assistance from a trellis of twine.

Opposite: Thick grapevine wraps around these posts, forming a sturdy support for the sweet-smelling moonflower.

Staking the sun

There are other plants that grow tall besides vines. This swamp sunflower towers above most perennials. It may grow 8 to 10 feet in height and can topple over when beaten by heavy rain. If you want to stake it, hammer three pieces of 8-foot rebar into the ground around the plant. Then wrap long shoots of elaeagnus around it and wire them to the rebar, creating a spiral enclosure. Now this leggy perennial has no choice but to stand tall.

flower garden
solutions

creative answers to landscape dilemmas

how to choose
long-blooming plants

Installing annuals and perennials is back-breaking work; digging each hole, watering, weeding, and fertilizing isn't easy. Make it easy for yourself when you go to the garden center. Select plants that bloom for long periods of time. Or choose reseeders, which are flowers that practically grow themselves.

There's no reason to plant flowers month after month. It's possible to make just one trip to the garden center each season if you purchase the right plants. Choose flowers or bright foliage plants that will shine for months at a time.

The least expensive way for gardeners to achieve long-lasting color for sunny locations is to throw out cosmos seeds after the last spring frost. Not only do cosmos come up quickly, but they also offer colorful spring and summer blooms. They need little care or water.

If you want a faster means of achieving color, look for cell packs or small containers of begonias, impatiens, lantana, petunias, melampodium, and narrow-leaf zinnias. These tried-and-true flowering plants are tough and have a lengthy bloom period.

There are also numerous foliage plants that produce long-lasting color. Caladiums, coleus, hostas, ornamental grasses, and purple heart add vibrant hues to the garden.

Lantana

spring color picks

Begonias These dependable annuals offer green or copper foliage with red, white, or pink blooms. The angel-wing type, 'Dragon Wing,' is not so compact and is an impressive bloomer. Begonias prefer full sun, but some selections will take a little shade.

Caladiums Choose from large pink, red, or white arrow-shaped leaves. These shade lovers mix well with ferns. They need warm nights and a soil temperature of 70 degrees to grow, so don't put them out too early.

Coleus This foliage plant comes in many colors from chartreuse to burgundy to multi-colored types. Most take the shade, but some new coleus are sun tolerant.

Cosmos Dazzling blooms range from white, pink, red, yellow, and orange. Plants vary in size, depending on selection. They like well-drained soil and lots of sun.

Hosta This showy-leaved perennial can range from blue-green to chartreuse. Variegated types have swirls of cream, gold, and white. They like shade and filtered light.

Impatiens This shade-loving annual blooms from spring till first frost. White, pink, lavender, orange, red, and purple flowers are available with minimal care.

Lantana This sun-loving plant thrives in summer droughts. Its large mounding form is topped with yellow, rose, lavender, and orange clustered flowers. It grows 1 to 4 feet tall.

Melampodium This underrated annual takes sun and light shade. Yellow to gold, daisylike flowers cover it from spring till frost.

Narrow-leaf zinnia *Zinnia angustifolia* comes in white, yellow, and orange. This is one of the most carefree long-blooming annuals. It grows 12 to 16 inches tall and needs a sunny, well-drained site.

Ornamental grasses Miscanthus and pennisetum are good for hot, dry, sunny areas. They range in height from 2 to 6 feet. Some pennisetums have burgundy foliage, and many of the miscanthus have showy white to cream stripes. Both grasses are topped with plumes in late summer and early fall.

Purple heart *Tradescantia pallida* 'Purpurea' has showy purple leaves that are tipped with tiny pink flowers. These plants like full sun and a well-drained site.

fall color picks

You know the end-of-summer blues, and so does your garden. It's the time when your summer-flowering annuals are as faded as your tan. Everyone thinks that autumn color comes only from the changing trees above, but look on the ground and notice all the plants that can make your garden beautiful. These fall annuals and perennials will put the color back into your garden.

Autumn Joy Sedum An all-time classic fall bloomer, it can be neglected and still reward you. Sturdy stems support coppery, broccoli-like blooms. Later in the season the large florets turn rusty red. Thick succulent leaves give this plant an interesting texture. A large sweep of sedum looks great in any garden and it combines well with chrysanthemums and ornamental grasses.

Aster This late bloomer will delight you with its true colors. Despite its name, New England aster *(Aster novae-angliae)* is native to the South. Also known as Michaelmas daisy, this species grows 3 to 5 feet tall, blooms in September and October, and bears purple flowers. 'Harrington's Pink' selection has daisylike blooms with yellow

Goldenrod

centers, characteristic of all asters. Full sun, consistently moist (but not wet) soil, and good drainage are the ideal growing conditions for asters.

Common ginger lily This perennial brings a tropical look to temperate gardens in the Lower and Middle South. Growing in full sun to partial shade, this 5-foot plant produces sweet-scented flowers that remind you of butterflies. It grows best in moist soil rich with organic matter.

Goldenrod Often taking the rap for the sniffles and sneezes of allergy season when ragweed is the real culprit, goldenrod should be one most wanted for its versatility. Plant it in either dry or moist soil in full sun. Like most perennials, goldenrod needs to be groomed after the flowers fade. Just cut the stalks back to the ground, and you'll have a tidy rosette of foliage.

Japanese silver grass Selections of *Miscanthus sinensis* have become very popular. As the summer's heat dwindles, these grasses send up tawny tassels that wave happily in the autumn breeze. Variegatus and Zebrinus are two variegated selections that will create an instant bright spot in your yard. Silver grass makes a nice specimen plant, adding instant height to any border.

Marigolds A nice alternative to mums, fall marigolds enjoy several advantages over mums. They bloom from the time you plant them right up until a hard frost. (Mums will bloom only three to four weeks.) Don't think of fall marigolds only as alternatives to mums. You can also use them to replace beds of summer annuals that have been hit hard by heat, drought, and insects. Marigolds suffer less from insects and disease in autumn than they do in summer. If you're tempted to plant mums and marigolds together, do so cautiously. Try not to mix too many bright colors unless you want your display to look like a homecoming float.

Marigold

Autumn Joy Sedum

Salvia

Patrina This perennial shows its stuff when summer drifts into fall. It produces billows of yellow or white blooms, depending on the selection. It takes full sun and well-drained soil.

Salvia These fall favorites can be a Southerner's salvation. All it needs is sun and well-drained soil, making it a plant that flourishes in heat and drought. Generally, salvias are annuals. They're tender perennials if you live in the Lower or Coastal South. Good drainage is a must. If you have heavy clay soil, add sand, fine gravel, or rich, loamy soil mixes. Plenty of water and a good, slow-release fertilizer are essentials.

Swamp sunflower *Helianthus angustifolius* looks like a black-eyed Susan on steroids. This towering perennial can reach 7 feet in height. Cutting it halfway to the ground in early summer will keep it more compact and manageable. From September through October, numerous yellow flowers top swamp sunflower, sometimes causing it to topple over; so staking it may be necessary.

what to plant for sun and shade

Sifting through the rainbow of choices at your local garden center makes the task of adding seasonal color complicated. Take the easy way out by choosing from our list of 10 reliable Southern favorites for sun and shade.

SUN WORSHIPERS

1. 'Gold Mound' lantana easily could have been named "gold mine lantana." The dazzling yellow blooms are a rich discovery for butterflies and gardeners alike. Plant this tropical shrub as you would an annual and you'll enjoy nonstop flowers throughout the hot months of summer. Be sure to give it plenty of sun and good drainage. The spreading form of gold mound, just 12 to 15 inches high, makes this selection a neater choice than some of its taller relatives. 'Gold Mound' is an excellent plant to spill over walls or along the edges of steps.

2. Dusty miller flaunts silvery gray foliage that shows off well beside just about any other color. It's quite drought tolerant, though you'll need to water young plants regularly to help them get established. Dusty miller prefers well-drained soil, so mix some sand into planting beds if you have clay soil. Remove yellow flowers in early summer to keep the plants producing foliage. Trim leggy plants in late summer to

enjoy renewed growth until frost. Most selections grow 6 to 12 inches tall.

3. Narrow-leaf zinnia will make you look like a gardening genius. Tiny daisy-faced flowers crowd together on each billowing plant, blooming nonstop right through the sizzle season. Unlike other zinnias that stand up straight, narrow-leaf zinnias form mounding cushions of flowers. Full sun and dry soil are all it takes to produce show-stopping color. Available in orange- and white-flowering plants.

4. Globe amaranth blossoms look like clover flowers dipped in Easter egg dye. The rounded flowers range in color from white, pale pink, and lavender to bright magenta, red, and orange. Plant a patch of globe amaranth (also known as gomphrena) in full sun for carefree color. Water young plants frequently for the first few weeks, then let rainfall do the rest. Selections vary in size from 8 to 30 inches tall.

5. Cosmos is so cooperative you need only to purchase seed packets to grow head-turning flowers. Scatter seeds in mid-spring on loosened soil in a sunny, well-drained spot; don't even bother to cover them up. In a month or so, you'll have blooms to

Lantana

Dusty miller

Narrow-leaf zinnia

Globe amaranth

Cosmos

Coleus   Melampodium   Caladiums

enjoy throughout the summer. Avoid the temptation to fuss with cosmos; too much fertilizer can produce more foliage than flowers. You can choose from a wealth of colors including white, yellow, orange, red, and any hue of pink you can dream up. Read the description of the seed pack for plant sizes, which may range from 2 to 5 feet. *Cosmos sulphureus* is a better choice for heat tolerance than *C. bipinnatus*.

SHADY CHARACTERS

6. Coleus is nature's answer to the crazy quilt. Foliage colors are available in a patchwork of rich burgundy, red, pink, white, copper, purple, and a most unlikely chartreuse. Variegated selections make the assortment of color combinations seem endless, giving shade gardeners an array of choices. Keep soil moist; coleus will wilt when roots get too dry. Pinch back blossoms to encourage production of the colorful leaves. Plant sizes range from 6-inch-tall dwarf selections to plants nearly 3 feet tall.

7. Melampodium supplies the shade garden with one of the few colors that impatiens can't—yellow. Though melampodium thrives in full sun, it is a valuable choice for dappled shade. Plant it in that in-between section of your yard where it's too sunny for impatiens but too shady for zinnias. You'll need to water melampodium only long enough to get young plants growing. Admiring the resulting mound of green and gold is all that is required of you for the rest of the summer. Expect flowers until frost. This plant often reseeds, so you

may find yourself enjoying it again next year. Like most annuals, melampodium prefers well-drained soil.

8. Caladiums deserve to be planted in every shady garden in the South. There's nothing like the nodding, colorful foliage to set the stage for lazy summer days. Plant tubers in late spring in rich, moist soil. Though some selections are suitable for sunny beds, most grow best in partial to full shade where plants aren't prone to drying out. (A layer of mulch will also help prevent the foliage from wilting.) Choose from heart-shaped, fancy-leaved caladiums or from arrow-shaped, lance-leaved plants.

9. Impatiens are the undisputed monarchs of the shade garden. Mounded plants covered with blossoms brighten shadowy garden spots with ceaseless color from spring until frost. Though impatiens require some morning sun to keep plants from getting too leggy, afternoon sun is too hot for these shade lovers. Don't hesitate to douse wilted impatiens with water; droopy plants will perk back up. Impatiens bloom best in soil that is kept evenly moist. Flowers are available in soft hues of pink, salmon, and white, or glowing shades of red, orange, and a particularly vivid violet color known as 'Lipstick.' Most plants grow 1 to 2 feet tall.

10. Wishbone flower grants three wishes for Southern gardeners: It loves humidity, it's easy to grow, and it blooms in the shade. Plant this Vietnamese native in a spot you can easily reach with a hose so you can keep the soil moist. Wishbone flower, also

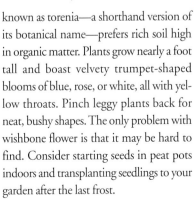

Impatiens

Wishbone flower

known as torenia—a shorthand version of its botanical name—prefers rich soil high in organic matter. Plants grow nearly a foot tall and boast velvety trumpet-shaped blooms of blue, rose, or white, all with yellow throats. Pinch leggy plants back for neat, bushy shapes. The only problem with wishbone flower is that it may be hard to find. Consider starting seeds in peat pots indoors and transplanting seedlings to your garden after the last frost.

MAXIMUM
impact with minimal effort

Flowers provide the finishing touch to a landscape, adding polish and personality. It takes time and a bit of money, but the results are worth the effort. But because of busy lives, opportunities to plant can be a luxury. So plan flowers for maximum impact with minimal expense and effort.

FRONT AND CENTER

"Put flowers where you want to focus your attention," says landscape designer Randy McDaniel, owner of McDaniel Land Designs in Mountain Brook, Alabama. "The entryway or front door is many times the most important focal point in the landscape."

Begin by looking at both sides of the front door. "Then, take steps back and look for places to put colorful flowers that will lead your eye along a path to the entry. The goal is to bring your eye ultimately back to the front door," Randy says. "Walk halfway through the yard and look; then walk out to the street. You might even go further, into a neighbor's yard, and look at your entrance from their vantage point. It helps to see your landscape from a distance for a little objectivity."

An entryway is not always visible. The door may be set back or positioned to one side. "If the front door is hidden from view, flowers can be used as a directional element," Randy says. "Put a little punch of color in an urn or in the ground to highlight the area."

The most pleasing landscapes are those where color is uncomplicated. Too many shades and hues do little to enhance a house. "Keep the color planting in your front yard simple," says Barbie Tafel Thomas, a landscape designer with Webb-Thomas in Louisville. "Generally, a lot of busy color in the front is not a good feeling. Use a single color for a calm appearance."

Flowers are not unlike a painting. A masterpiece is lost without the proper frame. The same is true in a garden. "Color is most effective when snuggled in next to something green," Barbie says. "Color needs that green backbone behind it to work well, and it should enhance your shrub base."

"Don't float your annuals out in the middle of the yard. They will get lost without a green backdrop, and the appearance is unorganized. Concentrate flowers by the front door and maybe by the mailbox," she suggests.

LEVEL THINKING

Plan flowers on more than one level. "Don't think of color on only one plane," Randy says. "Typically, people plant seasonal flowers in the ground and in a container or two. Layer it for more impact and bigger bang for your buck."

Below: Crepe myrtles frame this entrance, and their color is mirrored in containers near the door. White petunias and caladiums lead your eye up the front walk and complete this welcoming combination.

COLOR TIP: *To make a small space feel larger, place warm colors (red, orange, and yellow) in the front of a garden and cool colors (blue, green, and purple) in the back.*

Above: You don't have to plant large beds to make a statement. All eyes go to the front door with this vibrant pansy display. The containers provide impact and require minimal care. **Below:** Colorful windowboxes draw your eye to an interesting spot.

The Mediterranean-style house pictured opposite provides a good example of layering. Crepe myrtles planted along the sidewalk frame the entrance and introduce color at street level. That color then reappears on another plane, near the front door, in containers. In between, white caladiums and petunias add another color tier designed to draw your eye to the front door. The flowers are layered, from the street to the front entry.

BROADEN YOUR FOCUS

Look beyond your front door for other areas to use flowers effectively. "Windows are like steps between indoors and out," Barbie says. "A window box can add a terrific amount of softening. You can keep it pretty 365 days a year, and it will provide color and greenery where there is no other planting pocket."

A patio or deck can be another good place to focus color. "A terrace is a place to relax. Keep your color simple and easy to maintain," Barbie advises. "You don't want to feel compelled to deadhead and maintain when you really want to rest." Place the plants in containers for reasonable care requirements. "Do everything on your own terms. You certainly don't want to be a slave to what you've created," says Barbie.

find flowers that flatter your home

It's overwhelming and intimidating. Stop by a garden center in spring, and you're visually assaulted with color. There are so many shades to choose from, and each becomes a favorite. Whether or not those preferences are the best choice for your particular landscape is another matter. Many plantings miss the mark with color that's not quite right.

"Color unifies the house with the landscape," says Catherine Bowen Drewry, a landscape designer in Crawford, Georgia. "People spend a lot of time thinking about the colors inside their home and on the exterior. They need to factor landscape colors into the equation."

CHECK IT OUT

Take cues from your architecture. Roof, trim, and house colors are all factors in determining the best palette. Make note of mature trees and shrubs that bloom throughout the year. Their flowers should complement the overall scheme as well. "If your house is orange-based brick, ask yourself how that hot pink crepe myrtle is going to look against it," Catherine says. "Is it going to pick up a little pink in the brick, or is it really going to clash with it?

"A lot of the landscape is seen from indoors. If the dining room is soft yellow and you're looking out into the garden, you might want to see more soft yellow repeated outdoors. It helps make the garden feel like it's part of the house," she says.

THE BIG PICTURE

In the charming Victorian cottage pictured at left, the front door and brick dictate the color palette. "The door is a rich color, chosen to work well with the old brick. We had to find flowers to complement both and not compete," says Bill Nance, a garden designer in Huntsville, Alabama. "The salmon impatiens lead your eye up the stairs to the door and mirror its shade. The green ferns add inviting texture and prevent color clutter." The brick, door, copper light fixtures, and flowers are all planned to present a pleasing, unified presence.

An effective way to illustrate color is by ex-

Left: White flowers are the best choice for this crisply trimmed bungalow. The appearance is inviting and ample without overpowering the entry. Green ferns on each side of the door add warmth.

what about brick?

Brownish brick with yellow undertones is complemented by red, orange, and yellow flowers.

Pink-based brick works in harmony with rose, blue, and soft yellow. Neutral purple pulls them together.

This blue-gray facade can handle bold yellow and purple. The soft yellow prevents harshness.

COLOR TIP: *Warm colors are effective accents. Use them in small amounts to brighten up a cool color scheme.*

ample. The bungalow shown at right gets its color cues from crisp white trim. White flowers present a cool, unified look. They add ambience without being a distraction and complement the simple, elegant scheme.

A MYSTERY SOLVED

One of the most elusive color concepts is working with brick. Many homeowners struggle with the perfect palette to complement this popular facade. "With brick, you need to determine its base color," says Bill. "Take red brick—some of it has an underlying yellow base. This makes the brick color go toward orange. Other red brick has a blue cast. You must look for the base color and see if it goes to the orangy side of red, or the blue side."

"If your brick goes toward orange, choose warm-colored flowers such as oranges and yellows. If you have blue-red brick, go toward the blue and blue-violet flower family. It's when you combine the red-orange flowers with the red-blue flowers that you get into visual trouble," he says.

"When you have a brick home, be careful using azaleas as a foundation planting," Bill says. It is difficult to find a blooming shrub that works well with brick. Instead, he suggests planting boxwood or another evergreen as a buffer between the brick and azaleas. "I like azalea color against green. It doesn't compete with the brick, and green makes everything look good."

planting pitfalls you want to avoid

Once you've decided where to put color and which colors work best in your landscape, you must decide how to arrange the plants. When arranged properly, color flows through a garden like a well-orchestrated piece of music. In reality, there are numerous pitfalls to placement that can ruin a harmonious planting. Here are things to avoid and ways to go with the flow.

PITFALL #1: DOTS AND SPOTS
Avoid alternating colors, one by one.
A mass of one color creates more impact than a mishmash of several different plants. A collection of one color is usually known as a sweep. Consider tadpole-shaped beds of each flower type. Thicker at one end, these sweeps naturally provide a sense of movement in the flower border. It's easy to achieve this shape. Simply use a garden hose to lay out your color. Make a big loop, and then pull it so that it's longer than it is wide. Where the ends cross will be narrower than the curved side of the loop. If you plant several tadpole-shaped sweeps of color together, the garden will have an organized, tapestry-like appearance.

Repetition is important when combining plants in a design because it creates a sense of harmony. Identify a certain characteristic of one plant, such as texture or form, and repeat it in your design.

Below: Instead of stopping with a spot of color, plant a sweep. The black-eyed Susans were planted as if they were painted by the stroke of a brush.

PITFALL #2: SOLDIERS

Don't arrange bedding plants like soldiers, arms length apart. When planting annuals, keep them fairly close together, usually about 3 to 4 inches apart. This way, they will fill out and cover the bare bed in the first month or so. This ideal spacing prevents competition between plants and will shade the soil to keep out weeds. The flowers grow together to present a seamless, unified appearance.

PITFALL #3: DUCKS IN A ROW

Avoid planting annuals in neat and tidy rows all in perfect alignment. Plant in a staggered grid. Set out the first row, and then position your second row behind the first, but aligned between the ones in front. The third row will be directly behind the first row and so forth. Use the length of your trowel, or a portion of it, as a gauge to keep the spacing constant.

PITFALL #4: PERFECTION

Don't make things too perfect. The difference between a home garden and a commercial one is typically the element of surprise. Garden designer Ruthie Lacey in Columbia, South Carolina, says, "I like to mass plants and use curves. But then I like to put one plant out of place, so it looks natural." Add a visual blip to the garden to keep it from becoming static. A pot placed in a bed gives an unexpected thrust of height. Flowers spilling into a walkway soften a hard edge.

PITFALL #5: SITE UNSEEN

Don't plant flowers where they just won't grow. Although many flowers are easy to grow, some locations are simply unsuitable for flowerbeds.

Deep shade. It is just impossible to grow flowers in the dense year-round shade beneath evergreen trees such as hemlocks or magnolias. Not only do flowers lack light, but they also are unable to compete with the dense mat of tree roots for the soil's nutrients. In these cases, ground covers offer an alternative. To add color, you can punctuate the planting with a container of shade-tolerant plants such as caladiums or impatiens.

Here are a few more tips to keep your border beautiful, while keeping work to a minimum.

Go for good design. Make your flowerbed big enough to give you all the color you want, but don't bite off more than you can chew. Remember, the more flowers you grow, the more care they'll demand. If you're strapped for time, grow only as many plants as you can easily attend to in 2 to 3 hours per week. This may mean a smaller bed than you originally intended, but don't be discouraged. Just place this smaller bed in a high-impact area. You'll get a big effect for considerably less work.

Watch your back. While most flower borders have open space in the front, consider designing space in the back as well. This will allow you to groom plants from either side. Make the bed wide enough so that plant's won't be crowded, but not so wide that you can't comfortably reach the center from either side. If you opt for a wider bed, place stepping stones within it so you can step into the bed and tend plants without crushing them.

Shape up. The shape of the flowerbed is as important as the size. A border fashioned from long, flowing curves or straight lines is easier to maintain than one formed by squiggles and dips.

On the edge. If the bed is adjacent to the lawn, separate them with a mowing strip—brick or stone paving laid level with the soil surface along the periphery of the bed. By running your lawnmower atop this paving, you can quickly edge the bed.

Water wisely. To reduce the amount of water needed for your flowers, select drought-tolerant plants. Many such plants are highlighted throughout this book. Also mulch your flowerbed with 2 to 3 inches of pine straw or shredded bark. Mulch helps the soil retain moisture. Of course, sooner or later you'll have to water. Do yourself a favor, and place a water outlet close to your flowerbed so you won't have to move hoses across the yard.

Make a stand. Tall flowers, such as lilies, gladioli, and asters, often require staking and tying, particularly after a rain. A less time-consuming option is to place grow-through plant supports or tomato cages over the tops of young plants. As the plants grow, their stems will rise through the wire frames and be supported. And leaves and flowers will camouflage most of the wire.

Steep slopes. They require some leveling before they are suitable for gardening. Retaining walls made of stone or brick can turn a troublesome slope into a beautiful garden wall. Once the retaining wall is completed, you can grow plants at the top of the wall—the drainage there is often perfect. Slopes that are not stabilized are best planted with ground covers that help control erosion.

secrets to a stress-free landscape

***Southern Living* Editor** John Floyd shares the secrets that he incorporated into his personal garden.

I am an avid gardener who doesn't have time to garden. So when we built a new house five years ago, it was time for a reality check. How can I have a beautiful yard, still basically do it myself, and balance work as well as family issues that always seem to cut into my gardening time? There were some simple solutions.

SECRET #1: Don't do everything at once. I developed the garden over a period of years. (Even after five growing seasons I have some rough areas.)

SECRET #2: Simplify the landscape. I concentrated my efforts where I receive maximum benefit and enjoyment.

After I hired a contractor to build a retaining wall, add soil to the garden, and install a fence, I was ready to make the 30 x 80 foot space my garden. With these elements in place, I could start thinking about planting.

SECRET #3: Plan your garden to be at its peak during the times you are outdoors the most. At our old home, we enjoyed the garden more in late April through June and again from mid-September through October.

SECRET #4: Always define your garden edge. With that in mind, I chose yellow daylilies to form the border. I knew I wanted a clear yellow lily that blooms all at once in late spring, but I needed help choosing a selection. André Viette, owner of André Viette Nursery in Fishersville, Virginia, recommended 100 Suzie Wong daylilies. They bloom late May to early June. When the flower stalks fade, I cut them off and have lush green foliage as my edge until frost each year.

Because I didn't have a lot of time and it was late in the planting season, I set out color behind the daylilies the first year. It was a mixture of 10 flats (640 plants) of melampodium and narrow-leaf zinnias, but that was too much work.

SECRET #5: Plant only a few annuals each season. As fall rolled around, I knew from a maintenance standpoint that I needed to limit annuals to a few plants each season. Most of my color would come from shrubs, perennials, and reseeding annuals.

In the fall I planted three flats (196 seedlings) of reseeding Alaska daisies. Randomly placed throughout the daisies are 64 foxglove seedlings. I also planted 5 (1-gallon) containers of Japanese iris, 25 lily bulbs, and 25 (4-inch) pots of 'Newport Pink' sweet Williams. I knew that I could depend on color year after year from the Japanese iris, lilies, daylilies, and reseeding daisies. So I could replant the foxgloves and sweet Williams each fall, fertilize them with Osmocote (14-14-14) at planting and again early each spring with perennial booster (9-12-12), and have an outstanding spring display. Now, my total planting time is a Saturday morning any time in fall after a killing frost.

SECRET #6: Vary plant selections from year to year. In the future when I have more time, I will set out several nursery flats of orange pansies. Additional all-season color comes from 'Flower Carpet' roses that are carefree except for regular fertilization and winter pruning.

As the garden transitions from spring to summer, the display moves from full-color to a green palette with splashes of color. Summer-flowering Oriental lilies and Queen Anne's lace create focal points, while a white crepe myrtle and butterfly bushes provide additional summer color. If I have time, I'll sow a few seed packs of zinnias for cutting.

As fall approaches, I depend on the 'Flower Carpet' roses and a mass of perennial asters along with some late-flowering crinum bulbs to provide the flower color. There is fall foliage color from the crepe myrtle and 'October Glory' red maples.

While I know that I might like a more refined garden, this is one I can manage with a couple of hours a week in spring and fall plus a few Saturday mornings throughout the year. It gives the avid gardener in me satisfaction and peace.

As the garden transitions from spring to summer, the display moves from full-color to a green palette with splashes of color.

Top: In late spring as the daisies and foxgloves fade, daylilies and Japanese iris become the flower show.

Left: Spikes of foxgloves break up the mass planting of daisies.

Above: Lilies dot the landscape in summer.

A vibrant grouping of tulips enhances a circle of boxwoods.

when bulbs don't bloom

Follow these tips to common bulb problems and soon your yard will be filled with beautiful blooms.

Moving flowering bulbs to a new location is an easy job and not harmful to the bulbs if done at the right time. In late spring, after the bulbs have finished blooming and the foliage is beginning to turn yellow and flop over, hold the leaves in one hand. Next, loosen the soil under them with a spading fork. Then, lift them up and out of the soil by the leaves. If you know where you want to plant them, they can be planted back that same day. Just shake off the dirt, carefully untangle the roots, and plant the bulbs three times their height and three times their width apart. If you have to wait until fall to plant them, dry them as quickly as possible using a fan, and store them over the summer in an area that is dry and has lots of ventilation.

Daffodils that don't seem to bloom like they used to are usually missing one of their four requirements—enough cold weather, plenty of sunlight, adequate water, and good nutrition.

The maturing trees around your bulbs may be providing more shade than they used to. For best results, daffodils need at least six to eight hours of sunlight a day after the leaves are on the trees. Don't cut the trees, but they can be limbed up, providing filtered light for a more successful bulb bed. Also, spring bulbs need regular nutrition. Your best bet is topdressing with a slow-release fertilizer in the fall, but if you forget to do that, apply a 5-10-20 water-soluble fertilizer in the spring. Bulbs need about 1 inch of rain while they are actively growing, so if you experience a spring drought, a good watering once a week, especially with a soaker hose, will make a difference in the next year's blooms.

Planting bulbs in the lawn is fun, but caring for the bulbs and having a nice lawn at the same time takes some planning. Choose bulbs that are short and early blooming. Crocuses are the perfect choice because they finish blooming long before the grass needs cutting, come in many colors, and even have grasslike leaves. To encourage a crocus to grow leaves and replenish the bulb for next year's bloom, you need to set your lawnmower blade at the very highest setting so the grass can be cut at 3 inches or higher. Cutting your grass in this manner for the first few times will also encourage the turf to produce deeper roots and make it more tolerant of summer droughts.

When tulips vanish from Upper and Middle South gardens, there are several possible reasons and solutions. Choose selections that are more likely to be perennial. Normally, Darwin hybrids, Kaufmannianas species, and Scheepers hybrids (large single late or tetraploid types) are superlative choices. Deep planting is a must. Soil pressure at 8 to 10 inches is greater than at 5 to 6 inches and helps to keep the bulbs from splitting apart too soon. Because voles (underground bulb munchers) seldom tunnel that deep, it also helps to protect the bulbs.

Spray your tulip bulbs with Ropel before you plant them in the fall to ensure your efforts will be rewarded in the spring. Automatic sprinkler systems and overwatering during the hot summer months may cause dormant tulip bulbs to rot. It's best to plant your tulips with sedum or other drought-tolerant plants, requiring you to water them less.

Short on garden space? Try This.

Why would anyone take a perfectly nice plant and flatten it against a wall? Known as espaliering, this technique is not the earmark of compulsive gardeners with too much time on their hands or some strange form of horticultural revenge.

Classic espaliers use fruit trees or red-berried pyracantha and cotoneaster, but few take advantage of flowering shrubs and trees. Espalier, especially simple forms such as this gently fanned camellia (pictured on the opposite page), is actually beneficial to a flowering shrub and easy to train and maintain.

Even in partial shade, such as beneath the eaves of your house, thinning and spreading out your camellia allows light to reach every part, not just the outer branches. The classic fan shape also encourages the flow of nutrients along the branches, because there's not quite as much gravity to fight. As a result, the shrub is more likely to bloom from top to bottom and at multiple points along each limb.

If this encourages you to brighten up your own bare walls with a camellia espalier, you'll be pleased to know that this is not a major project. All you need is some nearly invisible 16-gauge galvanized wire and a hammer and nails (for wood surfaces) or, preferably, eyebolts (for wood or masonry surfaces) and a drill with the appropriate bit. Eyebolts make the trellis sturdier and hold the wires out from the surface of the wall a bit to allow more air to circulate around the camellia plant.

Set evenly spaced eyebolts into the wall a little higher than you plan for your shrub to grow. You can either measure the width of

Espaliering a camellia's branches exposes more of the shrub to sunlight, increasing the number and effect of vivid flowers.

the space so that the bolts divide it precisely, or simply give it your best guess because the wire won't be obvious anyway. Then set a single eyebolt at the bottom of the wall, below the lowest point where you'll attach a branch of the camellia. This bolt should be roughly in the center of the space to be covered by the espalier. Thread your wire through the top and bottom eyebolts to create a fan pattern, and then twist the ends thoroughly to secure and tighten the wire.

That's all there is to it. You now have a wonderful wire fan trellis. You just need some soft jute twine (available at home or garden centers) to tie the branches to the wires, and you're ready to espalier. Oh, and you do need the camellia, of course.

Plant a young, flexible shrub between 12 and 24 inches from the wall (for growing room and better access to soil nutrients and water), and prune branches that are growing in inconvenient directions or refuse to be bound to the wires. As your camellia grows, continue to clip protruding branches, or secure them to the fan of wires, making sure to allow room in the espalier for good air movement and access to sunlight.

You will be amazed at the abundance of flowers you'll have with this simple training method, and your friends and neighbors will be impressed by your gardening expertise.

fix up the front with flowers

A new home and an older one get facelifts courtesy of a few beautiful blooms.

HELP FROM A FRIEND

Dollars are definitely Steve Bender's nearest and dearest friends. It pains him greatly to part with any of them. So when his colleague Charlie Thigpen discussed ways to jazz up the front of Steve's new house, his first question was, "This isn't going to cost much, is it?" As it turned out, it cost around $100. That's a pain he can live with.

The impetus for the project was twofold. First, the front of the house looked as naked as a jaybird—well, actually "nakeder," since a jaybird has feathers. They needed to visually anchor the house to the site. And second, the retaining wall on the side of the house provided the perfect venue for innocent toddlers to dive face-first onto the driveway. That needed fixing pronto.

A fence solved both problems. Steve chose a split-rail one because it would look less formal than a picket fence, wouldn't need painting, and could be curved to fit

BEFORE

Below: When the Benders moved in, the front of their new house looked bare. And Steve was concerned about toddlers falling off the high retaining wall onto the driveway below. A new cedar fence and flower border solved both problems nicely.

AFTER

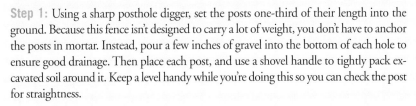

Constructing a fence like Steve's looks hard, but it's really easy. Our step-by-step instructions and the photos above and at right show you how.

Step 1: Using a sharp posthole digger, set the posts one-third of their length into the ground. Because this fence isn't designed to carry a lot of weight, you don't have to anchor the posts in mortar. Instead, pour a few inches of gravel into the bottom of each hole to ensure good drainage. Then place each post, and use a shovel handle to tightly pack excavated soil around it. Keep a level handy while you're doing this so you can check the post for straightness.

Step 2: Once the posts are set, attach the rails using 3½-inch lag bolts. Countersink the bolts so their heads won't protrude above the surface of the wood. Secure the lower rail about 2 feet above the ground and the upper one about 2 feet above that.

Step 3: Loop the copper tubing loosely around the post and rails, being careful not to bend it too sharply and crimp it.

Step 4: The copper will gradually develop a blue-green patina. To speed up the process, wipe on a liquid weathering compound, such as Maid O'Metal.

Step 5: The better the soil, the better your plants will grow. Steve's heavy clay soil needed to be amended. So he tilled in two (4 cubic-foot) bales of sphagnum peat moss, half a pickup truckload of topsoil, and half a pickup truckload of builder's sand.

Step 6: Stacked stones at the lower end of the bed keep rainwater from rushing down the front edge and washing the soil away.

the top of the wall. It would also furnish a pleasant background for flowers and a sturdy support for vines.

Charlie offered Steve some free Eastern red cedar rails and posts. This wood is great because it's rustic and slow to rot. You can substitute pressure-treated pine. You can also use Western red cedar. Use it for rails only—in the ground, it quickly rots.

After yanking up the Japanese hollies the builder had planted, they put up the fence in a single afternoon. Then Charlie came up with a wild idea—what if they wound flexible copper tubing around the fence to look like a grapevine?

They pressed one end into the soil next to a post, then curled the tubing around

the post and rails. To give the copper a weathered, blue-green patina overnight, Steve used an old rag to apply a liquid weathering compound he bought at an art-supply store.

It wasn't long before neighbors and passersby started scratching their heads in befuddlement.

"What you boys doin'?" asked a construction worker squinting from the window of his pickup.

"Oh, we just had a little problem installing our gas logs," Steve replied.

Steve's next-door neighbor inquired soon after. "What's with the copper tubing?"

"The washing machine is on the fritz," he said. "We're gonna hang laundry out here."

They didn't, of course, because they're respectable neighbors, as the new fence and garden prove. They dress up the front and deter accidental swan dives. Best of all, the whole thing cost Steve only 100 of his nearest and dearest friends.

SMALL HOME SHAPE UP

This tidy little house lacked charm and curb appeal but otherwise was in pretty good shape. A few problem areas needed to be addressed to make it more functional and attractive.

To begin with, there was no access from the driveway to the sidewalk, so you had to traipse through the yard to get to the front door. The spindly wrought iron railing on the porch looked dated, and the angular brick wall in front of the house was unattractive and served no purpose. Also, the downspout on the right side visually cut the house in two.

The landscape lacked personality as well. Sparse shrubs on the right side of the entry left the gas meter exposed. And without flowers, the front of the house was devoid of color.

Several small projects proved to be just what this house needed to spruce it up. The first order of business was to tear out the angular brick wall and then use the bricks to build a new, curving walk from the driveway to the front door.

The brick wall in front of the house was beginning to fall apart in places, so it was simple to knock down. Leaving some of the mortar on the bricks gives them an aged look.

A row of bricks set on their side creates a sweeping curved edging for the walk. Leftover and broken bricks were inset to form small patches of paving in the walk. Crushed stone fills in around the bricks and provides a hard-packed walking surface.

Next, the downspout on the right side of the large window was moved about 12 feet to the end of the house. But that left a hole in the gutter. A piece of tin sealed with silicon patches the hole nicely. This only took around 30 minutes to do. A large columnar growing 'Will Fleming' yaupon holly (*Ilex vomitoria* 'Will Fleming') camouflages the relocated downspout.

Replacing the wrought iron railing with a wooden railing and column updates the entry. The column, fashioned from a 6 x 6 with a little trim, makes a substantial support for the front porch. And 2 x 4s routed on the edges provide sturdy handrails. Pickets secure the steps and landing. Staining the new wood gray gives a fresh, clean look.

An iron crest added over the porch and iron pieces on the column lend character. Lots of garden shops sell old ironwork, and it looks great in the garden. Little touches like this give a house personality.

After the house and walk started taking shape, it was time to concentrate on the

Below: A little landscaping and an updated porch give this small house a big facelift.

BEFORE

AFTER

Above: New plants, a new walk, and an updated porch make this home more attractive and accessible. **Left:** Built with brick salvaged from the original wall, a gently curving path leads from the porch to the driveway. **Below:** This arbor topped with a red birdhouse creates a climbing surface for vines and a nice entry for guests.

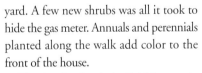

yard. A few new shrubs was all it took to hide the gas meter. Annuals and perennials planted along the walk add color to the front of the house.

The simple arbor is the finishing touch. It makes you feel as if you're entering a garden instead of a yard. The rapidly growing, tropical bleeding-heart vine *(Clerodendrum thomsoniae)* planted at the base of the arbor creates a colorful entry. Small climbing roses will eventually cover the structure.

It takes a little time and money to dress up a front yard, but improvements will make you feel proud every time that you pull into the driveway. It's also fun watching your neighbors strain their necks as they drive by trying to figure out what you're going to do next.

what to do with an unsightly side yard

Two homeowners share the secrets behind the gorgeous gardens they created on the side.

PUT IT ON THE LINE

The side yard may be the most overlooked spot on your property. But it doesn't have to be that way. Take a look at the garden Sherry Dahrling of Chattanooga, Tennessee, grows in the sliver of soil bordering her driveway.

It wasn't always inviting. When Sherry first started working on her side yard, it wasn't much more than a continuation of her neighbor's yard. The scene from her driveway, where family and friends formed their first impressions, was a grand view of the neighbor's swing set. But that didn't deter Sherry. She merely designed her own scalloped picket fence to grace the

BEFORE

property line. Though the fence isn't tall enough to provide total privacy, it neatly defines the side yard. A gate leads to the neighbor's yard, keeping things friendly.

Below: A fence built inside the property line left room for planting dogwoods along the back side. Annuals and perennials give the area color.

AFTER

Sherry saw the sloping soil as an asset. Filling it with flowers, she turned the empty bank into a gallery of color. Lilies, iris, and annuals thrive there. Dogwoods add a leafy canopy above the fence. A rusty, old bicycle propped beside the gate adds a touch of whimsy. Sherry lined its basket with sphagnum moss and potting soil and turned it into a planter.

Now the first thing visitors see when they drive up is a charming garden. It's worth a second look.

A NARROW ESCAPE

The owners of narrow lots know we're supposed to do something with the front yard and backyard. It's those narrow walk-through spaces on the side that stymie us; but they offer potential for an intimate and favorite garden retreat. It's all in the planning—as this charming Columbia, South Carolina, courtyard shows (pictured on page 74).

Duplex owners Billisue Hayes and Warren Light garden the area around the house. They had already developed the rest of the site. Only this narrow side yard remained. "I called it the last frontier because it was the last part of the garden we did,

Above: An old bicycle basket elevates flowers to new heights. **Below:** Oriental lilies find a home in the side yard.

side yard savvy

Don't be afraid to close in the side yard. Fences, trees, and evergreen shrubs can help define a narrow space and establish privacy.

Use your privacy screen as a background for added interest up front. Pathways, flowers, ground covers, and shrubs will focus attention on your side of the property.

Pay attention to the angle from which the area is seen. You may view it most often from a driveway, from the backyard, or from a window within your house. Add a flowering tree, bench, or sculpture to the most visible spot so you can enjoy it.

and it was so barren," recalls Billisue.

They put a lot of thought into what they wanted. They had measured it, made several conceptual drawings, and bought an old olive jar to use as a fountain, but many questions remained. It was time to

call in a professional to help site the patio and fountain, to define the boundary between side garden and back garden, and to handle the level change between the front and back.

Landscape architect George Betsill came

AFTER

BEFORE

Above: The owners' favorite retreat is enclosed by brick walls and planted with several types of hydrangeas. Creeping fig cloaks the house, and lush ferns frame the entrance where a bronze frog stands sentinel. An antique jar-turned-fountain serves as a focal point.

a **garden** *fountain*

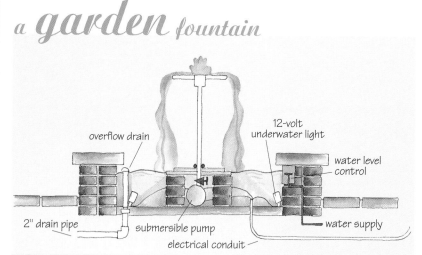

overflow drain

12-volt underwater light

water level control

2" drain pipe

submersible pump

electrical conduit

water supply

to the rescue, helping with the siting and the sizing of the 12-foot-square patio and the fountain pool, which measures 3½ feet square. He accommodated the change of level from front to back by placing a step just outside the gated entrance and used a knee-high brick wall with a 4-foot opening

to separate the courtyard garden from the one in back. By extending the low brick wall around the back garden in the form of raised planting beds, he provided plenty of seating and at the same time added an extra dimension to an almost flat lot.

With the hardscape in place, Billisue and

Warren selected plantings to suit their lifestyles. Early mornings, nights, and weekends are the primary times they use this garden. The cool color scheme of white, blue, and yellow glows at night. Variegated plants and mixed textures work well in the mostly shaded area.

Right: Antique wrought iron gates create an irresistible invitation into this courtyard. Aspidistra frames the entrance, while the foliage of elephant's-ears gives a tropical feel.

Bottom right: Ferns, hostas, hardy orchids, violets, and Lenten roses mix well with variegated plants such as coleus.

"We call this the hydrangea room," says Billisue, referring to the dominant plants here, including oakleaf, 'Nikko Blue,' 'Sister Theresa,' and variegated lace cap hydrangeas that contribute a long season of blue and white. The large foliage of elephant's-ears and yellow cannas add to the color theme and create a tropical feeling.

Layers of vines provide texture in narrow planting beds. In front of the wall covered in creeping fig, they planted fatshedera in one place and English ivy in another, adding a rich evergreen effect. In summer, annual or deciduous vines such as moon vine, potato vine, and hybrid clematis add flowers and more layers of color and texture. White wax begonias are used as fillers among perennials. A Japanese maple holds down one corner of the courtyard garden.

The fountain, designed by local water and lighting expert Glenn Clonts, is the undisputed feature of the garden. The lovely antique olive jar rests in its quiet pool as smooth sheets of water spill over the sides, mimicking the sound of a murmuring brook (see illustration at left). Lighting makes the fountain even more enchanting.

Warren enjoys the garden early in the morning while it's cool. Billisue loves to bring her dinner out because it's so peaceful. "I also love to read the paper here early on Sundays," she says.

Careful planning and the gardeners' personal choices make this hideaway a success. The antique wrought iron gates, found at an auction and adapted for the opening, hint that this is a special place. From the street, you are lured by the fragrance of a tea olive hedge along the side property line. Now step up to the gates and, with the sound of the fountain beckoning, look down the lushly planted walk. If the gate is ajar, who can resist going in for a peek?

a flower garden solves a common parking problem

A little hidden garden enhances a turn-around addition to a narrow drive.

Margaret Deimling's secret garden isn't around back. It's right in front of the house. But to see it, you have to walk a few steps up the driveway. It's all part of an ingenious solution to a common parking problem.

Her previous narrow driveway ran straight into the garage under the house. Cars that pulled in couldn't turn around—they had to slowly back out. So Atlanta landscape architect Bill Smith cut into the slope in front of the house and added a turnaround and

BEFORE

AFTER

guest parking area. Then he designed a small flower garden that's the first thing Margaret sees when she opens her front door.

But you can't see this sunken garden from the street. It sits about 4 feet below the front lawn. Only the top of a brick retaining wall hints at its presence—that and the blooms of 'New Dawn' roses peeking over the wall in spring.

Detail is everything in a garden this small. Bill didn't miss a trick. Here are some of the highlights.

• At the head of the turnaround, the brick landing ties together the retaining walls and new front steps.

• The white Chippendale bench that is placed against the brick wall matches the porch railing. It also acts as a focal point when you look down from the top of the steps.

• Dyed concrete in the driveway complements the colors of the house while also reducing glare.

Above: Cutting into the slope in front of the house allowed the construction of a new turnaround and guest parking area, plus a sunken garden hidden from the street.

Opposite, bottom: Imagine this much privacy without even a fence. Only the roses are visible from the street beyond. The Chippendale bench repeats the look of the porch railing.

• A strong backbone of evergreen shrubs and ground covers lends year-round visual interest.

Margaret's garden is such a hit with her neighbors that it won't be a secret long. "We live in a neighborhood where people walk a lot," she says. "And whenever I'm out in the yard, people always stop and tell me how much they love to look at the flowers."

small garden projects

great ideas for weekends

make flowers multiply

If you want to add to your plants without subtracting from your bank account, follow these techniques for propagating your plants by dividing, rooting, and layering.

Dividing

Above: Siberian iris *(Iris sibirica)* grow so thick after several years that they may begin to decline. Division invigorates them and provides plants for new flowerbeds.

1) Dig up a clump and wash or shake the soil from the roots. The roots can be teased apart by gently pulling. Some roots need to be cut apart.

2) Before you divide and transplant a plant, be sure that each division has young, viable roots (such as these rhizomes) and green, growing stems.

3) Plant the new divisions at a wider spacing. Look at the coloration on the shoots to determine how deep they were growing; replant them at a similar depth.

Divide these: **Hosta   Ajuga   Perennial phlox   Daylily   Iris**

Root Cuttings

Above: This autumn-flowering Mexican salvia *(Salvia mexicana)* is not easy to find in local nurseries. Like most salvias, its cuttings root quickly. Take cuttings in the fall so you can replant next spring.

2) Cut a few stems from the plant; then cut these stems into sections with two nodes each. A node is the point where a leaf attaches and where new shoots and roots emerge. Throw away the top-most cutting; it is too succulent and will wilt.

Root these: **Hydrangea   Rosemary**

1) Use a clean plastic pot; clay pots dry too quickly. Also, purchase a fine-textured, sterile potting mix labeled for starting seeds. Potting mixes that contain a lot of bark or sand dry rapidly. Ones with sphagnum peat and vermiculite hold moisture longer.

Above: Sprays of the polyantha rose called 'The Fairy' appear from spring until frost, making this little rose a favorite for gardeners to share. Although it can be propagated by rooting, layering is also effective.

1) Select a stem long enough and flexible enough to bend down and touch the soil. At the point where the stem contacts the soil, scrape off a bit of bark but leave the stem attached to the mother plant.

3) Remove the lower leaves so the nodes can be placed into the soil. Place four to five cuttings in a pot to form a multi-stemmed plant. Water the pot daily and place it in a shaded location until you see new shoots.

2) Mound soil over the wounded stem. Then lay a small rock or brick over the stem to hold it in place. In two to three months, remove the rock and give the stem a gentle tug. If you meet with resistance, the plant has rooted.

3) Use a trowel to lift the rooted portion, then cut the stem away from the mother plant. Pot the young plant, relocate it to another section of the garden, or share your good fortune with a friend.

Boxwood   Azalea   Fig   Salvia   *Layer these:* **Verbena   Forsythia   English ivy   Polyantha rose**

improve your soil for strong plants

Whether you're a seasoned gardener or just a beginner, one simple truth remains—the better your soil, the better your garden.

It's true. Good soil absolutely means lusher growth, less fertilizing, fewer pests, and stronger plants. Chris McDaniel found this out when he decided to redo the foundation planting in front of his house. His kindly builder had stripped away every ounce of original topsoil, and then generously applied a compacted layer of red clay subsoil over the entire yard. Plastic plants might have done okay in that stuff, but it's safe to say the living ones wouldn't be living for long.

Chris wanted to yank out all the old, scraggly plants and start over that summer. Then he decided to wait until fall. It is an ideal time for planting in most of the South, because while plants stop growing up top, down below they're still working on roots. By the time next spring rolls around, they have a head start on trees and shrubs planted in spring.

When starting out with awful soil, you have three options—dig out and replace the original soil (which can be both time-consuming and expensive); build raised beds filled with new soil atop the original soil; or improve the original soil. Chris chose the last option.

Chris's front beds extend out about 20 feet on either side of the steps. His first order of business was bringing in a truck filled with good topsoil and spreading half on each side of the steps. One tip for beginners—know the source of the topsoil and/or inspect it before you order it. You want good, clean, loose, dark earth—not clay, rocks, branches, and trash. Never substitute uncomposted cow or horse manure, unless you want seedlings of everything the animal ate coming up in your yard.

Topsoil isn't enough by itself. It usually lacks the organic matter that most plants crave. So Chris added sphagnum peat moss—about 1 (4-cubic-foot) bale for every 30 square feet of bed. Composted manure is an acceptable alternative. Some folks substitute pine bark, but it's not good to use it up against the house. Wood attracts termites, and you'd just as soon they schedule their picnic at somebody else's place.

After using a hard rake to spread the peat moss, Chris next added the final ingredient—sand. He spread 3 to 4 (40-pound) bags on each side of the steps. Though sand is inert, it loosens soil and aids aeration and drainage, as does organic matter. And when dealing with clay soil, good aeration and drainage are just what the gardener ordered.

Now it was time to mix together the topsoil, peat moss, and sand. Chris rented a heavy-duty power tiller for the job. These machines can be a handful to control, but Chris is a big, very macho guy. (Just ask him.) However, smaller tillers, weighing as little as 25 pounds, are readily available and more easily operated.

Blessed with practically perfect soil, Chris was now ready to plant trees and shrubs—and not a single one was plastic.

Above: High-quality topsoil is loose, crumbly, and brown. It shouldn't contain trash, clay, rocks, or limbs.
Above, right: Sphagnum peat moss is a good source of organic matter, which loosens heavy soil and enriches it.
Right: Tilling in sand improves aeration and drainage, making it easier for roots to grow.

add instant color
with annuals

Add some color to your yard this weekend. These tried-and-true tips will help you get great results.

When people buy annuals in flats or cell packs they tend to select ones that are tall and flowering. These two traits can mean that plants have been left in their flats too long. When this happens, annuals can't grow outward and spread, so they stretch for the sun and become spindly.

When selecting plants, choose short, stocky, nonblooming ones. If you wait too late in the season and have to buy leggy plants, here's what to do.

It's hard to tell someone who has purchased 10- or 12-inch blooming plants to cut them back to 3 or 4 inches and remove all the colorful flowers. But this will actually benefit overgrown plants. By cutting them back you eliminate the topgrowth, promote low branching, and encourage fullness.

Inspect the roots. Thick, matted roots should be separated with your fingers. Loosening these compacted masses will help them spread into the soil more readily.

Now your annuals are ready to be planted. Simply dig a generous hole in a prepared bed with a trowel or small pick. Set your plant in the hole at the same depth it was growing in the cell pack. Press the soil around your plant firmly, but do not pack it.

Water thoroughly until the root ball and surrounding soil are totally soaked. Repeat every couple of days for a few weeks, and then slowly wean plants so you'll have to water only once weekly.

To give your plants a boost, fertilize with liquid 20-20-20 or top-dress with a slow-release granular fertilizer, such as 12-6-6. When using a granular fertilizer, keep it off the plant's foliage. Water the fertilizer into the soil, and wash it off leaves immediately after it has been applied. Fertilizer left on leaves or stems will burn and kill plants.

Mulch and weed. Mulch makes your plants look better and keeps moisture in and weeds out.

Above: The bottom plant in this photo has a well-developed root system. If plants are root bound like the one on top, loosen and break apart the roots before planting.

Above: This flat of narrow-leaf zinnia has grown leggy from being in a constricting cell pack too long. If you plant them like this, you'll be disappointed.

Above: Cut annuals back before planting, and they will later develop into full, flowering adults. Plants also go through less shock when set out in the garden.

protect your pansies from the big chill

There are projects for the winter, too. The season's main challenge is to stay healthy. Life is no easier for pansies. These garden jewels suffer the ills of unpredictable weather as much as we do and can struggle to hold their flower heads high.

These plants flourish with moderation—when temperatures balance between the 30s and 40s. They need sunny days with a minimum of four hours direct sunlight. But winter has fickle habits, with temperatures that change dramatically from noon to nightfall and cold gray rain that seems to last a lifetime. These unpredictable patterns can cause healthy pansies to become stressed. Here are preventions, symptoms, and sure-cure remedies to help them through midwinter blues.

A BIG CHILL

Occasional warm days lure pansies into a false sense of spring. They produce new leaves and bloom profusely. Then the thermometer threatens to drop rapidly, way below freezing. Pansies need help to cope with the fast change. First, head into the garden; remove all the flowers, and bring them indoors for miniature bouquets. Then cover the plants with a light pine straw blanket. Use enough to insulate plants and soil, but don't flatten plants with excessive straw. When the thermometer is again above freezing, pull back the pine straw to expose the foliage to warm sunlight.

Even with pine straw, damage may occur. This is evident when yellow leaves appear at the base of the plants. Pinch or clip off all discolored or mushy leaves, and put them in the trash to prevent further decay and bacteria.

FEED THE COLD

Lack of sunshine stops flower production. When winter skies stay gray for weeks at a time, pansies go into hibernation. Remove all spent blooms, and

CONTAINER CARE

Pansies in pots suffer cold damage faster than those in the ground. Take these precautions to minimize problems when the weather gets tough.

- Cluster pots against the house for wind protection.
- Carry lightweight containers into an unheated garage for severely cold evenings.
- Water containers prior to a hard freeze.
- Large pots can be protected with a plastic trash bag. Tuck the bag's edges under the pot for a snug fit. Do not allow foliage to come in contact with the plastic. Remove it early in the morning, before sunlight heats the plastic.

Mix-and-Match Pansies

Pansies are true garden friends. They face winter head-on, and they hang with us Southerners from autumn through spring. But the sweetest side of these faithful flowers is the colors they offer through dreary winter months.

With so many choices, it's difficult not to want some of each. The challenge is to choose the best shades for your landscape. Make your own mix with the flowers on this page before you visit the nursery. Follow our tips to achieve the perfect look for your home.

Tip 1: Choose one dominant color. Take your cues from the surrounding structures and landscape. Whether it matches your house or trim paint or contrasts completely, that color is the beginning of the relationship with all other additions.

This beautiful blend illustrates how good color can be. 'Imperial Antiques Shades' is the dominant color, with 'Crystal Bowl Rose' and 'True Blue' added for depth.

color for softness. For example, a bed of bright yellow pansies can be blinding. Add soft yellow to the mix and the look is still cohesive, but it is easier on the eyes.

Tip 3: For a casual, mixed-color collection, add one or two different pansies to the dominant choice. More than three colors can become visually confusing.

Tip 4: Blue and purple are the graceful bridge between all other colors. Used solo, they recede and become lost in the landscape. But they have the ability to pull other unrelated colors together. Place a soft yellow pansy next to a rosy one. The colors don't clash but are also not exciting. Add a purple blossom, and watch how the trio comes alive.

Tip 5: Consider pansies with the dark blotch, such as 'Maxim' and 'Majestic Giant,' as two-tone blooms. A bed of 'Majestic Giant' yellow flowers is a mass of yellow and black. With the addition of one other blotched blossom, perhaps 'Majestic Giant' blue or purple, the combination presents itself as three colors. The yellow and blue are the primary and secondary colors, with the dark blotch as the third.

When incorporating other colors, use more of this principal shade. In a brick home, choose pansies that bring out the best of its base tone. Some bricks are red-orange, some can be pink, and others gray.

Tip 2: A one-tone planting presents a formal appearance. To keep things simple but less dressy, add different shades of the same

'Crystal Bowl,' 'Maxim,' and 'Imperial' pansies are widely available and offer many shades for a varied color palette.

give them a fertilizer boost. Feed weekly with a liquid fertilizer such as 15-30-15 to stimulate roots and to produce new leaves and flowers. Continue this routine until winter weather stabilizes, usually by late February.

THE WARM SIDE

We take such delight in those wonderful, balmy days during winter, and pansies do also. But continuous unseasonably warm weather brings its own set of problems. A growth spurt produces tender

stems, new leaves, and blooms like there's no tomorrow. Then the aphids arrive, with a feeding frenzy on every inch of lush new growth.

Act fast to save plants from these invaders. First, remove mulch that inhibits air circulation. Then saturate the leaves and buds with insecticidal soap. Pinch back leggy growth, and place insect-infested clippings in the trash. Once cool weather returns, feed pansies with a liquid fertilizer such as 20-20-20 to help them recover.

prepare flower beds for staking

Staking each stem is impractical, but support is a must to keep some flowers standing tall. With bamboo garden stakes and twine, you can create an attractive web to hold stems in place.

Few things are prettier than a flowerbed chock-full of zinnias or cosmos. Seeded directly into the soil, these annuals become a blooming carpet. But with summer's first shower, their heads become heavy with rainwater, and the blooms end up facedown in the dirt. With bamboo garden stakes and twine, you can create an attractive web to hold stems in place.

After preparing the soil for planting, install the support system. Arrange the garden stakes throughout the bed in a grid pattern or randomly if the bed is irregular. Allow only a foot between stakes, and push them deeply into the soil.

Tie one end of the garden twine to a bamboo stake, about a foot above the soil

Top: The second layer of twine provides support to flowers. **Above:** Wrap twine around each stake; then move on to the next. **Right:** Bamboo garden stakes and twine keep plants upright.

surface. Wrap it once around the pole to secure, and move on to the next. Weave between the supports, crisscrossing to create a web. Keep the string fairly taut, but avoid making it too tight as this will pull the stakes over. Repeat the process, starting about 2 feet above the soil surface. When you are finished, plant your flowers. Reach between the webbing to sprinkle and cover seeds, taking care not to poke yourself on the stakes. As the new flowers emerge, they will work themselves into the web.

Use the maze of bamboo stakes to add a whimsical dimension to your garden. In the large photo on the opposite page, colorful glazed ceramic spheres, that were found at a flea market, were placed on some of the stakes. They bobbed gracefully above the blooms, adding another shape as well as more colors to the bed. They were also a constant reminder to be careful of the pole ends when bending over to cut flowers.

The same effect can be achieved using plastic foam balls and spray paint. Use only one size with a single paint color, or go all out varying both the sizes and hues. The foam spheres should last through the summer season.

When the flowers reach their full summer stature, it's time to assess the height of the stakes. If the blooms do not come above the tops of the bamboo, use heavy-duty pruners to cut the stakes to the desired height.

Summer showers are rarely gentle, and the strongest stems can't stand a watery beating. Staking keeps flowers on their feet.

CREATIVE STAKING FOR CONTAINERS

If you've ever forced paperwhites you've probably watched their stems lengthen and the buds open. Shortly thereafter the stems and foliage begin to lean, and the flowers do a nosedive on the dining room table. Here are a few ways to avoid the dreaded flop.

Search around your yard for natural materials that can be used to create artistic-looking forms and structures. Common plants and vines such as elaeagnus, bamboo, wisteria, and grapevine make ideal

Above: Forms of elaeagnus, bamboo, and vine are simple to make and offer attractive, inexpensive toppings for emerging bulbs.

supports for top-heavy paperwhites. These props can actually enhance the looks of your containers by adding interest to winter's favorite forced fragrance. It's easy to loop, bend, or gently twist supple branches and vines over and around pots. Thin-gauge wire will come in handy holding the structures together.

The popular shrub elaeagnus (*Elaeagnus* sp.) is an excellent choice for creative staking because it has long, flexible, whiplike shoots. Copper-colored stems and silver-backed leaves also make elaeagnus an attractive material to work with.

Use vines, such as wisteria, honeysuckle, and grapevine, to loosely encircle the paperwhites. The brown horizontal lines contrast nicely with the vertical green lines

of the paperwhites. Once plants grow tall, they will gently lean on their viny boundaries.

Multiple loops of bamboo create a lovely dome shape over the top of a pot. Bend freshly harvested bamboo or cane to form a U-shape. Push the two ends into the soil along the sides of the container. These graceful yet sturdy arches will keep leaning flowers upright. Bamboo can also be used to build little tepees; small vines wrapped around the bamboo will support the flowers.

Forcing bulbs to bloom is a gratifying way to garden in the winter. Give the plants as presents or use them as a wonderful centerpiece for your table. Just don't let them lie down on the job.

give your mailbox a makeover

True, a mailbox can be a purely functional contraption. A simple black metal box on a pole will get the job done. But for most suburbanites, the mailbox is the first thing guests see when they drive up. It creates that first impression of your home. It can extend a warm, welcoming invitation or give them the cold shoulder. With a mailbox as plain as ours, even the mail carrier was tempted to drive by without stopping. Flowers give the area an updated look.

We began by clearing out the weeds around our old mailbox. Because the area was invaded with nutgrass, we first pulled the weeds, waited a week until the tender new sprouts appeared, and then sprayed them with a nonselective herbicide. We were careful to avoid spraying the existing Carolina jessamine (*Gelsemium sempervirens*), which was attempting to wind its way up the old mailbox.

Next, we dug around the existing corner bed, expanding it and creating a clean border edge. Then, using a garden fork to turn over the soil, we mixed in a little leaf mold to improve it. It's wise to measure the bed and sketch it out to estimate how many plants can fit in the space. Browsing through some garden magazines and books gave us clues of the plants we wanted. We looked for plants that would blend together well, not require much watering or other maintenance, and not block the view of the street from the driveway.

Ornamental grass makes a nice backdrop, and we liked the maiden grass (*Miscanthus sinensis* 'Gracillimus') in particular. Because some varieties of maiden grass grow as tall as 9 feet, we were careful to select a smaller variety and use it at the back so it wouldn't dominate the scene or obstruct the view. We decided some type of small evergreen, stepping down in

BEFORE

Above: Before, this mailbox extended a frightful greeting to arriving guests.
Opposite: Voilà! After the quick makeover, our mailbox presents a new attitude that has neighbors doing a double-take.

height, would stand out in front of the grasses and give the planting an accent during the winter. For added punch, we placed them in terra-cotta pots.

The existing Carolina jessamine vine climbing the post was a good idea, but because it was struggling to survive, we bought another one. The long blooming season and drought resistance of 'Autumn

Joy' sedum also attracted us. It is irresistible to bees, so if you are allergic to bee stings, consider another flowering perennial. We decided that a few 'Little Bunny' dwarf fountain grasses (*Pennisetum alopecuroides* 'Little Bunny') by the street would harmonize well with the taller maiden grasses at the back. Both grasses are drought resistant, and the tufted plumes look attractive as they emerge in mid-summer and last through winter as dried arrangements. For some color, we left small areas (approximately 2 x 3 feet) on either side of the mailbox for seasonal annuals.

We made a list for hardware (see page 90). With a plan and a list in hand, we visited a local home improvement center where we found nearly everything we needed. We also grabbed a rusted metal-and-glass firefly that was on sale. For annuals, we selected drought-resistant Mexican heather (*Cuphea hyssopifolia*), which features small but numerous purple flowers.

The store did not stock the dwarf grasses or specimen evergreens, so our next stop was a specialized landscape nursery that helped us complete our list. When we spied the bright green, relaxed branches of a compact Hinoki false cypress (*Chamaecyparis obtusa* 'Filicoides'), we knew we had found our specimen evergreens. The nursery confirmed that they are slow growing

AFTER

and make good container plants, although they require more watering than our other plants. We also bought a small copper vase as a finishing touch for the front of our post. It was time to head home and begin the real work.

With some difficulty, we pulled out the old, well-anchored mailbox and then cleaned out the hole with a posthole digger. If you select a wooden post as we did, dig deep enough to allow for a few inches of concrete in the bottom of the hole so it will not sit directly on soil. According to U.S. Postal standards, the bottom of your mailbox should be 42 to 48 inches from the road surface. When you have the hole at the proper depth, add a few inches of concrete mix; then set your post in. Gradually add water and concrete mix to create a thick mixture that will support the post. Use a level to check the front and side of the stake to ensure it is not leaning in either direction. If your concrete mix is too wet and the post won't remain vertical, you can nail scrap lumber to it for support until the concrete mix hardens.

Next, we added the copper post cap, brass house numbers, copper tubing, decorative copper vase, and the firefly. The copper tubing is sold in prepackaged coils, so we merely had to unwrap it, stretch it out, and wind it around the post. We then drilled a small hole at the top and nailed it to the top of the post. The bottom simply rests on the ground. With the hardware in place, we turned our attention to the plants.

First, we set the three concrete stepping stones in a semicircle behind the mailbox to use as stable bases for the potted Hinoki false cypresses. Next, we planted the three maiden grasses at the back. Although they were modest in size when restricted to their 3-gallon nursery containers, by late summer they filled out and peeked over the cypresses. Next, we added the jessamine and wound the streamer-like branches up our copper tubing. Three sedums went in the three corners, and the four 'Little Bunny' fountain grasses were staggered between the mailbox and the street. The two unplanted spaces were filled with the annual Mexican heather. We finished up with a 3- to 4-inch layer of pine straw mulch, and then gave all of the plants a thorough watering.

Now, instead of a mailbox that is the scourge of the neighborhood, we have the best dressed mailbox around, if we do say so ourselves.

SHOPPING LIST

- mailbox
- mailbox post
- copper post cap
- 1-inch nails
- 2 (40-pound) bags of quick-setting concrete mix (If you have a strong back, the 80-pound bag is a better buy.)
- house numbers (Screws should be included.)
- soft copper tubing (for a decorative twist)
- three terra-cotta urns
- one 2.5 cubic-foot bag of potting soil
- three 12-inch concrete stepping stones (large enough to support urns)
- one bale pine straw mulch

TOOLS YOU WILL NEED

- posthole digger
- level
- hammer
- drill and a ⁵⁄₆₄-inch metal drill bit
- screwdriver

to get this look

A maiden grass
B 'Autumn Joy' sedum
C annuals (Mexican heather)
D Urns with Hinoki false cypress set on stepping stones
E 'Little Bunny' dwarf fountain grass
F Carolina jessamine

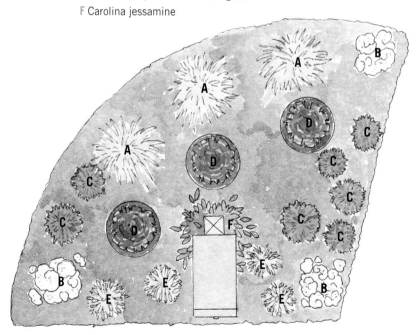

Step 1: A posthole digger is a valuable tool for this project. It allows you to dig a deep enough hole for the post in a fairly short amount of time.

Step 2: These smaller bags of concrete mix cost a few pennies more than the larger bags, but your back will thank you. You just add water directly to the hole and mix it with a shovel.

Step 3: After pouring and mixing the concrete, check your post to be sure it is level. Check it periodically until the concrete sets.

Step 4: Use plain concrete stepping stones to give your urns a stable base in the newly turned soil.

create a butterfly garden

Using scrounged plants, existing beds, and a few flats of annuals, you can make your garden attractive to these winged beauties in a weekend.

This homeowner was quickly growing tired of her all-green herb garden. Her good friend had grown tired of caring for her many containers of garden flowers. So they came up with a quick solution—this homeowner used her friend's extra pots to give life and color to her garden.

STEP 1:

They watered the garden the night before they were going to plant, so pulling up the mint and weeds was fairly easy.

STEP 2:

They'd decided to train a coral honeysuckle *(Lonicera sempervirens)* on the privacy fence as a backdrop for the butterfly garden. They stretched a piece of string between two nails to act as a level guide for the bottom of the trellis. Using a cordless drill, they drilled holes at roughly even intervals across the top and bottom of one panel of the privacy fence and up its two sides. Small eyebolts were screwed into the holes, using a pair of pliers. Then they threaded copper wire through the eyebolts and crossed it over and under itself to form a grid pattern. Two rolls of wire were all they needed.

Above: A butterfly rests on 'Buddy' Gomphrena.
Opposite: A variety of flowers attracts butterflies to this charming garden.

STEP 3:

Before adding some finely ground pine bark on top of the soil, they planted the large (5-gallon) coral honeysuckle in front of the trellis and tied its longest tendrils gently to the wire with soft pieces of jute. A lavender-flowered butterfly bush in a 3-gallon pot also went in at the back part of the bed, where it would have lots of room to grow and bloom. They planted three 1-gallon containers each of coreopsis, purple coneflower, and dwarf pomegranate, to establish the garden's perennial bones.

STEP 4:

They got a few flats of dwarf purple gomphrena and white narrow-leaf zinnia to fill in the edges and gaps. They set out the remaining small pots of flowers more or less where they'd be planted. After a few adjustments, they watered everything and stopped for the day.

STEP 5:

They chose a soaker hose to serve as the irrigation system. A Y-splitter valve is attached to the faucet outside the back door. A normal 25-foot hose leads from one side of the valve discreetly along the fence and up

BEFORE

AFTER

Top, left: An overgrown herb garden was the perfect spot for the butterfly garden.
Above: The finished garden at the end of May is full of blooms.
Left: Use string to train a coral honeysuckle on the privacy fence.

MATERIALS LIST

- gloves
- hammer and 2 long nails
- cordless drill
- eyebolts or nails
- pliers
- copper or galvanized wire
- jute string
- shovel
- Y-splitter valve
- 25-foot regular hose
- 50-foot soaker hose
- trowels
- fertilizer
- 8 bags of soil conditioner
- shallow pan with gravel

to the edge of the butterfly bed. The 50-foot soaker hose is attached to it and winds through the plants.

STEP 6:

They scattered fertilizer liberally around the beds, following the label directions. Then they spread 8 bags of ground-up pine bark labeled as "soil conditioner" for an all-purpose planting medium and mulch. The soaker hose vanished beneath the avalanche, and in no time at all the beds looked full, clean, and well-groomed.

STEP 7:

They'd finished the work that required tromping heavily through the beds, so they carefully tucked in all the little plants in cell-packs and 4-inch containers. Zinnias, gomphrena, lamb's ears, more pineapple sage,

more lantana, lots of basil for their pesto requirements, dwarf lavender pentas, and blue scabiosa were popped out of their containers and into the ground. The fine bark could be scooped aside with fingers or a trowel, then quickly smoothed back over each little root ball. This process also helped mix the fertilizer into the bark as they dug around in it. When finished planting, they turned on the soaker hose for deep watering and used the other hose to wash down the brick edging and themselves.

STEP 8:

They set out a saucer half full of sand and gravel, with enough water to keep it moist and to give the butterflies a place to drink.

They later hung some iron artwork to add interest to the fence until the butterfly bush matured. In late August, the

OUR TOP 10 PLANTS THAT ATTRACT BUTTERFLIES

1. black-eyed Susan (*Rudbeckia* sp.)
2. butterfly bush (*Buddleia davidii*)
3. butterfly weed (*Asclepias tuberosa*)
4. mist flower (*Eupatorium* sp.)
5. globe amaranth
   (*Gomphrena globosa*)
6. lantana (*Lantana* sp.)
7. Mexican sunflower
   (*Tithonia rotundifolia*)
8. pentas (*Pentas lanceolata*)
9. purple coneflower
   (*Echinacea purpurea*)
10. summer phlox (*Phlox paniculata*)

Above: Pineapple sage was included among zinnias, gomphrena, and lamb's ears.
Top, right: Butterfly bush. **Right:** Swamp milkweed.

basil, zinnias, and any other leggy plants got a haircut. They came back fat and happy, and also increased in bloom until the first frost hit in December. The visiting butterflies so far have included sulphur yellows, various skippers, swallowtails, monarchs, painted ladies, and fritillaries.

plants at a glance

the facts on flowers

'Annabelle' Hydrangea

From boring to beautiful in three easy steps. That may sound like an ad for a charm school, but it's also a good description of how to make a shady corner of your yard sparkle. Step 1: Buy a 1- to 3-gallon container of 'Annabelle' hydrangea. Step 2: Plant it and water regularly. Step 3: Stand back, and be prepared to accept compliments.

'ANNABELLE' HYDRANGEA
at a glance

Size: 3 to 5 feet tall
Light: partial shade to shade
Soil: rich, moist, well drained
Water: ample water during dry spells
Pests: few
Propagation: cuttings in July; division of clumps
Range: throughout the South

This hydrangea (*Hydrangea arborescens* 'Annabelle') isn't the shy, retiring type that blends into the background. Standing alone or as part of a border, it is a show-off that's sensational in woodland gardens.

It would be difficult not to notice dense, globular flower clusters up to a foot across, especially when they almost cover a shrub that quickly grows 3 to 5 feet tall and about 5 feet wide. Unlike many flowers that rapidly fade away in the South's heat and humidity, 'Annabelle's pristine white blooms lend a feeling of coolness to the landscape for at least a month.

'Annabelle' will feel right at home when planted in rich, well-drained, moist soil. It isn't the least bit fussy about pH, so it will be happy whether your soil is acid or alkaline.

In a border, good neighbors for 'Annabelle' hydrangea are impatiens, 'White Nancy' lamium, 'Francee' hosta, or a variegated carex such as *C. conica* 'Marginata.' If you've chosen a spot with a half-day's sun, consider daylilies as sidekicks because many of them bloom at the same time as 'Annabelle.' A lightly shaded walkway will make quite an impression with massed red or pink daylilies lining one side and 'Annabelle' on the other.

Care is simple: regular watering during dry spells and once-a-year pruning. To get the biggest blooms and more of them, cut 'Annabelle' back to within a foot of the ground in late winter because flowers are produced on new wood. This also helps keep the shrub compact.

The choice is yours. Settle for a sea of green in partial shade, or let 'Annabelle' light up the dark corners in spectacular fashion.

Below: 'Annabelle' hydrangea produces a spectacular display of enormous white flowers that last and last. This shrub looks great either in a border or standing alone.

A Sage Choice

This low-maintenance salvia is not just an attractive, reliable draw for pretty winged creatures. It's also a solid performer either as an individual plant or as a team player in a flowering border. The tiny blossoms, held aloft on airy stems, are deceptively delicate. From a few steps back, the sheer number of those little flowers massed together turns autumn sage into a mound of color. The palette ranges from red to pink and coral to crimson, which explains the alternate name "cherry sage." White forms of *Salvia greggii* are fairly common, as well, and even yellow selections are available.

In the Central, Lower, Coastal, and Tropical South, autumn sage is a nearly evergreen perennial that forms a small, woody shrub. Despite its name, this salvia

Birds do it, bees do it. There's no real data on whether educated fleas do it, but butterflies eagerly fall in love with autumn sage, and gardeners all over the South do, too—with good reason. It's one of the most colorful and cooperative perennials in the garden.

actually blooms from May through November. The autumn flowers are the most plentiful and richly hued of the year, however, which easily accounts for the common name's focus on fall. As a perennial, autumn sage gets more impressive every year. Replace plants every four or five years to keep them from getting too woody.

In the Upper South, cooler temperatures dictate growing autumn sage as an annual. Gardeners there will bless it for its rapid growth and quick onset of bloom. The bushy, slightly sprawling form with tidy little leaves also lends itself beautifully to containers. If you prefer the look of a groomed rather than a casual garden, occasional clipping back will stimulate autumn sage to thicker growth and even more bloom.

Make sure to give your plants good drainage and at least a half-day of direct sun. They cheerfully will earn the affections of butterflies, bees, hummingbirds, and, of course, gardeners.

Below: 'Pink Perfection' is a knockout next to an aromatic aster just coming into bloom.

AUTUMN SAGE
at a glance

Size: 2 to 3 feet tall and wide
Bloom: May to November
Light: full sun to partial shade
Soil: any, well drained
Water: once a week; drought tolerant when established
Pests: none serious
Propagation: cuttings
Range: hardy to 25 degrees as a perennial; entire South as an annual

Try This Geranium

How could anyone look at such a lovely plant and name it bloody cranesbill geranium? The tiny beaklike fruit it produces is said to be the inspiration for this injustice. Overlook the gory adjective and you'll find an enthusiastic little bloomer that comes back each year on its own.

Bloody cranesbills (*Geranium sanguineum*) are not what most gardeners think of when they hear the word geranium. The more familiar zonal geraniums sport clusters of flowers held aloft on stalks above rounded leaves. The blooms of bloody cranesbills are buttercup shaped and dot the foliage with color.

Flower hues range from white, pink, and red to the bright fuchsia blooms of the 'New Hampshire Purple' selection (pictured below). Though all bloody cranesbills bloom from early summer until frost, 'New Hampshire Purple' is known for nearly nonstop color during the hot months. Plants form low mounds of dense greenery about 1 to 2 feet high. Add bloody cranesbills to the front of your flower border for best viewing. Or try them along paths, tucked between stones, or creeping over the edge of a large container.

These plants can take the heat of summer, but they do need moist, well-drained soil. They'll bloom equally well in full sun or part shade. Blooming stops with the first cold snap, and leaves blush red before disappearing for the winter. New foliage will emerge in spring. Try bloody cranesbill. It's easy to grow, and the name is hard to forget.

BLOODY CRANESBILL GERANIUM

at a glance

Size: mounds about 1 to 2 feet high and 1 foot wide
Light: full sun to part shade
Soil: moist, well drained
Range: all South

Right: 'New Hampshire Purple,' a selection of bloody cranesbill geranium, will grow in sun or part shade, supplying bright blooms right through the hot months.

Cool Plumbago

Cape plumbago's soft blue flowers cluster in cool color during the hottest days of summer. In Coastal and Tropical South gardens, this woody shrub may grow 6 feet tall and wide, blooming all year long. For the rest of us, it's a handsome annual that blooms until first frost.

Dottie Myers, of Dottie Myers & Associates, a landscape architecture firm in Atlanta, frequently uses plumbago in containers for her clients. "This plant adds a flower color that is almost nonexistent," she says. "I find that plumbago is most effective when planted in containers that are viewed up close. The icy blue color is difficult for the eye to detect at a distance."

Cape plumbago is versatile in light preference. It blooms beautifully with three and a half hours of direct midday sun, but it is also tough enough to withstand all-day exposure. Diligent watering is a must as the amount of sun increases.

Sprinkle a small amount of timed-release all-purpose shrub fertilizer (12-6-6) on top of the soil when you plant. "We also recommend containers be watered with a liquid food every two to three weeks," Dottie says. Tip: Never fertilize a plant when the soil is dry. Water prior to feeding so the food will not burn the roots.

Mike Shoup, owner of the Antique Rose Emporium in Brenham, Texas, recommends an organic approach. "Amend the soil well with organic matter prior to planting. If necessary, supplement with an occasional watering with fish emulsion to keep the plant blooming," he says.

Plumbago is considered maintenance-free, but a little attention goes a long way. "This plant is forgiving and will flower without any extra care," Mike says. "It blooms on new growth and always has a sporadic cover of flowers. When it is pruned back, it will bloom with intensity."

One way to prune is to cut back the branches severely into a controlled shrub. This produces a tight mass of foliage and blue flowers. Or cut only the spent blooms from the tips of branches. This encourages new growth and flowers while maintaining the plant's flowing appearance in the garden. Always cut plumbago back directly above a set of leaves. If you choose not to trim it, plumbago will acquire a natural grace with arching branches.

Before first frost in autumn, cut your container plant back and bring it indoors. It will happily reside in a sunroom or frost-free garage until spring. Blooms are minimal during winter months, returning when the weather becomes consistently warm in late spring.

CAPE PLUMBAGO
at a glance

Light: half-day to full-day sun
Water: Keep evenly moist.
Fertilizer: Feed every two to three weeks with liquid blossom booster or fish emulsion.
Nice to know: There is also a white selection of plumbago, equally as lovely as the blue one.

Below: Graceful branches and showstopping blue flowers make Cape plumbago a valuable accent plant for containers and landscape.

One Tough, Showy Rose

It doesn't need spraying. It doesn't need watering. It doesn't need fertilizing. Frankly, it's beginning to sound like chestnut rose isn't a rose at all.

But, of course, it is. A large, gangly shrub growing 5 to 7 feet high and wide, chestnut rose *(Rosa roxburghii)* bears plump, showy blossoms of bright pink. The bush blooms heavily in spring, and then off and on throughout summer and fall. Pretty as they are, the flowers don't set this rose apart. That honor goes to curious prickles, reminiscent of spiny chestnut burrs. They cover both hips and buds, giving the plant its name. Chestnut rose's leathery green foliage is also noteworthy as it is immune to black spot and powdery mildew.

Once established, this rose is tougher than Grade D beef. It can easily live in a garden for a century or more with absolutely no care. Many years ago, Liz Tedder of Newnan, Georgia, received one from an old friend, Julia Blackburn. Julia had gotten her start from her mother years before. Liz says chestnut rose sends up suckers periodically, so it's easy to pass along.

Nice as it is, chestnut rose isn't perfect. For one thing, Japanese beetles love to eat the blooms, even though they aren't the least bit fragrant. Moreover, it's one of the spiniest roses around.

Despite these failings, it deserves a place in your garden. If you hate spraying, watering, and fertilizing, this is the rose for you.

CHESTNUT ROSE

at a glance

Size: 5 to 7 feet tall and wide
Bloom: heavily in spring, sporadically thereafter
Light: full sun
Soil: well drained
Fragrance: none to speak of
Pests: Japanese beetles
Propagation: separate suckers, root cuttings, or pin long canes to the ground until rooted
Range: all but Tropical South

Below: This large shrub makes a nice accent in the corner of a post fence.

Chinese Fringe Tree

Small trees bring a spectacular tier of flowers to the garden. Cherries and dogwoods proclaim the arrival of spring. But after all the petals have fallen, there's a lull in the garden. That's when Chinese fringe tree shows its stuff.

A close relative of the spectacular native fringe tree, Chinese fringe tree *(Chionanthus retusus)* is a favorite tree of landscape architect Ben Page in Nashville, Tennessee. "Chinese fringe tree is truly one of the great plants," says Ben.

Flowering begins in late April to May, depending on where you live, and can usually continue into June. Rounded green leaves are festooned with clusters of white-petaled flowers that are airy and light, like fringe.

After the flowers have faded, it remains handsome in its green summer cloak. The leaves turn yellow in autumn, and then drop to reveal its second best attribute after the flowers—its trunk. "The winter interest is wonderful," says Ben, "because of the way the winter sun strikes the leathery, sinewy bark."

Although Chinese fringe tree may appear as a shrub at the nursery, it makes a fine, multitrunked tree with a little help. Removing the lower branches as it grows taller gives the plant a treelike form. Ben recommends raising the canopy about 6 to 8 inches each year.

It will grow to 15 feet or more at maturity, producing a bountiful display of flowers in late spring, as if to answer as gardeners ask, "Is that all there is?"

CHINESE FRINGE TREE
at a glance

Size: 15 to 25 feet tall and wide
Light: sun
Pests: none serious
Range: Upper, Middle, and Lower South

Left: Chinese fringe tree offers its flowers just as much of the garden has begun to turn green.

Phlox of Color

Vibrant color adds impact to a summer garden. 'Common Purple' phlox blooms from July into the fall with flowers that butterflies find irresistible.

'COMMON PURPLE' PHLOX
at a glance

Bloom: July through fall; cut back spent blooms to encourage new flowers
Light: full to half-day of direct sun
Water: thoroughly, once a week
Fertilizer: spring: well-balanced timed-release fertilizer; mid-summer: liquid all-purpose fertilizer; late summer: liquid all purpose.

While the name might lead you to believe this plant is a ho-hum perennial, 'Common Purple' phlox (*Phlox paniculata* 'Common Purple') is quite above average. "It is gorgeous up close and from a distance, too. It blooms for such a long time during the hottest part of the summer and continues into fall," says Lella Bromberg, who grows it in her Birmingham garden.

Rick Berry and Marc Richardson, owners of Goodness Grows Nursery in Lexington, Georgia, discovered this phlox many years ago. "We were in Greensboro, Georgia, and found an old abandoned homesite. Growing against the foundation was this vivid purple phlox. It had obviously been there a long time and neglected for years. In the middle of the hot summer it was in full bloom, happy as you please," Rick says.

Plant this tenacious perennial in a location that receives at least a half day of full sun. In bloom, heavy flower heads require support. A round, plastic-coated metal grid on tall legs works well. Place the support over the plant in spring, and foliage will grow through the windows of the grid. (Look for these supports at garden centers.)

A common complaint among gardeners is the propensity of phlox to become covered with powdery mildew. 'Common Purple' phlox rarely has a problem with this fungus. Its leaves remain clean and healthy in most situations. Good air circulation helps keep this disease at bay, so plant phlox with some surrounding space.

Another way to control mildew is with deep, thorough watering. Rick's experience has shown that high humidity and dry soil are perfect conditions for mildew. "Phlox love evenly moist soil. Water the roots deeply at least once a week. If you use an overhead sprinkler, water early in the day so the foliage will dry before the plant becomes shaded."

Long-lasting flowers begin to appear in July. With proper pruning after the initial bloom, phlox can be coerced to bud several more times, adding rich color to late-summer and fall gardens. After the first flowers fade, cut the stem above a set of leaves one-third of the way down from the spent bloom. Within several weeks it will be budded again.

If there is a perfect summer perennial, this old-fashioned phlox is a strong and vibrant contender.

Below: This fragrant perennial produces one-inch-wide flowers in large, dome-shaped clusters all summer long.

Crazy about Daisies

There's nothing pretentious about daisies. You've loved these cheerful, common flowers ever since you learned to draw them in kindergarten. Perhaps it's because daisies grow in crayon colors: yellow centers ringed with white petals on plain green stems.

Shasta daisies *(Chrysanthemum maximum)* are the ones you probably remember from childhood. It's easy to add them to your own garden. Start with seeds or transplants in spring or fall. Autumn planting has the advantage of establishing root systems before flowering. Each 4-inch transplant you set out in fall will produce, at a fraction of the cost, roughly the same amount of blooms as a 1-gallon plant purchased in spring. But don't fret if you waited until spring to go daisy crazy; plants started now will continue to grow all year. If you leave spent flowers on their stems instead of trimming brown seedheads, your daisies will reseed.

Daisies are perennial, so consider your patch an ongoing addition to the garden. Dig up large clumps of them every other year around October, and cut roots apart to divide them. This will keep crowded roots from smothering each other and will offset the natural decline that occurs after two to three years. Set divisions 10 to 12 inches apart in full sun, or share them with friends. You can also dig seedlings from beneath parent plants in fall and replant them. Seeds purchased in packets may be sown in fall or spring.

Bed down Shastas for winter by tucking mulch around each plant, taking care not to cover leaves. The rosettes of foliage stay green year-round in much of the South. 'Alaska' is a selection named for its tolerance for icy weather; this 2-foot beauty produces 2-inch flowers nonstop for at least a month in the spring and sporadically until cold weather returns. For a shorter Shasta, try 'Snow Lady,' a hybrid measuring 10 to 12 inches high. Give plants a good drink of water during summer's dog days.

Shasta daisies will reward you with bright bouquets filled with heart-warming blooms.

Below: The Antique Rose Emporium in Brenham, Texas, collected Shasta daisies from an old homestead to start its patch.

SHASTA DAISY

at a glance

Size: 10 to 24 inches high
Light: full sun
Soil: moderately fertile, well drained
Range: all South
Nice to know: great cut flowers

Dazzling Daylilies

Daylilies have been called the lazy gardener's flower because few perennials give so much for so little. But this depends on which daylily you choose.

Of the hundreds of selections, some are grown strictly for their outstanding, prize-winning flowers, while others are perfect for durability in the landscape. If you choose your daylilies carefully, it is possible to enjoy them six to ten months of the year.

Thanks to plant breeders, daylilies are no longer limited to the tawny daylily, the well-known tall plant with orange blooms that is found along roadsides at many old homesites. Today's hybrids come in nearly ever color—cream, yellow, orange, apricot, pink, lavender, red, near-black, and bicolors. Even when daylilies are not in bloom, the fan-shaped foliage of many selections lends its green, grassy, curving lines to the landscape. And once they have put their hardy roots down in well-drained soil, the toughest selections require very little care, only occasional division.

In the landscape, daylilies are classics in a cottage garden when planted in drifts in a border of mixed flowers or shrubs. Tall selections work best at the back of the border or against a wall or fence. Lower-growing selections add impact when planted in neat clumps and are often used in foundation plantings.

Daylilies are also popular for mass planting, and many of the tougher selections will spread dependably to naturalize an area or to form a stable ground cover. Because their roots help stabilize the soil, daylilies are effective ground covers on steep slopes in full sun. Compact selections work well in containers on decks and patios or when it is used for spots of color near stairs, doorways, or garden features. Select fragrant daylilies to plant near a favorite outdoor sitting area.

While this lazy gardener's plant is remarkably trouble free, when pests do strike, they can be deadly. Just keep away the aphids, slugs, and spider mites.

DAYLILY
at a glance

Size: 8 inches to 4 feet
Light: full sun to partial shade
Soil: well drained
Water: medium
Pests: aphids, spider mites, slugs, nematodes, thrips
Range: perennial throughout South
Nice to know: easy summer color, good for ground cover

Right: Few flowers rival daylilies for giving so much beauty from so little attention.

Fountains of Forsythia

Forsythia seems like it's been around forever. But in fact, it didn't arrive in the South until around 1900.

That it spread so quickly to so many gardens is due to a trio of factors. First, for most people this shrub grows easier than mildew. Second, rooting it takes no brains at all. Just weigh a lower branch to the ground or—simpler yet—cut off a branch and stick it into moist earth. Third, forsythia, often called yellow bells, is the herald of spring. It blooms with the year's first mild weather. Cut branches that are taken indoors bloom as early as January.

Now you'd think something so popular would earn great reverence and respect, but not so. All over the South, otherwise gentle, rational people regularly seize their hedge-trimmers and butcher this graceful shrub into balls, squares, trapezoids, and other bizarre, unnatural shapes. They forget that an innocent-looking, 1-gallon plant can grow 8 feet tall and wide in the time it takes to fetch the morning paper. So they plant it in all the wrong places—under low windows, beside the steps, and at the very edge of the driveway. Butchery soon commences, ruining the next spring's bloom.

This heinous practice must end. To look its best, forsythia needs lots of elbowroom. So let it blanket a hillside; cascade over a wall; or form a billowing, unclipped hedge. If your garden is too cramped for this, try one of the new, compact selections that seldom need pruning. 'Minigold' grows 4 to 5 feet tall and wide, while 'Gold Tide' grows a mere 20 inches tall and 4 feet wide. Both feature showy, bright yellow flowers. Please stop the madness of forsythia butchery. Tell your neighbors to stop it, too. Then maybe by the time another century passes, we'll have one thing we can count on. Forsythia everywhere will be beautiful and golden.

Below: From late winter to early spring, the branches of these fountain-shaped shrubs are covered with yellow flowers.

FORSYTHIA
at a glance

Size: usually 8 to 10 feet tall and wide; some selections smaller
Light: full sun for best flowering
Soil: moist, fertile, well drained, acid or alkaline
Pests: none serious
Growth rate: fast (up to 4 feet per year)
Prune: Immediately after flowering in spring, if necessary; use hand pruners, not hedge-trimmers
Propagation: cuttings, layering
Range: Upper, Middle, Lower South

Impatiens Handle the Heat

Blooming nonstop from spring until the first frost, impatiens find their way into more gardens than any other summer annual. Low-maintenance, tropical hybrids, they need only a few hours of sun to produce dazzling mounds of flowers for five to seven months.

Impatiens come in more than 15 different colors—from shimmering whites and pale pinks to vivid purples and bright oranges. Faithful bloomers in the shade, impatiens are by far America's best-selling bedding plants.

This versatile annual enlivens evergreen shrub borders, or looks great massed for waves of color. It can also strategically fill holes in shade gardens with a few plants.

Or let impatiens colorfully cascade from hanging baskets and containers near an entry, a terrace, or a deck. Impatiens work well as a ground cover in woodland settings, mixed with ferns, caladiums, and other shade lovers for a cool effect.

The easiest way to start impatiens is to purchase transplants after the last frost. Plant them in the shade or in areas that are shaded in the afternoon. Although

IMPATIENS

at a glance

Size: 6 to 26 inches talla nd wide
Light: shade to partial shade, morning sun
Soil: moist but well drained
Pests: slugs
Nice to know: 'New Guinea' impatiens tolerate full sun, all impatiens grow well in partial shade

many selections can tolerate sun, they will need an excessive amount of water during the summer. No matter where they grow, impatiens need a lot of water during dry spells.

The introduction of new hybrid impatiens, derived from plants found in New Guinea in 1970, brought a new look to American gardens. With dark, variegated foliage, bigger flowers, and the ability to tolerate full sun, new selections of impatiens are being continuously developed, causing many different forms, sizes, and colors to be available to gardeners. Dwarf types are great for hanging baskets and ground covers in shady and wooded settings. The 'Twinkle' series produces bicolored flowers with a white central star, and the 'Super Elfin' series comes in many solid colors.

So if you're looking for unstoppable, perennial-like blooms, consider the cool look of impatiens. There's a huge selection to choose from—and they'll last from late spring well until fall.

Left: A sweep of impatiens borders a shaded fountain.

Easy-Care Lilies

As Southern days stretch smoothly from spring into summer, increasing warmth brings stately blue lilies into bloom.

Ann Donnelly, head gardener at Longue Vue House and Gardens in New Orleans, notes, "That first warm day, you'll see blue buds on the Nile lilies. Then they all start opening and put on a show for a month or more."

Lilies-of-the-Nile, also known by their botanical name, *Agapanthus,* are not true lilies and come from South Africa rather than Egypt. But Southern gardeners care more about their elegance and ease of culture than about such details. These flowers are so useful in containers, borders, and vases, that it's impossible not to like them.

Fortunately they are easy to grow anywhere in the South. Some species are more cold hardy than others, and the different forms have mingled in the nursery trade, so the easiest way to sort them out is by winter foliage. If they have leaves in winter, they're evergreen and will prefer to occupy flower borders in the warmer zones. Deciduous lilies-of-the-Nile, whose straplike foliage dies back in winter, should be cold hardy in the ground through the Middle South.

Ann points out that the gorgeous blue border at Longue Vue needs only minimal care. These plants require good drainage and plenty of water during the early part of the growing season, but once established they'll keep blooming even through a drought. "The Nile lilies here have probably been in the ground about 15 years. They bloom reliably every year from late April or early May, whenever the temperature gets really warm, into June," Ann says. "They don't require much special attention."

Occasionally, according to Ann, the leaves can get a little fungus late in the summer, after the bloom season. Instead of spraying the plants, she just cuts them back. "It's easy, and they come back with foliage when it's cooler.

"Basically they do exactly what they're supposed to do every year, with almost no effort from me," Ann says. "They're really satisfying. *Agapanthus* is supposed to be Greek for 'flower of love.' I can see that."

Below: Airy blue flowers of lily-of-the-Nile cool off the summer borders at Longue Vue House and Gardens in New Orleans. **Right:** 'Peter Pan,' a popular dwarf selection, is only 18 inches high.

LILY-OF-THE-NILE

at a glance

Bloom: six weeks or more in summer
Soil: rich, well-manured soil with excellent drainage
Water: well in spring and summer; lightly in fall and winter
Fertilizer: slow-release fertilizer or compost after blooming
Sun: full sun to light shade
Range: Lower, Coastal, and Tropical South in the ground; Upper and Middle South in containers
Nice to know: Don't divide too often. *Agapanthus* will bloom best if left undisturbed and a little crowded.

Lovely Loropetalum

Loropetalum (pronounced lor-o-PETA-lum) may be hard to say, but it sure is a pleasure to grow. This large, handsome shrub is a native of China and Japan, but it's pretty happy growing here in the South.

Gardeners who want to avoid trying to say loropetalum may simply call it by its common names: Chinese witch hazel and Chinese fringe.

The white-flowering type, *Loropetalum chinense*, has been around for years and is truly a good dependable shrub, but it has never been widely grown. A pink-flowering version, *L. c. rubrum*, a relative newcomer to garden centers, has really popularized the plant. Some of the pink bloomers can be found under names such as 'Blush,' 'Burgundy,' 'Sizzlin' Pink,' 'Razzleberri,' and 'Rubrum.' Their airy ribbonlike blooms are striking, and some selections sport showy purple-green to burgundy foliage.

When you see knee-high plants at the nursery, don't be misled. At maturity some selections will grow up to 12 feet tall and 6 to 8 feet wide. They tend to have a vaselike shape. You can remove lower limbs from older shrubs to make small trees. Read the label or tag on the plants you buy for guidelines and spacing recommendations. They don't waste much time filling out and can grow up to 3 feet in a season.

These shrubs prefer loose, well-drained, acid soil. Full sun to partial shade is needed for plants to maintain a full shape and bloom heavily. Some of the burgundy-leaved selections have high fertilization requirements and need lots of sun to retain their dark foliage.

They seem to perform best in the Middle to Lower and Coastal South. Subzero temperatures can kill or knock plants back to the ground. In cooler climates apply a thick mulch to protect roots, and plant in a protected area.

Loropetalum makes a nice accent plant in a large container or planted in a shrub or flower border. Be careful using them in foundation plantings—many of the pink selections are so new that their mature sizes are unknown.

Their name may be hard to say, but these plants are easy to grow, and they're a great addition to any landscape.

Below: The flowers and foliage of this pink loropetalum border a fence and stand out against the white azaleas.

LOROPETALUM
at a glance

Size: 12 feet or more tall, 6 to 8 feet wide (Mature sizes of some new selections are unknown.)
Bloom: stringy pink or white blooms in spring
Light: full sun to partial shade
Soil: needs well-drained nonalkaline soil
Pests: no major insect or disease problems
Nice to know: works great in borders, containers, hedges, specimens

Ice Blue Salvia

Imagine a typical, sweltering summer day. Then imagine a light frost descending through the blistering heat and humidity. Ice blue mealy-cup sage *(Salvia farinacea)* in a sunburnt border works like a floral plunge into cool water.

MEALY-CUP SAGE
at a glance

Size: 2 to 3 feet tall and 1 to 2 feet wide
Light: full sun to partial shade
Soil: any, well drained
Pests: none serious
Propagation: seed, cuttings, or division
Range: annual throughout the South

The flowers and stems are covered with tiny hairs that make them look as if they are dusted with a coat of frost. For practical purposes, these little hairs insulate the plant's surfaces from heat and slow water loss. Visually, the effect is restful in the daytime and luminous in moonlight.

Whether grown as an annual or a perennial, mealy-cup sage stands out as an individual performer, but it's also a great team player. The silver and blue colors make nearby flowers of orange, red, and yellow burn hotter. The same icy shades blend beautifully with pastel blossoms.

Care is simple. Plant it from seed in early spring, or transplant it at any time during the year. It enjoys sun, needs minimal water and fertilizer, and doesn't care about the soil as long as there's decent drainage. In a large border, this plant can be left alone to bloom from midspring until frost. Then either replace it, or prune it to the ground early in the following spring, before the new foliage pushes through.

If you can't get the species form of *S. farinacea,* look for a selection called 'Strata' to get the same effect. There are also white selections ('Porcelain,' 'Silver,' and 'Cirrus') and the darker blue 'Victoria' or 'Blue Bedder.'

Left: Attractive in any setting, mealy-cup sage is one of the best blue flowers for the hottest part of summer.

Zinnia's New Look

If you expect a bed of zinnias to have the primary colors found in a fistful of helium-filled balloons, look again.

NARROW-LEAF ZINNIA

at a glance

Size: 12 to 15 inches tall
Light: full sun to light afternoon shade
Soil: amended, well-drained garden soil
Water: Irrigate when dry.
Pests: mildew resistant, some spider mites in hot, dry weather

Unlike the stand-up habit of their bright cousins, narrow-leaf zinnias lie down in their bed, making a carpet of color that lasts all summer. And the golden orange blooms among blue-gray leaves appear like a meadow in full flower.

Narrow-leaf zinnias *(Zinnia angustifolia* or *Z. linearis)* are long lasting. Plant them in full sun atop a raised bed, and give them good drainage and adequate moisture; they will hardly droop a leaf on the hottest day. In fact, narrow-leaf zinnia will bloom steadily from the time it is planted in spring until frost nips it in fall. You don't even need to snip off the faded flowers.

While other zinnias succumb to summer's mildews, narrow-leaf zinnias take no notice and grow on with scarcely a blotch on a leaf. The naturally bluish tint to the abundant foliage sets the flowers apart, creating a harmony rarely enjoyed between blossom and leaf.

Narrow-leaf zinnia is readily available from garden centers among the spring and summer bedding plants. Look for orange ('Golden Orange'), golden ('Star Gold'), and white ('Crystal White') forms.

Choose a location where it can trail over a wall, or place it along the front of a border. Plants will grow about 12 to 15 inches tall, but little more. They won't be seen

Below: Narrow-leaf zinnia blooms all summer in a cascade that fills an entire bed or the front of a border. Practically carefree, it's a busy gardener's choice for a sunny spot.

behind taller annuals and perennials, so put them out front. Set transplants 12 to 15 inches apart, and any gaps will be filled in only a few weeks.

Narrow-leaf zinnia is also an ideal choice for a plant to trail over the edge of a container. Plant it in large pots that contain upright shrubs or small trees, and it will soften that hard edge with a drape of summer flowers.

Before setting plants out, amend garden beds with organic matter to improve the drainage in clay soil and help sandy soil retain moisture. Incorporate a slow-release fertilizer into the bed at planting time to ensure vigor through the long growing season.

Reawakened Rose

'NEW DAWN'

at a glance

Fragrant flowers that are the delicate pale pink hue of clouds blushed by the early morning light on a plant you couldn't kill with a highway department roadside mower—that's a combination that makes a good garden rose. And the modern climber 'New Dawn' has been one of the best ever since its introduction in 1930.

An exquisitely beautiful rose, 'New Dawn' climbed the plant popularity charts as the everblooming offshoot of the existing favorite 'Dr W. Van Fleet.' The original rose had an outrageous spring display, then shut down while its offspring produced the same lovely flowers throughout the growing season.

'New Dawn' received the first plant patent ever granted, and this bit of historical trivia secured the rose a place in the horticultural record books, but its performance as a climbing rose secured its place in the hearts of gardeners. Because both 'New Dawn' and 'Dr W. Van Fleet' are still grown and can sometimes be confused, it's a good idea to buy from a reliable nursery or purchase the blooming rose in the fall to

Size: 15 to 20 feet tall and wide
Light: full to partial sun
Soil: tolerates a wide range of growing conditions
Growth rate: vigorous, lots of thorns
Pests: none serious
Range: Upper to Coastal South

ensure that the desired variety is chosen.

A full-size climber, 'New Dawn' throws out long canes that can eventually reach 15 to 20 feet in any direction. The dark green, semiglossy foliage is rarely troubled by pests or diseases. The prickles are healthy, too. But scratches aside, 'New Dawn' is an easy rose to train if you start with a young plant. The flexible canes can be arranged in attractive patterns before they stiffen with maturity.

As with any climbing rose, training the canes to the side (or letting their own weight arch them over) helps produce greater quantities of bloom, with flowers at every leaf axil. And climbing roses never need to be pruned back, just cleaned of dead canes and unattractive branches. If you decide to plant 'New Dawn' in a natural area where it will mound over meadow fences or clamber into the trees, you don't have to do any grooming at all.

If 'New Dawn' has a flaw, it's the tendency of the pale pink flowers to fade white under strong sun. Otherwise, this fragrant, vigorous rose tolerates most soils, blooms often, requires little feeding or watering once established, propagates easily from cuttings, and is at home from Upper to Coastal South.

Below: The glorious blooms of 'New Dawn' enhance a fence.

Pearlbush Makes the Heart Beat Faster

To love a pearlbush takes a special person. One with a beating heart. Yet for some strange reason, few gardeners grow pearlbush or even know it exists. You almost never see it for sale. About the only way to obtain one is to get a start from a friend.

Flora Ann Bynum of Winston-Salem, North Carolina, got hers that way. She received a seedling from a friendly gardener. "Pearlbush just drips seeds, and little plants come up everywhere," she explains. "As a gardener, you don't want to throw them away, so you look around for somebody to give them to. It's definitely a pass-along plant."

In Columbus, Mississippi, Margaret Sanders tells much the same story. "A friend gave me lots of little sprouts," she says. "Now they've gotten big, and baby plants come up all around. I like to find them a good home."

Named for expanding flowerbuds that resemble pearls, pearlbush *(Exochorda racemosa)* ranks among early spring's showiest bloomers. But gardeners should remember that it often grows bigger than its name indicates. Although a compact hybrid called 'The Bride' remains 4 to 5 feet tall, the common form assumes an open, fountain-like shape, reaching 20 to 25 feet tall. Unremarkable when not blooming, pearlbush looks better in a corner, a naturalized area, or back of the border than in a prominent place.

Flora Ann grows hers in a rear corner of a small garden dedicated to heirloom plants. She yearly removes its lower branches, transforming it into a small tree. "It's really spectacular in spring, with its upper branches drooping down," she says. "And now I have room to plant underneath it."

Though overlooked by mass merchandisers, pearlbush owns a place in the hearts of charitable gardeners who are happy to share. Each time its blossoms open in spring, those hearts beat a little faster.

PEARLBUSH
at a glance

Size: 15 to 25 feet; 'The Bride' grows 4 to 5 feet
Light: full sun or very light shade
Soil: moist, well drained
Pests: none serious
Prune: immediately after flowering
Propagation: seedlings, division in late winter
Range: Upper, Middle, Lower, Coastal South

Right: One of the first large shrubs to bloom in the spring, pearlbush is a Southern heirloom that's passed along from gardener to gardener.

Perfect Pentas

Easy to grow and a favorite of hummingbirds and butterflies, this flower blooms nonstop in colors of red, pink, lavender, and white.

Are you a shameless creature of habit? Have you been setting out marigolds and scarlet sage ever since the Beatles disbanded? Then it's time you tried something new. And we have just the thing. It's a flower called pentas that simply does everything well.

It blooms nonstop in warm weather. It attracts hummingbirds and butterflies. Its cut flowers last a long time in water. Its cut stems root easily in soil or just plain water.

The point is, this is one terrific plant. Native to Tropical Africa, pentas *(Pentas lanceolata)* grows 2 to 3 feet tall and wide. Flat clusters of red, pink, lavender, or white starlike flowers appear atop dark green, deeply veined leaves. Perennial in the Coastal and Tropical South, it's an annual elsewhere. Of course, you can pot it up and take it indoors to a sunny window for the winter.

Although some folks prefer to mix the colors, mass plantings of a single color show up better in flowerbeds. Pentas makes an excellent container plant, too. Periodically removing spent flowers and shortening stems keeps this champion performer bushy and floriferous.

You'll find pentas at most good nurseries and garden centers.

PENTAS
at a glance

Size: 2 to 3 feet tall and wide
Light: sun or light shade
Soil: moist, fertile, well drained
Pests: spider mites in hot, dry weather
Propagation: seeds, cuttings
Range: perennial in Coastal and Tropical South; annual elsewhere

Left: For the most impact, mass a single color rather than planting one of each.

The Joy of Primrose

Roll up your sleeves if you plant this wildflower. You could be in for a tussle.

Adding a beautiful perennial to your garden doesn't usually require inordinate courage. But pink evening primrose isn't like other perennials.

Consider that this native wildflower grows happily through cracks in the pavement. Consider it flourishes in any well-drained soil, from the parched caliche of West Texas to the red clay of Georgia to the sands of South Florida. Consider that planting it in good soil among well-mannered perennials is akin to leaving your Pekingese in a pen with a hungry wolverine.

So why plant it? When it blooms from April to June, it's an unquestioned joy to behold. Also known as showy primrose, Mexican evening primrose, and in some parts buttercups (because if you playfully shove a flower onto the end of someone's nose after asking him to smell it, the pollen leaves a yellow smudge), it bears hundreds of pink or occasionally white blossoms. With a unique, cruciform style (female reproductive part) in the flower's center, each magenta-veined blossom looks like a satellite dish. Well-informed ants reclining below are probably tuning in to CNN.

Despite its name, pink evening primrose *(Oenothera speciosa)* blooms during the day. The 1½-inch-wide blossoms appear atop a sprawling mat of foliage that's 10 to

PINK EVENING PRIMROSE
at a glance

Size: 10 to 12 inches high
Light: full sun
Soil: any, well drained
Pests: none serious
Propagation: seed, division
Range: throughout the South

12 inches high. The plant spreads rapaciously both by seeds and underground stems. Poor, rocky, or highly acid soil slows its progress to a saunter. However, in loose, fertile soil, it attains warp speed. After finishing blooming, it dies back a bit and appears to rest. But don't be fooled—those innocent-looking seeds and stems have ideas.

The safest spot to grow pink evening primrose is where it can spread to its heart's content without hurting anything—for example, a wildflower meadow, naturalized area, or informal lawn.

But if you prefer this plant in a traditional border, beware—it will insinuate itself between bricks and stones and devour finicky flowers. One solution, says garden designer Edith Eddleman of Durham, North Carolina, is to combine it with tall perennials it can't engulf, such as Russian sage or Siberian iris. Or we suggest planting it among other perennial thugs, such as hardy ageratum, obedient plant, or common yarrow, and let these bad boys duke it out. "Even then, on the whole, *Oenothera* will win," she warns.

Unfortunately, hungry wolverines won't triumph either. They will just wind up with funny little yellow smudges on their noses.

Below: Hundreds of showy blossoms decorate pink evening primrose in spring. Despite its name, the flowers open in daytime.

Drops of Rain Lilies

Rain lilies are sometimes called summer's crocus because they look similar and are about the same size. August and September rains trigger starry white blooms.

As summer's heat takes its toll on the garden, plants curl, crumple, and give in to the searing sun. Few plants thrive late in the season, but one tiny flower shines.

Rain lily *(Zephyranthes candida)* usually begins to bloom in late July. This tough little bulb grows naturally in the marshes of South America. Its common name refers to the blooms that magically appear after rains. It may bloom several times during the season, and it peaks in August and September. The white flowers are sometimes edged in pink. Bright yellow stamens spring from their centers.

Rain lilies look small and delicate, but they are extremely tough. Most pests leave them alone. A site with rich, moist soil is preferred but they will also grow in heavy-clay soils. The bulbs suffer if the soil around them becomes completely dry for prolonged periods. Keep bulbs moist during summer droughts.

You can sometimes find bulbs growing in containers at nurseries, but you may have to mail-order them. Once established, rain lilies will multiply at an alarming rate. Small offshoots form on bulbs, making new plants. They also propagate by reseeding.

Rain lilies look great in irregular-shaped drifts. As they multiply, they will appear as if they are native plants that have formed loose colonies. The versatile little bulbs look at home edging a small pond, sprinkled through a woodland garden, or in a formal border. They even work well in containers.

Plant a few of these delightful bulbs in your garden. Their goblet white blooms will perk up your landscape in the heat when many plants are melting in summer's heat. They're easy to grow, and after a summer shower you can watch your garden rain lilies.

RAIN LILIES
at a glance

Size: 10 to 12 inches tall
Bloom: late July through September
Light: sun to partial shade
Nice to know: will grow in boggy as well as heavy-clay soils

Below: These little bulbs make a nice addition to a late-summer garden.

Red Hot Yucca

If you've been looking for a plant that is tough, that produces attractive flowers for many months, and that can go weeks without irrigation in the summer, consider red yucca.

RED YUCCA
at a glance

Size: 5 to 7 feet tall
Light: full sun to partial shade
Soil: not particular
Water: drought tolerant
Pests: Deer love the flowers.

The name is a bit deceiving, because botanically it is not a yucca at all; it's a hesperaloe *(Hesperaloe parviflora)*. And although the foliage is slender and spiky, it is not dangerously sharp like some of the true yuccas. This shrub is one of the most attractive plants for gardeners in Texas or anywhere heat and drought are a challenge. Cold hardiness is not a problem because it will endure in all but the coldest areas of the Upper South.

The long, slender leaves are stiff and gray-green in color, and they form stemless clumps. The leaves sprout fine, white threads from their edges, but the real drama comes with the flowers. Gracefully leaning stalks reach 5 to 7 feet tall and bear coral-pink flowers from May through early fall. The individual flowers are about 1½ inches long and continue opening for many weeks. It is not unusual for mature clumps to have six or eight flower spikes during the season.

Red yucca is not particular about soil; it flourishes in alkaline or slightly acid conditions. It also tolerates fairly moist sites and thrives as a low-maintenance container plant. This shrub revels in full sun and reflected heat. When given a half-day of shade it may bloom less. About the only maintenance necessary for this shrub is to remove the old flower stalks at the end of the bloom season.

Another appealing quality is its attractiveness to butterflies and hummingbirds. The long flowering season allows plenty of time to lure these colorful creatures into your garden.

This shrub is readily available at garden centers. One-gallon container plants usually bloom the first year they are planted, although growth is rather slow. For the best effect, use it in drifts of three or more. Water well at planting and every few weeks the first growing season if rains are infrequent. After that, just sit back and enjoy the colorful flowers and interesting texture, as well as the butterflies and hummingbirds that—like you—will find the flowers irresistible.

Below: The leathery leaves of red yucca form a nondescript clump, but when the 5-foot flower stalks emerge, the plant makes a statement.

Sunny Shower-of-Gold

How many shrubs do you know that bloom continuously? Here's one.

Shower-of-gold does two things that Southerners love—it keeps its leaves year-round and blooms almost all of the time. So it's a bit of a mystery why more gardeners aren't growing it.

One reason may be that those who know it still call it "thryallis," a holdover from when the plant's botanical name was *Thryallis glauca.* So when they see it in the garden center labeled with its new botanical name, *Galphimia glauca,* they think the nurseryman is out to lunch and buy a gardenia instead.

That's too bad because shower-of-gold has a lot to offer. True to its name, showers of showy, golden blooms continuously pour from its branches in warm weather. It also features handsome, bright green leaves with reddish leaf stems and twigs. Native to Mexico and Guatemala, this shrub grows 4 to 8 feet tall and wide and suffers no serious pests. It can get a bit leggy with age, but a little pruning restores its bushiness.

Thanks to the blooms, shower-of-gold makes a fine accent plant for focusing attention on a particular part of the garden. You can also mass it to create a big splash of color or use it as an informal screen. Just remember that its brittle twigs break easily, so don't plant it where people will constantly brush against it.

If shower-of-gold has one major fault, it's susceptibility to cold. This semitropical plant isn't winter-hardy north of the Coastal South. If you want to grow it elsewhere, do so in a pot that you can take indoors for the winter. Give it plenty of sun and warm temperatures and watch the flowers come raining down.

Below: Use shower-of-gold in masses to create a big splash of color and an informal screen. The golden blossoms, which attract butterflies, appear nonstop in warm weather atop handsome evergreen leaves.

SHOWER-OF-GOLD

at a glance

Size: 4 to 8 feet tall and wide
Light: full sun
Soil: moist, well drained; tolerates some drought
Growth rate: moderate
Pests: none serious
Salt tolerance: takes mild salt spray if planted well back from dunes
Range: Coastal and Tropical South

Wonderful Weigela

Those who appreciate a fine antique will love old-fashioned weigela. This shrub has been flowering in Southern gardens for more than 100 years with little more to recommend it than its flowers and its hardy nature. In shades from white to pink to red, it carries on, spring after spring.

Weigela *(Weigela florida)* makes a statement in bloom. Depending on the selection, it will grow 3 to 9 feet tall and 4 to 12 feet wide. Give it full sun to partial shade and well-drained soil; then stand back. It will be a gratifying grower.

Because weigela recedes into the green backdrop of summer once flowering ceases, plant it as a background feature or in a mixed border of shrubs and small trees. It does not have a lot to offer in the other three seasons, so don't make it a focal point of the garden. Let it be, and when it blooms, weigela will call attention to itself.

In addition to a variety of flower colors, some selections offer plants with colorful foliage. This can be an asset in shrub borders where plants of varying textures need to stand out from one another. For variegated foliage, try 'Variegata' or 'Variegata Nana.' Golden-leaved forms include 'Rumba' and 'Rubidor.' Keep in mind that burgundy-leaved plants such as 'Java Red,' 'Minuet,' or 'Alexandra' will develop their best color in full sun.

For white flowers, look for selections such as 'Candida' or 'White Knight.' Red selections are much more plentiful, with names such as 'Evita,' 'Minuet,' 'Bristol Ruby,' 'Red Prince,' 'Rumba,' and 'Nain Rouge.' For pink blooms, plant 'Pink Princess,' 'Polka,' 'Java Red,' or 'Variegata.'

To keep your plant vital and attractive, lop out the oldest canes immediately after flowering. This will thin the plant, encourage new growth, and keep it flowering. While you're at it, cut away any dead wood. It is typical for some branches to die from time to time.

A little pruning isn't much to ask. The rest of the year, weigela takes care of itself. And for your trouble, you'll have flowery rewards, generation after generation.

WEIGELA
at a glance

Size: spreading 3 to 9 feet tall, 4 to 12 feet wide
Light: full sun to partial shade
Soil: well drained
Range: Upper, Middle, Lower South

Right: Spreading wider than it is tall, weigela offers a fine display of spring flowers, as it has for generations.

Showy Shrimp Plant

One of the great things about gardening is that every year you have the chance to try something new. Granted, some experiments don't pan out. But others succeed magnificently, and you're richer for it.

A recent personal triumph for one of our garden editors involved a plant unfamiliar to most folks—yellow shrimp plant *(Pachystachys lutea)*. It's semitropical, meaning that it's perennial in the Coastal and Tropical South, but elsewhere you treat it as an annual. He wanted something different and eye-catching to supply color in front of his house throughout the summer. Boy, did he make the right choice.

Like many tropical and semitropical plants, yellow shrimp plant blooms continuously in warm weather. The bloom you notice from a distance is not a true flower, but a cone of overlapping yellow bracts. The true flowers are white and creep out of the bracts like ghosts emerging in the night. Even though the blooms aren't red, hummingbirds like them just the same.

Caring for yellow shrimp plant is simple. You don't have to remove spent flowers because they drop off automatically to make way for new ones. All the plant basically wants is full sun and well-drained soil. To get a bushier plant and more blooms, cut back the main stems by several inches after planting. Always cut back to a node (the point where leaves sprout from the stem). Each cut stem will produce two new stems. Feed it every two to three weeks with a high-phosphorus, bloom-booster fertilizer.

Look for yellow shrimp plant at local garden centers, home-center stores, and greenhouses. You'll probably see it recommended as an indoor plant only. Don't believe it. A plant this showy needs to be seen out front.

Below: Yellow shrimp plant is easy to grow and supplies bright color in the garden from spring until frost. Red lantana makes a good companion.

YELLOW SHRIMP PLANT
at a glance

Size: up to 3 feet tall and wide in most locations
Light: full sun
Soil: moist, well drained, fertile
Pests: occasional scales, mealybugs, spider mites
Prune: early spring
Range: winter-hardy only in Coastal and Tropical South

A Cherry for the South

Imagine yourself on a fine, early-spring day when the lawn chair beckons insistently. As you sit reading a book, you notice a light fragrance in the air. Tiny, translucent, pale pink petals are drifting down onto the pages. It's like being in a wonderland. How can you put yourself into this picture? Just plant a Yoshino cherry tree.

Yoshinos became popular in this country after the Japanese government presented a gift of their nation's favorite tree to the people of the United States in 1912. Pictures of Yoshino cherry trees blossoming along the Tidal Basin in Washington, D.C., soon became an annual harbinger of spring for all Americans.

Yoshino cherry (*Prunus yedoensis*) blooms in early spring with the forsythia. Slightly fragrant, ethereal, white blooms with a pink center usually appear before the leaves, giving the effect of a pale pink cloud. They are followed by inconspicuous purplish-black fruit. Ranging in size from 20 to 30 feet (with a possibility of 50 feet) in height and a spread of 20 to 30 feet, Yoshinos will give you shade in a very short time. Smaller selections are available, so it's important to know the ultimate size of the one you choose. Trees can have multiple trunks or a single one with a canopy that spreads out like an umbrella. The blooms look especially pretty with a tall evergreen background. In summer, the tree's deep green leaves fade into the background until fall, when its leaf colors of gold and orange put on another show.

Full sun, a moderate amount of moisture with good drainage, and pruning to remove any dead wood or suckers on their trunks are all that Yoshino cherry trees ask in return for their spring extravaganza. If your soil is very acidic, adding some lime would help. A soil test can tell you how much lime you need. Because it tolerates pollution, Yoshino makes a good city or street tree.

You can grow this cherry in the Upper, Middle, and Lower South. Bill Welch, an Extension landscape horticulturist at Texas A&M University does not recommend it for Texas gardeners, nor does Kristin Pategas of the Disney Institute in Orlando suggest it for Florida gardeners. There's just not enough cold to set blooms. Elsewhere in the South, Yoshino thrives.

John Ruter at The University of Georgia Coastal Plain Station in Tifton, Georgia, is conducting a trial of cherry trees. He says, "The Yoshino requires around 900 chilling hours to bloom reliably. That means it will not bloom well in the warmest parts of the South, but I would grow it here in South Georgia just for its fall color."

In the central South Carolina city of Orangeburg, former city horticulturist Jon Mason, who oversaw the care of a large citywide planting, says, "If I were going to plant a cherry tree, I would choose Yoshino."

YOSHINO CHERRY
at a glance

Bloom: early spring
Light: sun
Soil: average soil, good drainage
Water: medium
Pests: subject to borers, stem canker, and bacterial canker
Range: Upper, Middle, and Lower South
Features: mildly fragrant pink to white blooms, fall colors of gold and orange

YOU HAVE A CHOICE

Akebono: (also known as 'Daybreak') Single, soft pink flowers; 25 feet high x 25 feet wide
Shidare Yoshino: White flowers and weeping habit. This is the tree known as the weeping Yoshino; 20 feet high x 30 feet wide.
Cascade Snow: Pure white flowers; more resistant to disease; 25 feet high x 20 feet wide

If you've always wanted an allée of trees but can't wait for live oaks, this cherry tree may be your answer. It won't live as long as an oak, but it grows up to 2 feet a year. In 8 to 10 years you will have a canopy you can walk under. Be the envy of the neighborhood at cherry blossom time.

Left: Yoshino cherry blossoms open from pink buds and then quickly fade to white. They are typically used as accent trees in a lawn.

Southern classics

favorite flowers for the region

native plants for your landscape

John Gutting is a passionate advocate for native plants. So when this landscape architect from Church Hill, Maryland, was presented the task of restoring a formal walled garden, outfitting it with tightly clipped rows of boxwoods wasn't an option. He stuck with his passion, and the results are beautiful.

The garden is only 100 feet square. It consists of two equal sections— a sunny upper garden devoted to meadow plants and a semi-shaded lower garden for moisture-loving types. A central pathway, sheltered by a handsome wood-and-metal arbor, leads you through a gateway from one section to the other.

The plantings represent a selection of species native to the Chesapeake Bay region. In the upper garden, trumpet honeysuckle *(Lonicera sempervirens)* and crossvine *(Bignonia capreolata)* drape the arbor with bright scarlet blossoms. Dwarf-eared coreopsis *(Coreopsis auriculata* 'Nana'), blue star *(Amsonia tabernaemontana),* gold-

en star *(Chrysogonum virginianum),* and other wildflowers carpet the ground. In the lower garden, cheery yellow blooms of golden groundsel *(Senecio aureus)* mirror in the beautiful waters of a perimeter pond.

But this is not a one-season garden— John planned it for a succession of bloom. "From April to November, there's a symphony of colors, flowers coming in and bowing out," he says. "This is what happens in nature all the time." For example, late summer and autumn give witness to joe-pye weed *(Eupatorium purpureum),* goldenrod *(Solidago* sp.), asters, cardinal flower *(Lobelia cardinalis),* and swamp

Below: The garden is home to a variety of sun-loving wildflowers planted in rectangular beds connected by gravel paths. Crossvine and trumpet honeysuckle decorate the central arbor.

Southern Natives *at a glance*

Interest in native plants has skyrocketed in recent years. But before you rush out to create a completely native garden, keep in mind a couple of points. First, the South is a big, big place. Just because a plant is native to the Southeast doesn't mean it will grow well in the Southwest. Second, native plants aren't always easier to grow than exotics. The key to any successful garden is choosing the right plant for the right spot. Here's a glance at a few Southern natives that grow well in any region.

OAKLEAF HYDRANGEA

Size: 4 to 10 feet tall, 10 feet wide
Light: partial shade, full sun in mountains
Soil: rich, well drained, slightly acid
Moisture: low
Pests: none serious
Range: all
Bloom: large flowers, fall color, peeling bark
Nice to Know: one of the loveliest deciduous ornaments

BLUE PHLOX

Size: 12 to 15 inches
Light: partial shade
Moisture: medium
Pests: powdery mildew
Range: all
Bloom: early spring perennial; showy flower clusters; low, mat-forming habit
Nice to know: naturalizes in woodland settings

Trumpet honeysuckle   Redbud

TRUMPET HONEYSUCKLE

Light: sun to shade; will bloom heavier in sun
Moisture: medium
Range: all
Bloom: late spring into summer produces showy, unscented orange-yellow to scarlet flowers
Nice to know: this semi-evergreen with a twiny vine will become shrubby if not given support

REDBUD

Size: 20 to 30 feet tall; 25 to 35 feet wide
Light: full sun to partial shade
Soil: variety
Pests: canker
Range: all
Bloom: bright magenta flowers before leaves appear in early spring
Nice to know: one of the most widely adapted native trees in the country

Hydrangea   Phlox

sunflower (*Helianthus angustifolius*) in bloom. Many of the flowers play host to butterflies and hummingbirds.

The trick when using all native plants, John says, is getting people to recognize your creation as a garden. There's a danger that unrestrained masses of blooms, stems, and leaves might simply look wild.

To avoid this, John took advantage of existing formal elements, then added a few

of his own. The restored brick walls define the shape of the garden, while the arbor he designed acts as a unifying element. Gravel paths crisscross each other at right angles, edging rectangular planting beds. "All the human-made details give the garden a crisp structure that people respond to," he notes. "I created a botanically diverse community under controlled circumstances." You could call the finished product beauty by design.

DESIGN TIPS

When using a wide variety of plants, use walls, arbors, paths, and gates to give the garden structure and form.

Emulate nature. Plan for more than one season of bloom.

Native doesn't always mean nice. Some wildflowers (such as golden groundsel) spread rapidly in moist, fertile soil, so you'll need to keep an eye on them.

start spring with
daffodils

Sunny symbols of spring, these flowers are pest free, low maintenance, and easy to establish in your garden or landscape.

W e can't help being partial to daffodils," explains Brent Heath. "Yellow is a wonderful color, and daffodils put up these big yellow flowers to attract early spring pollinators, so they grab our attention and win our admiration at the same time." Brent would know. His family has been growing daffodils in Gloucester, Virginia, for more than 100 years. The fields of yellow, brilliant now in early spring, are part of Brent's heritage as well as the backbone of Brent and Becky's Bulbs, the business he runs with his wife.

Daffodils are among the easiest plants to grow. "You don't have to do anything if you just want a one-time spring display," says Brent. "Bulbs, daffodils in particular, are pretty resilient and typically adapt to whatever situation you give them." For your daffodils to come back year after year, however, Brent has a few suggestions that will increase your success.

First, be sure of the sunlight. Choose a site that gets at least six hours of sunlight after the leaves are on the trees. It can be morning, afternoon, or constant dappled light, but the daffodils must have light for their leaves. Otherwise, they can't replenish the nutrients in their bulbs for the next blooming season.

Secondly, plant so your bulbs have water during their growing season and good drainage all the time. Brent points out that most of the South has less than ideal soil for bulbs, which need to stay especially well drained during the summer so they don't rot. Daffodils would prefer sandy loam, but Southern gardeners are more

likely to be wrestling with thick, sticky clay.

The easiest way to deal with heavy soil, Brent says, is to build your beds on top of it. "Improve just the top layer of soil by turning or tilling in well-composted organic material. Plant the bulbs shallowly; then add several inches of clay, or even coarse builder's sand, on top. Bulbs grow up through the clay or sand just fine, put out their roots in good soil, and get all the drainage benefits of a raised bed."

The third requirement for happy daffodils is to fertilize your bulbs every fall with a timed-release organic or encapsulated product (such as Holland Bulb Booster or Brent and Becky's Daffodil Fertilizer), broadcasting it over the bulb beds according to instructions on the bag. "The ideal fertilizer for daffodils would have an N-P-K balance of 10-10-20," Brent says. "We recommend feeding in the fall when roots begin to form, but it's actually never too late to make a difference unless you wait until after they bloom. In early spring, you can't count on the nutrients leaching down to the roots quickly enough, so if you wait till then, use a fast, water-soluble fertilizer."

If you follow Brent's advice, you not only get beautiful drifts of daffodils every spring, but also you get a much better looking landscape after the burst of bloom is over. "You're left with nice, healthy foliage that normally stands upright and remains green as long as it's still actively supporting the bulbs underneath through photosynthesis," says Brent. He goes on to add that it's only if

Above: Floods of golden flowers wash across sunny gardens and reliably return year after year in greater beauty.

Opposite: These bright yellow blooms alert Southerners that spring is on the way.

Above: Daffodil blooms shine underneath the sunlight.
Right: Plant several of these long-lasting daffodil selections to enjoy vibrant yellows, or oranges and pinks, as well as suitable pastels.

there's a shortage of three critical elements—sunlight, moisture, or nutrients—that the foliage weakens, flops over, and becomes unattractive. "Then gardeners want to tie it in knots, braid it, or fold it over and pin it to the ground, all of which suffocate the leaves and starve the bulbs."

After the foliage begins to turn yellow, you can cut, mow, or cover it with mulch if it isn't neatly hidden by companion perennials growing around the daffodils. That's also the time to dig, divide, and transplant bulbs. Until then, leave your daffodils alone. They need to gather all the sunlight they can, blending it with moisture and nutrients to make starches and sugars, stored in their bulbs for next year's joyful yellow blooms.

LONG-LASTING BEAUTIES

The first daffodils stirring in the garden are among the most welcome visitors of late winter and early spring. Once the daffodils arrive, we want them to linger. Experienced gardeners have learned that certain selections produce flowers that are actually a bit thicker than most and have an almost waxy texture. These daffodils are more resistant to the elements, living in the garden for as much as a week longer than other selections. When picked shortly after blooming, the flowers will last an extra two to three days.

The Heaths have known the selection of 'Ceylon' to last six weeks in the garden and up to two weeks after being picked. But if the weather is too warm or dry, they do not last as long.

In addition to 'Ceylon,' the Heaths recommend these selections for long-lasting blooms:

'Bravoure'—Large yellow-and-white blooms, 18 to 24 inches tall
'Saint Keverne'—Golden white flowers with a slightly frilled cup, 16 to 18 inches tall
'Ice Wings'—Two to three nodding ivory blossoms per stem, 12 to 14 inches tall
'Pink charm'—White petals encircle a large cup banded in orange and pink, 16 to 18 inches tall
'Redhill'—Red-orange cup inside ivory petals, 16 to 18 inches tall
'Gigantic Star'—Very large saffron-yellow blossoms with a vanilla fragrance, 18 to 20 inches tall

When these flowers appear in the garden, be sure to pick a few to enjoy indoors. Cutting daffodils can damage the foliage; instead, just pick them with your fingers. The upper part of the daffodil stem is hollow and won't hold moisture. Reach down to the white portion of the stem, and snap it off. Be sure to leave the foliage intact.

Daffodils exude a liquid that is harmful to other flowers. Before arranging with other flowers, place the stems in 6 to 8 inches of lukewarm water for an hour or so; change the water, and let them stand another hour or more.

Daffodil stalks won't penetrate florist foam easily; instead, place glass marbles in a vase to hold the stems in place. In an opaque vase, use crumpled chicken wire or floral bases to anchor the stems.

Be sure to keep arranged flowers cool, out of direct sunlight, and away from dry heat so that they will thrive longer. Cooler night temperatures also help keep them fresh. Place them near a window at night; they can tolerate temperatures to about 28 to 30 degrees.

20 EASY DAFFODILS

early

'Rijnvelds Early Sensation'
'Barrett Browning'
'February Gold'
'Gigantic Star'
Narcissus odorus (a.k.a. 'Campernelle')
'Tête à Tête'
'Saint Keverne'

mid-season

'Bravoure'
'Carlton'
'Ceylon'
'Erlicheer'
'Ice Follies'
'Trevithian'
'Accent'
'Avalanche'
'Flower Record'
N. jonquilla (a.k.a. 'Simplex')
'Quail'
'Sweetness'

late

'Geranium'
'Hawera'
'Ice Wings'
'Pink Charm'
'Redhill'
'Thalia'

tigers in the garden

You can't miss these distinctive felines. Flashy curls of orange petals dappled with dark spots, a long sweep of stamens, and a 3- to 6-foot-tall stem make these lilies an outstanding addition to any planting. It's no wonder that gardeners have adored these striking flowers for the last 200 years.

Tiger lilies *(Lilium lancifolium, formerly L. tigrinum)* are a traditional cottage-garden favorite. Despite their fierce name, tiger lilies are surprisingly easy to grow throughout the South. They're much less fussy about soils and moisture and having their roots shaded than many of the Oriental and Asiatic lilies, so they're a perfect first lily for beginners. They're also super for a child's garden, because they're gaudy and nontoxic—and have an undeniably great name.

For the quickest results, plant tiger lily bulbs either in fall or early spring, in a sunny site with good drainage. With prepared garden soil containing plenty of organic matter, they won't need any extra fertilizer. Plant the bulbs 6 to 8 inches deep, and space them about 8 inches apart. You can also start tiger lilies by planting the tiny bulbils that form during blooming season. These look like fat purple seeds tucked in where the leaves join the stalk. Collect some of the bulbils a few weeks after flowering, and plant them 1 to 2 inches deep to increase your own tribe of tigers. Or share the spares with friends. Tiger lilies take several years to reach maturity if grown from bulbils, but the price is definitely right.

With up to 12 vivid flowers adorning each stalk, dramatic tiger lilies are among the long-blooming delights of the summer garden. If you haven't grown them for a while, perhaps it's time to get some back into your flowerbeds.

THE TRUTH ABOUT TIGERS

Easy-to-grow tiger lilies are highly resistant to mosaic virus, but they can still carry it. Tigers should be planted far enough away from other lilies (beds on opposite sides of the house, for example) so that aphids can't spread any infection from one to the other.

Tiger-spotted lilies are now commercially available in several different colors. While these are in the Asiatic lily group and not quite the same as the true tiger, they have a similar effect. Try one of the white, yellow, red, pink, or salmon selections. There's even a new, more compact Asiatic lily selection called 'Tiger Babies,' with large salmon-peach flowers and a chocolate-pink reverse. These tiger-type lilies are a little more demanding than the true tiger, but all have endearing dark freckles.

TIGER LILY

at a glance

Size: 3 to 6 feet tall
Light: sun to partial shade
Soil: garden soil, well drained, lots of organic matter
Moisture: Water sparingly.
Pests: none serious
Propagation: Plant bulbs in fall or early spring; plant bulbils a few weeks after flowering.
Range: entire South
Bloom: roughly May through June in Lower South, June through August in Middle South, July through September or later in Upper South

pass along a French hollyhock

This is the hollyhock with a difference, a petite long-bloomer that adds a debonair touch to any garden. Its flowers of pale lilac striped with dark mauve are tucked in above every leaf, resembling boutonnieres in a row of buttonholes.

French hollyhock *(Malva sylvestris Zebrina)* grows to a modest 2 to 3 feet high and blends charmingly with other annuals and perennials in the garden. This useful little plant reseeds energetically and offers multiseason value. Its bright blossoms present a charming contrast to the broad foliage throughout the summer months. In winter, barring a hard freeze, the distinctive clumps of deeply lobed leaves stay vivid green, giving a look of lushness to otherwise barren months.

French hollyhock is a traditional Southern pass-along plant with a place in both formal borders and casual cottage gardens.

It's a particular favorite of Arkansas gardener Nancy Porter, who grows it at her home just outside Little Rock.

"They reseed all over the place; that's why I love them," she says. "I like a natural-looking garden—helter-skelter—I don't like things all lined up. I've grown French hollyhocks probably 20 years. I ordered seeds from a catalog, just because I thought they looked pretty. Once I had them going, they stayed.

"They hop and skip all over the garden, wherever the seeds fall, even in the paths," Nancy explains. "If I notice them before the taproot gets too deep, I can move them

FRENCH HOLLYHOCK
at a glance

Range: thrives in all but Tropical South
Light: full sun to light afternoon shade
Soil: not choosy—may actually flower best in poor, well-drained soil
Moisture: tolerates drought but flourishes with a weekly watering
Bloom season: late spring through early summer, continuing sporadically into fall
Propagate: by seeds or cuttings

Below: French hollyhocks are framed by white flowering tobacco and purple butterfly bush at the New Orleans Botanical Garden at City Park.

where I want. If they get too big, they don't transplant as well, and I have to just pull them up. But I have so many I can easily spare a few. They bloom just about all summer, because different ones come on at different stages, all over the garden. I have a lot better luck with them than I do with regular hollyhocks. They really are beautiful and very easy to grow."

While French hollyhocks don't live very long (only a year or two), as old plants die, new ones come up. They are more resistant to rust, spider mites, and leaf miners than are the taller hollyhocks and are even quite tolerant of alkaline soils. As a result, this versatile and persistent flower is welcomed as a desirable addition to gardens everywhere.

lenten roses

Blooming in winter, Lenten roses push nodding buds through chilled soil to join the season's earliest bulbs.

Unlike other flowers that fade within days, Lenten rose *(Helleborus orientalis)* stays colorful for several months. Not a rose at all, but an evergreen perennial, it blooms in subtle shades of white, pink, and rose that fade to green as spring progresses. Thanks to recent breeding efforts, their flowers are getting even showier. Lenten rose hybrids have graced the shaded beds of Southern gardens for generations. Gardeners treasure their winter foliage, early flowers, and seeds that drop and grow into seedlings for transplanting or sharing.

"You don't have to water or fertilize, and deer won't eat them," says Sam Jones of Piccadilly Farm in Bishop, Georgia. Sam, alongside his wife, Carleen, runs a nursery that specializes in Lenten roses. These plants' sturdy character and long blooming season have meant ever-increasing popularity. They make a hardy evergreen ground cover in shaded areas. Naturally drought tolerant, they endure the summer and then put on a flush of new growth in fall and again after flowers appear in late winter and early spring.

With greater demand comes opportunity for nurseries to make improved selections. Judith and Dick Tyler of Pine Knot Farms in Clarksville, Virginia, started with the Piccadilly Farm Mix and continue making crosses and strains using Lenten roses they bring home from annual visits to England. Through work with this breeding stock, they have been able to offer the Ashwood hybrids, plants with more vivid and varied colors and flower forms. Exciting innovations include doubled and anemone-flowered blossoms, outward-facing flowers, picotee flowers (a lighter or darker edge),

LENTEN ROSES

at a glance

Light: shade of tall trees
Soil: organic, well drained
Moisture: tolerates drought, but not wet
Spacing: 30 to 36 inches between plants
Propagation: transplant seedlings in fall
Nice to know: deer and vole resistant

brighter pinks and whites, and new colors such as green, yellow, apricot, and dark velvety purple.

Success with Lenten roses requires some advance planning. Here are a few guidelines to aid your endeavor.

Choose the right spot. Lenten roses need light shade and well-drained soil. Plants prosper from the Upper to Lower South and into Central Texas. North Florida and coastal gardeners need to provide full shade, fertile soil, and perfect drainage. Sam says that calls from customers who have lost plants usually reveal that they have used automatic sprinklers that kept the roots too wet.

Don't plant too deep. The crown of the plant should be sitting on the surface of the soil. If set too low, the plant will decline. Years of heavy mulching or a buildup of fallen leaves will have the same effect.

Give them a good start. Prepare the soil deeply. Work plenty of organic material, such as compost, mushroom compost, soil conditioner, sphagnum peat moss, or rotted manure, at least a foot deep into the planting bed. Also mix in a timed-release fertilizer at the rate recommended on the label. If your soil is acid, add a half-cup of dolomitic lime per plant as well. In winter every year after, sprinkle a handful of lime around the plant.

Left and above: Shade-loving Lenten roses bring the waning days of winter into full bloom.

Because Lenten roses multiply by seed, conscientious growers sell only after seedlings flower and show their colors.

Choose the right colors. Although the dark purple or slate (sometimes called black) Lenten roses are intriguing, they don't show up well in the garden. White flowers carry the best at a distance. Pink and rose colors add interest during a season when flowers are so rare.

Groom plants in small gardens. If your plants are close to either a walk or a terrace, remove any ragged foliage that has been damaged by harsh winter weather. The flowers will show up better, and you can expect that new growth will quickly emerge.

Above: An astonishing variety of blooms is available among Ashwood hybrid Lenten Roses.
Right: One of the finest ground covers for shade, Lenten rose combines handsome evergreen foliage with lovely, late-winter flowers.

fabulous Southern roses

Bred in the South and perfect for our gardens, historic Noisette roses are delighting a new generation of gardeners with their beauty, fragrance, and ease of care.

Born in Charleston, South Carolina, they were sent to France for that extra bit of polish, then brought back in triumph to fill the South with their charm and beauty. Since that time in the early 1800s, Noisette roses have been the easy, graceful, fragrant fulfillment of everything a Southern rose should be. Their shapely flowers, filled with silken petals in shades of cream, pink, yellow, apricot, or white, are produced with open-handed generosity on big, healthy, amazingly adaptable plants that thrive in the warmth and soils of most Southern gardens. Cherished specimens have been handed down via rooted cuttings for so many generations that they've become genuine living heirlooms. Still, they all originated from one rose.

'Champneys' Pink Cluster' came from a marriage between two great rose families—in the Southern sense of family, that is. Its "people" were the centuries-old, cluster-flowered European musk rose *(Rosa moschata)* and the more recently introduced ancient pink Chinese rose 'Old Blush.' The pair shared two important traits. Both loved warm climates, and, in a day when most roses bloomed just once in the spring and then quit, these prolific roses flowered periodically all summer and again in the fall.

Right: Ruth Knopf, of Charleston, South Carolina, harvests from her bounty of roses.

'Lamarque'

'Rêve d'Or'

NOISETTE ROSES
at a glance

Bloom: heavy in both spring and fall, scattered flowers in summer

Range: all South—though some may be tender in Upper South

Light: at least six hours direct sun

Soil: any well drained

Moisture: Soak root zone with about 1 inch of water weekly during growing season.

Fertilizer: Apply a slow-release fertilizer (such as Mills Magic Rose Mix) at pruning times (usually February and August). Apply a liquid fertilizer (such as alfalfa tea or fish emulsion) every two weeks when rose is blooming heavily. Do not feed after October.

Nice to know: Noisette roses, while not impervious to black spot, thrive without being sprayed.

'Natchitoches Noisette'

'Blush Noisette'

ONES TO TRY

'Aimée Vibert': white climber, 6 to 10 feet, thornless

'Blush Noisette': light pink shrub or bushy climber, 4 to 8 feet

'Bouquet d'Or': soft gold climber, 10 to 12 feet

'Champneys' Pink Cluster': pink shrub or bushy climber, 4 to 8 feet

'Crépuscule': apricot climber, 6 to 12 feet

'Madame Alfred Carrière': blush white climber, 12 to 20 feet

'Rêve d'Or': tawny yellow climber, 10 to 12 feet

'Céline Forestier'

The floral union produced what all families hope for—progeny showing the most attractive traits of their mingled bloodlines. 'Champneys' Pink Cluster' featured myriad dainty bunches of the palest pink, perfumed petals, blossoming in successive waves over a large, sturdy bush. Best of all, the new rose was completely at home in the Southern region, standing up to heat, humidity, irregular winters, and sandy and clay soils with endearing ease.

Only genealogists—or seriously addicted rosarians—will be interested in following the travels of 'Champneys' Pink Cluster' and its seedling, 'Blush Noisette,' across the ocean to rose breeders in France. It's of more interest to the average gardener today that their heavy-blooming progeny returned to us enriched with a broader range of colors, fatter flowers, and some climbing habits. Both the early bush-style Noisettes and the later big, buxom climbers are perfectly adapted to our Southern climate—and perfectly magnificent in the modern garden. From spring to fall, these roses prove their lasting worth by producing armloads of fragrant flowers to share and enjoy.

Fortunately, Noisette roses are no longer just pass-along heirlooms. They are now readily available at many nurseries that specialize in old-fashioned roses, and their beauty is featured in a number of rose display gardens. All across the South in the spring, Noisette roses will be coming into exuberant blooms. You can watch and applaud. Or you may decide to join the growing ranks of rose lovers who are inviting these Southern beauties back into their own gardens.

secrets to gorgeous roses

Steve Bender may be older than King Tut's underwear, but that doesn't mean he can't learn something new. Case in point: Until he met Pam Cunningham, he never knew roses were low-maintenance plants.

"Madness!" you cry, having heard horror stories about incessant spraying, grooming, feeding, and weeding of roses. But Pam swears she gets beautiful flowers year-round with little effort.

Her garden in Ocala, Florida, was designed by a local landscape architect for vegetables and herbs. But she found the upkeep to be overwhelming. "We had to completely replant the garden every season," Pam explains. "And our plants were getting killed by insects. Then I had the idea that I should garden organically, so my daughter and I would go out and remove caterpillars from broccoli by hand and fill paper cups. It was disgusting."

Out went the vexing vegetables and herbs. Then, aided by a local horticulturist, Pam rededicated her garden using the original design. "We dug up the beds; amended the clay soil with sand, peat moss, and manure; and edged the beds with Japanese boxwoods," she recalls. "Then we planted roses. And they were so much easier."

Several factors determined the kinds of roses. "I wanted great color and a lot of variety," she says, "some antique-looking roses, some long-stemmed ones like 'Mr. Lincoln' and 'Tropicana,' others like 'Playgirl' that have just a few petals, and small-flowered

Opposite: Pam tends roses with daughters Ellison and Kelli.
Below: Japanese boxwoods edge formal beds linked by paths of brick and gravel. Drip irrigation lines keep thirsty roses watered.

ones like 'Summer Snow.' When 'Summer Snow' is in bloom, you can cut it and make huge bouquets of flowers."

But what of the unending toil and high anxiety we all know beautiful roses demand? It's a myth, insists Pam. She simultaneously feeds her roses and fends off insects by sprinkling RosePride Systemic Rose & Flower Care 8-12-4 around the base of her plants every six weeks. She doesn't bother spraying for black spot or mildew. Instead, she simply picks off any diseased leaves she spots. To retain soil moisture and inhibit weeds, she mulches with pine bark chips several times a year. Finally, a drip irrigation system supplies necessary water without wetting the foliage, which would promote disease.

"What I like most about the garden is the continuous flowers," Pam states. "I cut the roses back around Valentine's Day, they grow back, and I have flowers all year long." Her daughters, Ellison and Kelli, enjoy the roses too. "They've taken a real interest," she notes. "They'll cut a rose and call it theirs. I think they'll grow into an even greater appreciation of gardening than I have myself."

And they won't have to stick with just the selections Pam grows now. Other easy-to-grow roses include 'Souvenir de la Malmaison Rouge,' 'Hansa,' 'Heritage,' 'La Marne,' 'Pet Pink,' 'St Patrick,' 'Moonstone,' and 'Cécile Brunner.'

"Gardening isn't a big secret," Pam concludes, admiring multitudinous blossoms. "Maybe it seems easier because I have good soil and an irrigation system. But I think that plants require very little care, other than food and water. And if you give them that, they'll thrive."

'Tropicana' 'Peace'
'New Dawn' 'Playgirl'

getting started with roses

For beautiful roses in the South, follow these tips.

- Plant in full sun. The more sun your roses get, the more flowers you'll get.
- Roses prefer fertile, well-drained soil that contains lots of organic matter, such as sphagnum peat moss, garden compost, ground bark, chopped leaves, and composted manure. Organic matter is especially important in sand or clay soils.
- Water roses deeply once a week, thoroughly soaking the soil. Do not wet the foliage.
- If you don't like spraying, try the roses mentioned here, as well as 'Louis Philippe,' 'Mrs. B.R. Cant,' 'Bonica,' 'Carefree Beauty,' and 'Carefree Wonder.'

Below: Running beside the house, the garden contains about two dozen kinds of roses, as well as a variety of perennials. Its modest size makes for easy maintenance.

a garden of rhododendrons

If you've ever tried growing rhododendrons in the South, you know the procedure consists of five easy steps. Buy your rhododendron. Plant your rhododendron. Cry over your dead rhododendron. Throw away your rhododendron. Surrender. Plant a holly instead.

Why do rhododendrons give us fits? Because they're suited to the more temperate regions of the world, where folks seldom fry catfish on their foreheads in July. Rhodies prefer cool summer nights, regular rainfall, and practically perfect drainage.

That doesn't sound like my garden—and probably not yours either. But don't give up. You can still enjoy beautiful rhododendrons by heeding the following instructions.

Choose the right one. Nurseries sell hundreds of different selections, but relatively few grow well in the South. Stick to the tried-and-true ones (see the chart on page 144). These combine cold hardiness, heat tolerance, and disease resistance.

Buy Southern. Many rhododendrons sold at garden centers come from the Pacific Northwest. Because the heavy soil they're shipped in doesn't allow enough oxygen to reach the roots in the South's more stressful climate, the plants sometimes get diseases and die. One way to prevent disease is to plant rhododendrons correctly (see below). But you should also favor plants grown in the South and East over those grown in the West. If you're unsure where rhododendrons in your garden center came from, check the tag or ask the nurseryman. As an alternative, order plants.

Find the right spot. Although some rhodies tolerate full sun, most do best in light, dappled shade. But don't try to plant them beneath maples, beeches, willows, or magnolias because these shallow-rooted trees steal moisture and nutrients. And don't plant them beneath a black walnut, as the roots of this tree release a chemical that is toxic to rhodies. These shrubs will grow much better beneath oaks, pines, tulip poplars, and hickories.

Avoid western exposures. Planting on the western side subjects plants to hot, drying summer sun and cold, drying winter wind. Plant on the north side of your garden instead.

Keep in mind that, with the exception of the Bonneville Salt Flats, the worst spot for a rhododendron may be up against your house. The soil there often reeks of clay and lime and alternates between desert and swamp. Also, snow and ice falling from your roof will snap the shrub's brittle branches. Better locations include shrub borders and the edge of a woodland.

Plant rhododendrons correctly. They need a loose, acidic (pH 4.5 to 5.5), fertile soil containing lots of organic matter.

Left: 'Roseum Elegans' lives where other rhododendrons die. These 12-year-old plants decorate the Atlanta garden of Jack and Russell Huber.

Forget about planting in heavy, red clay.

Jeff Beasley, owner of Transplant Nursery in Lavonia, Georgia, suggests the following regimen for planting a rhododendron: Dig a hole at least 10 inches deep and twice as wide as the root ball. Mix equal amounts of excavated soil and plain pine bark (make sure the bark does not contain lime). Fill the hole with this mixture; do not tamp it when finished. Place the rhododendron atop the filled hole. Then mix one part excavated soil to three parts bark, and mound soil around the sides of the root ball, leaving the top of the ball exposed. Cover the ball with 1 or 2 inches of pine straw.

Go easy on the fertilizer. If the leaves become chlorotic (yellow between the veins), use a product such as Miracid that supplies chelated iron. Otherwise, just sprinkle a half cup of cottonseed meal or 1 tablespoon azalea-camellia food around the dripline of the plant in spring.

"Always water thoroughly," cautions Willis Harden a rhododendron expert in Commerce, Georgia. "Rhododendrons don't respond well to light, daily watering. They need a deep soaking of 1 to 2 inches per week. Water them in the morning, never at night. The leaves need to dry prior to evening or they'll get fungal diseases."

That's it—all you need to know to successfully grow a rhododendron. Of course, that leaves you with a new problem. Now where are you going to plant that holly?

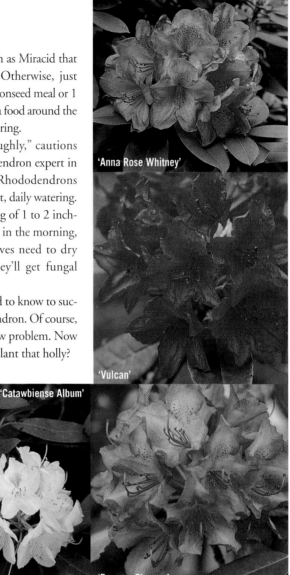

'Anna Rose Whitney'

'Vulcan'

'Scintillation'

'Catawbiense Album'

'Roseum Elegans'

RHODODENDRONS FOR THE SOUTH

Plant	Flower Color	Height after 10 Years	Comments
'A. Bedford'	lavender with purple blotch	6'	sun tolerant, handsome leaves
'Anah Kruschke'	rich purple	5'	glossy foliage, sun tolerant
'Anna Rose Whitney'	deep rose-pink	8'	fast grower, trouble free
'Bibiani'	bright bloodred	6'	glossy, deep green leaves; very heat tolerant
'Caroline'	light pink	6'	fragrant, disease resistant, very heat tolerant
'Catawbiense Album'	white with chartreuse blotch	6'	vigorous, adaptable, tough
'Cynthia'	rose-crimson	5'	sun tolerant, extremely durable
'Dora Amateis'	white with green spots	3'	fragrant flowers; compact; small, shiny leaves
'Mrs. Tom H. Lowinsky'	white with orange-brown blotch	5'	orchidlike blooms; glossy, dark green leaves
'Roseum Elegans'	lavender-pink	6'	fast grower, dependable, real survivor
'Scintillation'	light pink with light brown blotch	5'	extremely handsome foliage
'Trude Webster'	pink	5'	huge flower trusses, easy to grow
'Van Nes Sensation'	orchid-pink with yellow center	5'	fragrant flowers, heat tolerant
'Vulcan'	brick red	5'	most popular red for the South

The high, dappled shade of tall tulip poplars provides the perfect light for 'Scintillation' rhodedendrons.

azaleas by the bunches

Take a look around your neighborhood in the spring. If you live in a warmer section of the South, chances are you won't have to travel very far to spot confectionery clouds of pink, white, red, or lavender blooms surrounding a home.

Evergreen azaleas are not native here, but they've been welcomed with open arms since they arrived in the early 1800s. It's easy to see why the South overflows with these plants. For starters, they're evergreen, which is always a nice quality. Second, they offer a mind-boggling variety of flower form, color, and size.

Whether you're contemplating a new landscape plan, adding to your existing garden, or just looking for tips on caring for the azaleas you already have, here are some guidelines offered by Hank Bruno, trails manager at Callaway Gardens in Pine Mountain, Georgia. This 14,000-acre garden, nestled in the southernmost foothills of the Appalachian Mountains, could be called the Super Bowl of azaleas. It features hundreds of types of azaleas that can be grown in the Southeast. Hank conducts workshops teaching visitors how to grow them. As it turns out, this is not astrophysics. Actually, growing azaleas is easy.

BEGIN WITH GOOD DESIGN

"What I'm seeing in the home landscape is a lot of people are not being very judicious in their use of color," Hank says. "When you've got the vibrant colors that azaleas have, I recommend people select different hybrid groups with different bloom times so they aren't blooming side by side at the same time. Either that or try to harmonize the colors, which is what we're doing here with our plantings. But what I worry about is that people start clashing colors, and the yard looks like a cacophony instead of a concert."

If you want to put together a first-rate symphony, a conductor can tell you that you need to group your instruments; scattering everything randomly would not lead to harmonious music. It's the

same with azaleas. Mass plantings of a single color will lend a graceful appearance to your garden. (If you're into heavy metal music, you might not be afraid of mixing lavender and orange blooms.) Pastels are easier to work with because the colors tend to harmonize well.

Opposite: No matter what color your home, white azaleas are always a good match.
Right: Plant azaleas in graceful sweeps rather than spotting them here and there. Keep combinations to no more than two colors, such as these 'Pink Pearl' and white 'H.H. Hume' azaleas.

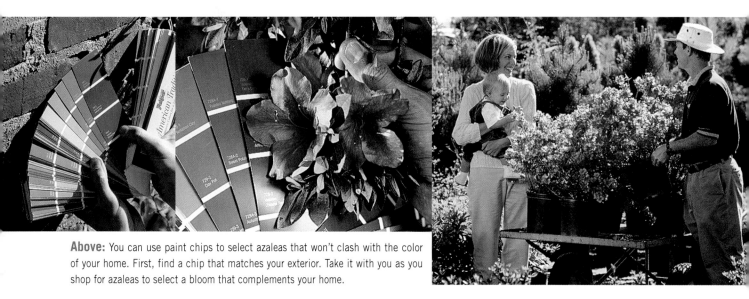

Above: You can use paint chips to select azaleas that won't clash with the color of your home. First, find a chip that matches your exterior. Take it with you as you shop for azaleas to select a bloom that complements your home.

Another design strategy that keeps Hank awake at night is alternating red and white azaleas as a foundation planting, especially against a redbrick house. "If you want to use two colors, put them in blocks rather than alternating them," he says. "We try to encourage a color scheme that appeals to the individual homeowner. We're not trying to dictate the color; we just try to emphasize a little bit of discretion."

PLANT IT RIGHT

If you want your azaleas to enjoy a long and healthy life, you need to give them a good start. "Soil is the key, as with any plant," Hank says. "They like acid soil with a pH of 5.5 to 6. You have to plant them in well-drained soil with lots of organic matter. Drainage is paramount."

Hank recommends preparing a raised bed for your azaleas, tilling or forking in aged pine bark, leaf mold, and compost. This is

particularly important if your soil has a lot of clay. "Individual holes usually end up acting like sinks in our clay soils, and you pay the price," he cautions. "You get water held in the bottom of the hole and that sends root rot right on up to the crown." Once the soil has been properly prepared, add fertilizer before planting. Work in a slow-release variety such as cottonseed meal at the rate of 1 cup per plant. You can also use one specifically formulated for azaleas. Apply at the rate recommended on the label.

When planting azaleas, Hank leaves about 2 inches of the root ball above the ground. He then mounds soil up to (but not on top of) the root ball and finishes up with 2 to 4 inches of mulch to hold in moisture, prevent weeds, and protect the tender new plants from cold. They'll need a thorough soaking at least once a week for the first year while they get established. They also appreciate highly filtered shade, such as that from tall pine trees, to protect them from the full brunt of the sun's rays.

Below, left: Before planting your new azalea, water it thoroughly. **Below, middle:** Measure the dimensions of the hole before planting. Dig the hole two times as wide as the container. **Right:** The top of the root ball should be slightly higher than the soil surface. Mound the soil around it, and mulch. Thoroughly water at least once a week for the first year.

Small pruners are fine for trimming pencil-width stems, but long-handled loppers are the tool of choice when cutting branches ½ inch to 1½ inches in diameter. The handles provide the leverage needed to make clean cuts.

Below: If you see pale, fuzzy buds curled tight on the tips of branches, it's too late to prune azaleas without cutting off next year's flowers.

Above, left: A grouping of pink azaleas is just the right height and color underneath this window.

MAINTAIN YOUR AZALEAS

Once your azaleas are on their way, they are relatively easy to maintain. "Azaleas are not heavy feeders," he says. "As they're sending out those new roots, if they come in direct contact with fertilizer it will burn them." In spring after the plants have flowered, he adds a slow-release fertilizer such as a 12-5-9.

To keep your azaleas blooming and to maintain their shape, prune them after they've finished blooming. "I usually tell folks if you haven't done it by July 4th, it's too late," Hank says. "If you prune later than that, you're going to lose flowers next year." The only other time to prune is to remove dead or diseased wood, which can be done anytime. Simply prune back the dead branches until you find green wood. If you suspect a disease, sterilize your pruner blades with rubbing alcohol or a 10% bleach solution between each cut to prevent spreading the disease. The caution is worth the time, because anything you can do to keep your azaleas happy means a few more jubilant blooms hailing springtime in the South.

To see the efforts of Hank Bruno and his garden staff, visit the Callaway Brothers Azalea Bowl at Callaway Gardens in Pine Mountain, Georgia. For information call 1-800-225-5292, or visit www.callawaygardens.com.

SHAPING YOUR AZALEAS

Shaping your azaleas is like getting a good haircut; the improvement is noticeable but the amount removed isn't. With a little attention, your plants will be as pretty as a picture. Artful pruning can get these shrubs in shape and keep them that way.

If you trim azaleas during the wrong season, you will cut off next year's blossoms. That's because azaleas bloom on old wood, so they produce flowerbuds on last year's growth. You won't hurt the plant by pruning during warm months, but if you want flowers, hide your clippers after spring. The best time to trim azaleas is just after they've finished blooming.

Never prune azaleas with electric shears. Hand pruners are essential for doing the job right. If your shrubs haven't been shaped for a while, they've probably grown long woody stalks with clusters of foliage at the tips. Reach inside the plant to cut these stalks off where they join each branch. Not only will all cuts be hidden by surrounding foliage, but this technique also allows sunlight to penetrate to the center of the plant, encouraging new growth and flowers. (Flat-topping your azalea by trimming only the ends of branches results in dense twiggy growth with sparse foliage.)

Though you may end up with an alarmingly large pile of cut-off stalks, don't worry. Your azaleas won't look like they've just been butchered. That's because this pruning method allows the shrubs to maintain their natural, airy shape.

Tips for Texas

What do armadillos and evergreen azaleas have in common? Answer: They're not native to Texas, but they don't seem to know it. In fact, they're almost everywhere.

While armadillos fend for themselves, you can't say the same for azaleas. Indigenous to Japan, China, and Korea, these evergreens need special care in the Lone Star State, or you can kiss them goodbye. Fortunately, providing that care doesn't require a brain the size of DFW airport. Just follow these guidelines.

CHOOSE THE RIGHT AZALEA

Many types of azaleas exist, and they vary in their cold hardiness and heat tolerance. For example, the large, semi-tropical Southern Indica azaleas won't take the cold winters of the Panhandle, while the smaller, cold-hardy Kurume types won't like the heat of Corpus Christi. Your local nursery can point you toward azaleas that thrive in your area.

PREPARE THE SOIL BEFORE PLANTING

Azaleas prefer acid, well-drained soil that contains lots of organic matter. Few parts of Texas, though, have soil like this, so you'll probably have to improvise. Most East Texas soils should be fine. Steve Brainerd, former president of the Azalea Society of America and a resident of Rowlett, Texas, advises planting azaleas in a raised bed, about 15 inches deep, atop existing alkaline clay soil. Set the plants no deeper than they were growing in the pots.

Steve and the Dallas Chapter of the Azalea Society recommend using Azalea Mix, manufactured by Vital Earth Resources in Gladewater, Texas, in the raised beds. This product consists of a pre-wet mixture of 60% finely milled pine bark and 40% coarse sphagnum peat moss with added micronutrients, such as iron, sulfur, and manganese. The peat moss gives the mixture an acid pH of 5.0 and supplies organic matter. The pine bark improves drainage, adds organic matter, and suppresses root rot fungus.

You can make your own azalea mix from sphagnum peat moss and pine bark, but you need to thoroughly wet it before using. Fill a wheelbarrow with the mix; then slowly add water while stirring vigorously with a stick or handtool. Continue until the mix is evenly moist. If you fail to do this before using, water will run off the mix like raindrops from a duck's back, and your soil will always be dry.

Most Central and West Texas water is alkaline, so the pH of the azalea bed will slowly rise as you water. To keep the pH in the preferred range of between 5.0 and 6.0, apply 1 pound of 3 parts garden sulfur and 1 part iron sulfate to 100 square feet of bed. This should lower the pH by 1 point. While young plants require acid soil, older plants gradually adapt to a higher pH. "I have seen established plants 8 to 10 years old in soil with a pH of 8 without any sign of chlorosis [yellow leaves with green veins]," claims Steve.

WATER BOTH ROOTS AND LEAVES

When you water, thoroughly wet the root zone and the leaves. "Azaleas take up a lot of water through their leaves," explains Steve. Overhead watering with sprinklers works well, but do this in morning so that the leaves dry by the afternoon to prevent possible fungus problems. Avoid using drip irrigation, because it doesn't uniformly wet the root system.

MULCH, PRUNE, AND FERTILIZE IN SPRING, RIGHT AFTER THE BLOOMS FADE

Mulching in fall holds heat in the ground and also delays the onset of dormancy, so plant stems remain full of water. "Then when you get a quick freeze," says Steve, "the water expands and the bark splits." Pruning in summer, fall, or winter removes flowerbuds for the next spring's blooms, and fertilizing before blooming in spring encourages leafy growth at the wrong time. (When you do fertilize, use a slow-release, azalea/camellia food that contains iron, sulfur, and manganese.)

A winding line of azaleas graces the drive.

fashionable hydrangeas

With a look as old-fashioned as grandmother's garden, or as stylish as the latest summer fashions, hydrangeas have become a renaissance flower in our landscape. As Elizabeth Dean of Wilkerson Mill Gardens in Palmetto, Georgia, says, "There's a newfound madness about hydrangeas."

The well-known mophead selections are only the beginning of what this family of flowering shrubs has to offer. "When people come in to buy a hydrangea, they want one of two things," she says. "They either want a hydrangea just like their grandmother grew, or they want anything but what their grandmother grew." Either way, they have plenty of choices.

French hydrangeas *(Hydrangea macrophylla)* have luscious, round, globelike flowers also known as mopheads. These are our grandmother's hydrangeas. Ranging from deep lavender-blue to pure white with a healthy assortment of pinks and reds in between, these dense flowers make a colorful splash in the garden.

Lace caps are a prissy sister of mopheads. These lesser known hydrangeas have flowers that seem to float in flat, delicate-looking clusters above the foliage. Their appearance is light and airy, with gentler colors than the voluptuous mopheads.

WINTER WOES

If these hydrangeas suffer a down side, it's their eagerness to break dormancy and leaf out in late winter. This is especially true in the Lower and Middle South where warm days in late January and February are not uncommon. Then, along comes a cold snap, and tender new leaves are burned or destroyed. "A lot of hydrangeas have been de-

veloped for the florist trade," says Elizabeth. "They are grown quickly in a greenhouse and put in a pretty container to be sold for Mother's Day. They grow in controlled conditions and have beautiful flowers. But they may not necessarily be garden-hardy selections and may not know how to go dormant. You will find these hydrangeas available in nurseries even though their cold hardiness is questionable."

Through years of experience, Elizabeth and husband Gene Griffith have identified several selections that are more inclined to stay dormant until spring. "We've found Générale Vicomtesse de Vibraye to be slow to produce its foliage and begin spring growth. It is a large mophead with electric blue flowers. Lilacina is a lace cap that also waits until spring to leaf out," Elizabeth says.

EXTENDED FAMILY

H. serrata is an excellent choice for gardens in the Middle and Lower South where variable late-winter temperatures lure hydrangeas out of dormancy. "They seem to be more able to go dormant and stay there," Elizabeth says. They also flourish in the Upper South where temperatures are more constant throughout winter.

Their overall size is more petite than their macrophylla cousins, making them a good fit for small gardens. They are even happy in pots.

Left: Each branch of Nikko Blue mophead hydrangea bears a bouquet of blooms.

You will find both mophead and lace cap flowers in this family. Preziosa has demure, mottled-color mophead blooms, while Blue Billow produces lace cap flowers.

Elizabeth and Gene recommend that you, "Look for the best size plant for your garden. Then choose the bloom type that you prefer. Whether you decide to do a mixed bed of all sorts of hydrangeas or just one kind, enjoy them for their flexibility, versatility, and their great summer color."

Opposite page: Given the right growing conditions, hydrangeas bloom pink rather than blue. **Below:** This Blue Billow has reached mature size and is an excellent choice for a small garden.

Top, left: Lilacina sports lovely lace cap blooms. It is also an excellent choice for Lower South gardens where winter days occasionally warm up.

Top, middle: Générale Vicomtesse de Vibraye, with its electric blue mopheads, is less susceptible to cold damage because it remains dormant throughout winter.

Top, right: Close up blooms of Lilacina

Above: The mophead flowers of Preziosa deepen in color as they mature.

the charm of camellias

Azaleas aside, no plant of foreign soil has so totally rooted itself in Southern culture as the camellia. Through two centuries, camellias have accompanied Southerners on their journeys through life.

Camellias were the flower of choice for winter weddings and holiday centerpieces. They adorned tuxedo lapels and upswept hair with equal frequency. The faithful brought baskets of colorful blooms to church for the altar. And always you would find a short-stemmed blossom floating in a shallow bowl on a parlor table.

The cherished flower of Northern conservatories, camellias flourish beneath tall pines in deep South gardens. Here, as in the camellia's native Japan and China, mild winters afford both shrubs and gardeners crisp outdoor days filled with flowers.

Like so much we take for granted until it is gone, many of those old camellias have become scarce, replaced in the nursery trade by the newest and best. While enthusiasts continue to produce exciting new camellias, many of us long to grow the blossoms of old family favorites.

It's good to hear the names again: 'Lady Clare,' 'Alba Plena,' 'Debutante,' 'Purple Dawn,' and 'Magnoliaeflora.' They drawl in our memory's ear as they fell from our forebears' lips, bringing not only the recollection of a flower, but a day spent with a beloved parent or grandparent.

They were called "japonicas," referring to the species, Camellia japonica, as opposed to "sasanquas" (C. sasanqua). The handsome, evergreen shrubs would be desirable if they never bloomed, but they do.

One of the earliest camellias to appear in Southern gardens was 'Alba Plena.' Arriving around 1800, it is still a favorite today. The problem is that, like so many old selections, it is difficult to locate.

The number of selections on nursery lists grew throughout the 19th century. During the 1930s, 1940s, and 1950s,

Opposite: Vibrant pink flowers brighten the winter landscape. **Below:** The graceful blooms of 'Magnoliiflora' ('Hagoromo') 1859 bring beauty to the garden.

The camellia buds are swelling and salvation is at hand.
—George Wright

interest in camellias was keen. Every town had a camellia show, and gardeners competed for ribbons.

Meanwhile new selections continually appeared, fueled by widespread enthusiasm and the lust for a prize at the show. But by the early 1960s gardeners' interests had turned to foundation plantings and lawns, rather than gardens. Now Southerners are rediscovering their ancestors' appreciation for the camellia.

"I had never seen a camellia before the winter of 1983," says George Wright of Wintergarden Nursery, referring to the time when he moved to Fairhope, Alabama. "I was in awe. Most of the neighbors could not answer my endless inquiries, but they would direct me to people who could—mostly elderly people, carryovers from the camellia craze. I decided I was going to grow camellias, for I couldn't install a garden in good faith without camellias. It's like serving salad without dressing. And their availability was becoming very limited."

George and business partner Bobby Green began to take cuttings from old garden sites, at times snatching them from the path of a bulldozer. "Houses are being squeezed in where gardens once flourished," George says. "Man is the primary cause of camellia death; the plants can survive for hundreds of years." Today their collection numbers more than 1,200 selections.

But even in the South, cold snaps are perilous. "I don't think there's anything prettier than 'Alba Plena,'" says landscape architect Robert Marvin of Walterboro, South Carolina. "But they were all killed in this part of the world in 1951, when we had the most severe freeze in my life."

Robert grew up with camellias, his father owned Wildwood Nurseries. "I used to know 40 or 50 of them by their leaf, without having to see the bloom. 'Professor Sargent' and 'Duchess of Sutherland.' 'Elegans' was easy to kill in the cold, but it was a good camellia. 'Pink Perfection' was a wonderful one."

The old-style gardens required enough space to plant 20 to 40 selections beneath trees. Robert recommends creating a camellia walk where you have camellias on both sides of a path. "They ought to be at least 12 to 15 feet apart because they grow pretty big." Gardeners can also plant these evergreens as screens or large specimens in their suburban landscape.

Gardeners in borderline areas can look to the more cold-tolerant selections of the old camellias or new cold-hardy types. It helps to locate them in a sheltered nook such as near a masonry wall. A canopy of trees also offers protection.

The history of camellias in the South reveals an enduring passion. It reaches to the core of who we are.

"I think everybody would be much happier in their life if they had a collection of camellias," says Robert. "There is nothing to equal it in the middle of the winter when little else is blooming."

cold-tolerant *choices*

Based on 20 years of studies by the American Camellia Society, the following are some of the more cold-hardy japonicas.

'Berenice Boddy'
'China Doll'
'Coquetti' ('Glen 40')
'Doncklaeri'
'Drama Girl'
'Dr. Tinsley'
'Governor Mouton'
'Imura'
'Magnoliiflora' ('Hagoromo')

Opposite: Winter brings big blooms and lots of them. No wonder Southerners' enthusiasm for camellias has spanned the centuries. **Above:** 'Coquetti' ('Glen 40') 1839 received an award of merit from the Royal Horticultural Society in 1956.

dynamic dogwoods

Every spring, a Southerner's heart becomes a little crowded because a dogwood takes up half the space.

That Southerners love flowering dogwood (*Cornus florida*) was never more evident than when we asked *Southern Living* readers to send us remembrances and interesting facts about this native tree. Mail flooded in. Envelopes held photographs, short stories, and even a flower or two.

Talk about interesting facts. You know dogwood's reputation for being delicate and temperamental? Alice Pryor of Jefferson City, Tennessee, tells of her 50-year-old white dogwood broken off at the ground by careless construction workers. Not only did it live, the regrown tree now sports pink and white blooms!

In Winnsboro, Texas, Pete Forshee remembers splitting rails for fences as a boy. He used wedges and chisels made from dogwood. Only the wood of hickory is harder, heavier, and more durable. William Thomas of Oak Ridge, Tennessee, stresses the ecological importance of dogwoods. He says they serve as "calcium pumps" by absorbing large amounts of this nutrient from the subsoil, concentrating it in their leaves, then bestowing it to the soil surface. When the leaves drop in fall, dogwoods feed their neighbors.

These trees enrich the spirit too. Paula Rogers of Chesterfield, Virginia, remembers two desolate years living in the Arizona desert. Finally, her family was called back to Virginia. On the drive home, white dogwoods laid out the welcome mat in Tennessee. "The dogwoods that lined the roads all the way back to Richmond . . . were my Southern sentinels," she writes. "They reminded me of all I had missed about the South: the refinement, the grace, the beauty, the glory of the spring. I knew I was back home."

A dogwood is more than a tree. It's a symbol of hope, fidelity, friendship, and renewal.

Quite a few readers told us how dogwood blooms celebrated anniversaries. Jerry Bigner of Shreveport, Louisiana, recalls the letters her grandfather, a traveling salesman, sent to her grandmother. "He wrote, 'I'll be home to get you when the dogwoods are in bloom,'" she says. "And every year [he] would bring from the woods bouquets of dogwood as a reminder of his love." Their marriage, born on Easter Sunday, 1903, lasted 67 years.

For many, the cruciform blossoms of dogwood symbolize hope, renewal, and rebirth. Gelynda Underwood of Carthage, North Carolina, is one. On July 11, 1995, she found a yearling dogwood, growing by the side of the road, that was due to be mowed down. She wanted to transplant it, but her husband warned it would surely die if dug in summer.

"[That] really shook me," she says. "You see, a year to the day had passed since our third child was born 15 weeks premature, and we were told then he would not live. Well, our miracle child did live, so I decided to plant [this dogwood] for him on his first birthday. After two weeks and lots of care, the tree was still alive, and we took Dillon's picture with his tree."

Above: Fall sees glorious color, too—leaves turn bright red and crimson before dropping.
Opposite: This pink specimen graces Louise Hammond's garden in Anapolis, Maryland.

DEALING WITH DOGWOODS

Flowering dogwood will not grow in the Tropical South, unfortunately. Elsewhere, it needs moist, acid, well-drained soil. Full sun is fine, if the soil is deep and fertile. Otherwise, plant it beneath tall pines and hardwoods, so it receives afternoon shade. Be sure to water during summer droughts or the leaves will scorch badly. Watch out for anthracnose, a deadly disease that begins as purple-rimmed spots or tan blotches on leaves and flowers. To control it, apply Daconil 2787 once a week from the time the first blooms open until the leaves are fully expanded.

Most trees grow 15 to 25 feet tall and wide, but some get bigger, and in a few cases, a lot bigger. A dogwood in the yard of Margaret Thurmond in Charleston, Missouri, stands 37 feet high with a spread of 49 feet and a trunk circumference of 5 feet, 7 inches. It's the Missouri State Champion.

Nursery-grown dogwoods sometimes struggle to adjust to people's yards. Michael Murphy, a certified arborist in Beaufort, South Carolina, thinks he's discovered a remedy. He says that after inoculating the root zones of two dogwoods in a city planting with mycorrhiza—beneficial soil fungi that help roots to absorb nutrients—the trees responded "with incredible results. In every aspect, they were superior to the other trees." How can you get mycorrhiza? Scoop up a jarful of woodsy soil beneath a natural stand of dogwoods. Add it to the soil mix when you plant your tree.

If you want to try growing dogwoods from seeds, follow the advice of Mary Coleman in Prescott, Arkansas. Gather berries in fall, scrape off the red pulp, and dry the seeds. Around December 15th, plant the seeds atop the ground, covering them with pine straw or oak leaves; then lay wire screen atop that. Remove this covering in mid-March. Seedlings will sprout shortly. Mary, an active gardener in her nineties, has grown 18 dogwoods this way.

Below: Like clouds tethered to the ground, dogwoods adorn the South each spring. In full sun, they grow rounded and dense; in shade,

colorful crepe myrtles

We Southerners share certain memories—the smell of a freshly mowed lawn, the high-pitched cry of cicadas on sweltering days, the juicy taste of sweet watermelon, and the vision of huge crepe myrtles bent low by the weight of their blooms.

lthough native to China, crepe myrtles have set deep roots in our Southern soil, becoming a part of both our landscape and our traditions. This time of year they dress up historic cities such as New Orleans, Savannah, and Charleston. They also grace many of our own private gardens, a sign of their enduring popularity.

And why not? These easy-to-grow trees possess many outstanding features. Sinewy and strong, crepe myrtles have gray, tan, or cinnamon-hued branches that bear glorious clouds of colorful, long-lasting blooms starting in June. In the fall, they dependably produce radiant foliage in reds, oranges, and yellows. Winter reveals their exfoliating bark, which makes their naturally sculpted trunks look like living works of art.

Crepe myrtles boast year-round appeal, but in the heat of summer they show their true colors, from red and pink to lavender, purple, and white. Widely available, they can be found at most any nursery or garden center, and summer is a great time to purchase them because you can see exactly what color you're getting. Just remember, if you plant them in the summer, give them lots of water to help them adjust to the garden and promote new root growth.

Above: Watermelon red is a popular color of crepe myrtle. They also come in pink, purple, lavender, and white.
Opposite: Crepe myrtles sprinkle their paper-like blooms onto this sidewalk. These old trees also provide shade from the hot summer sun.

THEY KEEP ON BLOOMING

Unlike spring's cherry trees, with delicate flowers that may last only a week or two, crepe myrtles can bloom all summer. Light tip pruning or snipping off old blooms will encourage more flowers. Although tip pruning may be recommended, heavy cutbacks in late winter or early spring are never a good idea. Many people who don't know better cut back trees in February or March, leaving only 4- or 5-foot trunks sticking up out of the ground. This ruins the natural shape of the trees. It also causes multiple shoots to sprout from the cut-back point. Trees then grow so thick that air circulation is reduced, making the plants more susceptible to aphids, sooty mold, and powdery mildew. The numerous branches also create too heavy a load, which can cause them to split or crack during heavy rains or high winds.

Know a crepe myrtle's mature height before you plant it. If you don't want it to be too big, look for a low-growing selection (see chart on page 167). Crepe myrtles range in height from 2 feet to 30 feet. Trees such as 'Natchez' or 'Tuscarora' reach 25 to 30 feet in height. 'Sioux' and 'Regal Red' are medium-size selections that will grow only 12 to 15 feet tall. These medium trees are perfect for a small courtyard or patio. Breeders

also market dwarf selections. Some of those, such as 'Chickasaw' and 'Pokomoke,' have been around for a while, and many new dwarf selections have been introduced in recent years. A number of trees grow less than 3 feet tall.

Crepe myrtles have many landscape uses. They can be planted together to make a large hedge or screen, or a single tree can act as a specimen to create a distinctive focal point. Some of the smaller growing selections even look great in large containers.

These trees do need a sunny site to grow full and bloom heavily. Left in the shade, they become leggy and produce few flowers. Crepe myrtles also may suffer from cold damage in cooler climates, so if you live in the Upper South, be sure to plant cold-hardy selections such as 'Acoma,' 'Centennial Spirit,' or 'Hopi.'

If you've already planted a crepe myrtle that's overgrowing its boundary, you might want to move it. These trees may be transplanted easily, and only a small root ball is needed for success. It's best to move them in late fall or winter, when they're leafless and dormant.

When you need a small tree and have a sunny spot, make a point to try a crepe myrtle. This classic plant will beat the heat and make your summer garden more colorful and memorable.

pruning myrtles

Once crepe myrtles have bloomed and shed their flowers, they will set seed. The small round seedpods or capsules usually weigh the limbs down, making them sag.

Using a sharp pair of clippers or hedge trimmers, cut off the seedpods. New shoots with buds will quickly appear, and you will get a second bloom.

Sometimes people are hesitant to remove seedpods because they think the round capsules are flowerbuds. This is not so. The seedpods are larger than the flowerbuds and are extremely hard.

If temperatures stay warm into the fall and you continue to remove spent flowers, you may even get a third or fourth bloom out of your crepe myrtles.

Crepe myrtles send up suckers from the base of the tree. Remove them any time of the year. Cut suckers off as close to the soil level as possible.

CREPE MYRTLES IN THREE SIZES

large

'Centennial Spirit': 20 feet tall, dark red flowers
'Muskogee': 20 feet tall, lavender flowers
'Natchez': 30 feet tall, white flowers
'Tuscarora': 23 feet tall, dark coral flowers

medium

'Acoma': 10 to 14 feet tall, white flowers
        15 feet tall, bright pink flowers
'Yuma': 15 feet tall, lavender flowers
'Regal Red': 12 feet tall, deep red flowers

small

'Centennial': 3 feet tall, bright purple flowers
'Chickasaw': 3 feet tall, pink flowers
'Pixie White': 24 inches tall, white flowers
'Worlds Fair': 24 inches tall, deep red flowers

beautiful
gardens

from the readers of *Southern Living*

a Southern heirloom garden

This family homestead, which spans generations, nestles among heirloom plants that have their own stories to tell.

They are to this day the sure image of the South: grand old homes graced by glorious gardens. Such seasoned homesteads still anchor our region, in big city and small town alike. Most contain heirloom plants that have endured the elements—and possibly neglect—yet they flourish every spring. When they do, they serve as windows through which we can see the past and glimpse our heritage.

Mrs. Gertrude Gibson McGehee gives us a look back in time by strolling the grounds of Oakside, her childhood home in Verbena, Alabama. Her grandfather, Major Joseph Carr Gibson, built the house in 1873. In later years, her father, Sidney Lanier Gibson, and mother, Mary Lee, lovingly planted the gardens. Mrs. McGehee's aunt, Mrs. B. B. Comer, assisted in the planning. Together the three, none of whom had any formal training, fashioned a timeless garden that complements the fine home. Today, Mrs. McGehee and her sister, Judith Gibson Robinson, maintain the home and garden.

A lichen-covered rock wall that is nearly consumed by English ivy surrounds the property. Mrs. McGehee's father pulled the stones from a nearby creek and used a mule to deliver them to the front yard. The wall must have been built well, for it is very much intact. Massive roots from large trees nearby have heaved it up in places, making it tilt, but it refuses to tumble.

Once through the waist-high walls and past the oversize finials, one can look beyond the boxwoods and see the stately home towering majestically over the flowers and shrubs. Massive oaks frame the house, which makes it easy to see where Oakside got its name.

At times a train whistle can be heard in the distance with a loud rumble that grows closer. Major Gibson intentionally built the home near the tracks because, at the time, rail was the only means of transportation other than horse and buggy.

An old well lies directly outside the front door. Not just a garden ornament, it was where water was drawn for cooking and cleaning.

In front of this fair house where two roads meet
And come together as good friends would greet,
Two sweetheart oaks grow, pressing lip to lip
And join their leaves in happy fellowship.
from "Oakside" by Clifford Lanier

Above: Azaleas and dogwoods cover the landscape and wrap around the old well. **Below:** Snowdrops and bluebells are so content, they have multiplied beyond their original boundaries. **Opposite:** A reproduction of the original gate makes an inviting entrance when surrounded by spring flowers.

The distinct odor of boxwoods permeates the garden, but tea olives, winter honeysuckle, roses, and numerous bulbs help sweeten the earthy smell. Bulbs bloom so thickly that a visitor once asked Mrs. McGehee how in the world her mother planted all of them. Mrs. McGehee chuckled and replied, "Mother didn't plant all those bulbs; they have multiplied over the years."

Many of the things her family planted are still popular today. During the dead of winter the dark green boxwoods form the bones of the garden, creating little hedged rooms across the yard. In January the camellias and quince buds burst open on sunny days. There is a collection of camellias that nestles quite happily underneath long-armed water oaks. February reveals tuliplike blooms that unfurl on the stems of sprawling, deciduous magnolias. Winter honeysuckle's discreet flowers scent the chilled air.

As the soil warms in spring, daffodils, narcissus, snowdrops, and bluebells fill the beds. White and purple iris blooms pop out from clumps of fanned, swordlike foliage. Pink, red, and white azaleas look like blotches of watercolors dabbled across the landscape. Numerous dogwoods grace the air with starry blooms.

This third-generation house and garden become harder to maintain as the years pass. Painting, replacing rotting wood, tugging on the escaped wisteria vine, and

The little imperfections around the 127-year-old Southern home and garden add character and charm.

weeding are never ending. The little imperfections around the 127-year-old Southern home and garden add character and charm.

When Mrs. McGehee reflects about growing up in this beautiful place, she smiles. Her stories are filled with fond memories of a simpler time. Afternoons weren't spent in front of the T.V.—they were spent relaxing on the front porch where the landscape could be admired and the children could be seen.

Fridays were always special because her father would hire a young lady to tell stories and play games with the children in the village. The young ones would gather at Oakside to romp around on the grassy lawn. You can just imagine them playing hide-and-seek, peeping out from behind a tree trunk, or balancing atop the stone wall with arms spread like an airplane. You can even picture a young Mrs. McGehee grinning as she presents her mother with a handful of freshly picked daffodils. It is a beguiling image of her and of this garden's past.

Above: Stones from a nearby creek form a low wall that surrounds the homestead.
Below: Quince puts on a show in early spring.
Opposite: Snowdrops and quince stand guard outside an old shed.

a blooming Charleston garden

In Peg and Truman Moore's garden, beauty stems from careful planning—and hiding Truman's pruners.

When you call Peg and Truman Moore, expect the phone to ring a few times. They're probably out in their Charleston, South Carolina, garden. Maybe they're enjoying a glass of wine on the porch. Maybe Peg is busily clipping spent blooms. Or, maybe Truman is yanking weeds along the walk, trying to impress Peg with his usefulness.

These two own an amazing garden. Though relatively small—just 45 x 100 feet—their garden abounds with blossoming plants. No season, no month, or no week passes by that does not see something in bloom. Just as impressive as the flowers is the clean, formal framework of lines, vistas, and focal points that reins in this boisterous assembly.

Which noted landscape architect designed the garden? If you're as creatively challenged, you'll cringe at the answer. Peg and Truman leafed through some garden books, grabbed pencil and paper, and did the whole thing themselves.

Newcomers to the Lowcountry, the Moores moved from New York into their historic home (built in 1786) eight years ago. They chose Charleston, says Peg, because "we wanted to live in a sophisticated city, but a smaller city. And because we were very involved in historic preservation, we wanted to live in a place that values its history. Charleston does."

They also coveted a garden. "I wanted a place to garden year-round," she explains. "Our real estate broker understood this. I told her I didn't care about the kitchen or living room—the first

Above: Peg and Truman relax on their porch. **Opposite:** An arch of roses beckons guests to a garden fountain.

thing I wanted to see was the garden."

Or rather, the potential area for a garden. "The yard was pretty much a blank slate," Peg recalls. "Nothing but fire ants and grass." But this did not bother the Moores, who preferred starting from scratch than tearing down an old garden. Truman, noting existing features, carefully measured every inch of the yard to create a base plan. He also studied the area's sun and shade patterns. Then Peg embarked on a series of roughly 30 ever-evolving design sketches. She based the earliest ones on the works of renowned landscape architect Loutrel Briggs, who designed many great gardens in Charleston.

"His gardens were symmetrical and formal," Peg notes. "But it's hard to have a symmetrical garden when one half is sunny and the other is shady, like our garden. Even if the same plants survive in both places, they don't grow to the same size. So I gave half the garden the Loutrel Briggs look—the formal lawn, the brick walks, the loquat hedge, the herb parterre—and then the other half, the sunnier part, I did in the looser cottage garden style."

The color scheme evolved as well. "Like many people, I started out with the whole pink-blue-and-white bit," Peg says. "But here in Charleston with our intense sunshine, that palette tends to be too pale. So I added a lot of reds and oranges." Indeed, at this moment in early May, the bright reds and oranges of verbena, petunias, geraniums, gerbera daisies, daylilies, and pot marigolds catch your eye and carry it throughout the garden.

Peg and Truman live in Charleston all year—they don't flee to cooler climes when the weather gets hot. So their garden, unlike many in the city, needs color beyond the spring. To accomplish this, they grow dozens of flowering plants in pots that Peg keeps along the brick terrace. Some bloom in spring, some in summer, and some in fall and winter. Whenever and wherever she needs color, she plugs them into the garden at an appropriate spot.

Such gardening can be exhausting, but the payback is worth it. "It's a joy to have things growing and blooming year-round," Peg

Above: Enclosed by walls, the Truman's garden rests on a long, narrow lot behind their house.

declares. "You don't have to endure nine months of nothing, like you do up North."

Rich, generous soil is key to a garden like this one. "Someone told us that during World War II, the owner here kept chickens," Peg says. "So actually, we started with pretty good soil." To make it even better, she and Truman hauled in many truckloads of compost in the garden's early stages. And they amend the soil with compost and manure every year.

Every successful gardening partnership demands that each partner accept a role. Here, Peg is the master gardener—the planner, the planter, the artist. As for

Above: Details, such as this tiny birdbath tucked behind magenta petunias and white serissa, make the difference.

Above, right: Scarlet petunias atop an ornate pedestal provide a dazzling focal point.

Right: The fountain edge was designed at just the right height for sitting.

Opposite page: Herbs, perennials, and annuals thrive on the herb parterre at the head of the lawn. A pot of red petunias atop a pedestal serves as a distant focal point, emphasizing the line of the walk.

Truman, he's the "under-gardener," a position he has held ever since he committed the cardinal sin of pruning the roses without asking Peg. Truman: "I thought we understood we were going to hard-prune 'em." Peg: "He cut off 45 rosebuds that were just about to open. I couldn't believe it."

With Truman's duties now redefined, all is well at the couple's house. "I'm Doctor Death," he announces proudly. "I get rid of weeds and bugs. I'm good for fungus, Florida betony, dandelions, and stuff like that. If it needs to be killed, I'm the guy."

But that stuff will have to wait. Right now, the only liquidation Truman is contemplating is a glass of red wine with Peg.

an Eastern Shore hideaway

When you own a piece of tranquility, what better place for a garden? Come for an autumn visit to Maryland's Eastern Shore.

You feel it as you cross the Chesapeake Bay Bridge onto Maryland's Eastern Shore—a palpable timelessness, a sense that what you see, hear, and feel remains essentially pure and unchanged since the day explorer John Smith first mapped the area in 1608. Each day, The Bay's waters rise and subside with the tides, as if the great estuary were breathing. Blue herons prowl soupy marshes. The dying sun rouges a virgin forest of oak, tulip poplar, and dogwood.

Here, in 1972, Caroline and Chuck Benson decided to make their home, settling beside Leeds Creek near the Miles River. They bought a brick manor house that was built in 1810 by the family of Charles S. Winder, a brigadier general during the Civil War under the command of Stonewall Jackson. Nothing but cornfields lay between the house and water. Caroline wanted a garden.

She asked Kathleen Cowgill, a self-taught garden designer, to lay out the beds. "Kathleen never drew a plan," recalls Caroline. "She just walked around and said, 'This should go here and that should go over there.' " The finished design established four large, rectangular parterres divided by 30-foot-wide cross paths. "She felt it should be a formal layout, appropriate to the period of the house," explains Caroline.

Classic, mixed borders of perennials, shrubs, and trees, the parterres are dedicated to two separate color schemes. Those on the right feature pink, red, white, and blue; those on the left showcase purple, yellow, and white. To maintain these classic themes throughout the seasons, Caroline weaves together a complex tapestry of different flowers and foliage. For example, blues may come from lilacs in spring, chaste tree in summer, asters in fall, and blue spruce in winter.

Left: Flaming borders of pineapple sage burn off the fog as the October sun rises on Caroline Benson's garden. **Above:** Caroline Benson gathers flowers for indoor arrangements.

Above: Dew-laden yellow crabapples rake moisture from the autumn air.
Opposite: An espaliered pyracantha adorns an old smokehouse turned into a toolhouse.
Below: The setting sun hangs over Leeds Creek.

Close proximity to the water moderates temperatures, making Caroline's garden a horticultural nexus where South and North meet. "We have a wonderful climate, USDA Zone 7," she says, "so we're able to grow a lot of Southern plants that aren't hardy north of here—crepe myrtles, camellias, gardenias, chaste tree, and some jasmines." Cold-weather plants, such as peonies, lilac, and dwarf conifers, thrive, too. "Almost all perennials do extremely well," she adds. "About the only ones that are hard are

delphiniums. They don't like our hot summers. I use them as annuals."

Another reason plants flourish here is

soil richer than cheesecake. But it didn't start out that way. "Our soil has lots of heavy clay," Caroline notes. "Fortunately, it's easy to amend." It's particularly easy because Chuck and Caroline raise Thoroughbreds and so they have a ready supply of manure. The fact that they double-dug the beds prior to planting didn't hurt either.

Proof of good soil is the startling rate at which the plants have grown in for over 25 years. "Everything started small," says Caroline. "I could carry

every tree that we planted myself."

Some years ago, Caroline opened Garden Treasures, a prospering garden center in the nearby town of Easton. Stocked with a fine array of shrubs, native plants, perennials, and ornaments, it hums with activity. Yet watching her as she drives home this day past dignified, old cedars and soybean fields turned golden brown, you sense she's found her refuge. "It's very tranquil most of the time," she observes. "You never hear another car."

Opposite: Almost everything—including salvia, hydrangea, viburnum berries, mums, asters, crabapple, hyacinth bean, ornamental grasses, and even brussels sprouts—in Caroline's arrangements comes from the fall garden.

Right: Purple and white Mexican bush sage peers over the brick-colored blossoms of Autumn sedum joy.

Below: This mare and foal will never ride off into the sunset. They're topiaries formed by clipped English ivy trained onto a wire frame.

garden of youth in Texas

In Little Elm, Texas, two sisters know the secret to a long, happy life. They rediscover it each day in the garden.

"I feel sorry for people who do not like to grow things and get their hands dirty," Shirley Welch says earnestly. "I think it was intended for us to keep our hands and bodies close to the earth."

Today, as she does almost every day, Shirley will have lunch with her sister, Marie Caillet (pronounced Cal-YAY), who lives across the quiet country lane that separates their yards. They'll talk about the usual things—who called this morning, which iris beds need digging, and how long it took Marie to drive 600 miles to New Orleans and back. There's nothing really notable about this, until you consider their age. They've been gardening together on the shores of Lewisville Lake, 45 minutes north of Dallas, for the last 30 years.

The sisters attribute their interest in plants to French ancestors who arrived in Texas in 1855 and counted botanists among their ranks. Marie and Shirley's mother, Laura, inherited the "green gene" and started her own nursery at their home on Lover's Lane in Dallas in the late 1920s. She raised bearded iris and sold them for up to a dollar a piece, earning enough money to buy her first car. "Bearded iris were very popular," recalls Marie, "but many were introduced at a high price. I remember once our mother paid $25 for one. That was a lot of money back then. She put a little fence around it."

The girls routinely helped weed and water the garden. "We lived in the country and didn't have a lot of close neighbors or playmates," remembers Shirley. "So our mother and father saw to it that we enjoyed the outdoors. Gardening wasn't a job for us. We had fun."

Reaching adulthood, the sisters went into teaching. Shirley served as an elementary school principal for 23 years. She was so popular with her students that they addressed her as "Aunt

Left and above: Sisters Marie Caillet and Shirley Welch grew up gardening. **Top, right:** If forced to pick a favorite iris, Shirley might point to 'Beverly Sills.' **Top left:** Unlike bearded iris, Louisianas like wet and steamy weather. One of Marie's favorites is 'Purple Professor Ike.' **Opposite:** Shirley prefers growing bearded iris on her higher ground because they multiply with abandon.

Shirley." She married Clyde Welch (who died several years ago) and moved to her present home on family land in 1960. Marie taught at the University of Southwestern Louisiana in Lafayette for 33 years. She retired in 1972 and moved next door to her older sister.

Special irises from Marie's former garden accompanied her. They weren't bearded iris, which disliked the Louisiana climate. Instead, they were Louisiana iris, hybrids of five species of iris native to the South. Louisianas bloomed in every color of the rainbow. Unlike the beardeds, they relished hot, steamy weather and soggy soil. Few people knew about them, however.

Marie decided to change that. She helped found the Society for Louisiana Irises and co-authored a book, *The Louisiana Iris*, which has become a standard reference. She also planted hundreds of selections in her garden. Photographs of Marie's iris, gleaming like multicolored jewels above the inky water of her small pond, did more to popularize these plants than almost anything else. Scores of selections are now available. A blue one bears her name.

Shirley, however, stuck with the bearded iris that her parents had planted years ago. In fact, the only Louisiana iris she owns is 'Aunt Shirley,' a huge, pink bicolor named for her. She explains the situation like this—she has the high ground and good drainage, which beardeds prefer; Marie has the low ground and the pond, just right for Louisianas. In spring, the spectacle of both gardens draws scads of visitors. "It's a good thing we're real sociable and love company," notes Shirley. "But that's how we've made some of our best friends."

Contented iris multiply like the proverbial loaves and fishes. So if friends play their cards right, they will likely be granted an iris or two. "We have plenty to give away whenever people stop," says Shirley. "Marie scolds me and says there's a special time when bearded iris should be dug. But I just dig them anytime somebody comes by."

Shirley has slowed a bit. Marie, meanwhile, buzzes from project to project. She believes keeping mentally and physically active after retirement is key to a long, fruitful life.

"A lot of my friends have no hobbies, no outside interests, and they don't know what to do," she laments. "It's pitiful. I just went to a funeral last week of a lady who was younger than I am, and I'll bet she never walked any farther than from the house to the car."

Gardening may extend life, but it can't prolong it forever. Shirley and Marie find satisfaction in the fact that so many of their plants thrive in family and friends' gardens. Plants, like children, let gardeners glimpse immortality.

And who knows, perhaps many springs from now, someone in Texas will spy a pair of iris plants, vigorous and exuberant. Once again, 'Marie Caillet' will bloom beside 'Aunt Shirley.'

Right: Louisiana iris, yellow flags, pink penstemons, white spider lilies and poppies adorn Marie's garden.

an unforgettable Georgia garden

Once threatened with disaster, Liz Tedder's garden weathered a storm to become a treat that is long remembered.

Certain images stick in your mind like gum to your shoe. Such is the case with Liz Tedder's garden.

Jane Bath, a friend of *Southern Living* Garden Writer Steve Bender and a garden designer in Stone Mountain, Georgia, had told him of a new garden near Newnan, about 40 minutes southwest of Atlanta, that he just had to see. So Steve called Liz that spring and drove out for a visit. As he pulled up to the house, he feared his call had been a harbinger of doom. A huge tree lay sprawled across the garden, crushing peonies and irises beneath its limbs.

Liz walked across the grass, calmly stopping now and again to tidy the destruction. "A tornado hit last night," she said matter-of-factly. "Fortunately, it didn't damage the house. Oh well, I'd been meaning to take that tree down anyway. I guess God did it for me."

As Liz calmly surveyed God's handiwork, Steve carefully surveyed her borders. She had the prettiest tornado-ravaged garden he'd ever seen.

In the decade since, the garden has blossomed like a debutante, growing lovelier with each passing year. Every time Steve visits, he can't wait to stroll the length of its borders, admire their composition, identify heirlooms that he'd like starts of, and marvel how a single peony plant in bloom can make you forget the rest of the world. But to truly appreciate the scope of Liz's accomplishment requires some elevation. Looking out from a third-floor window between twin brick chimneys reveals the essence of her creation.

Formal mixed borders of perennials, shrubs, and seasonal annuals extend 100 feet from a terrace on the house's south side. Between them, a rectangular fescue lawn, chosen for its green winter color and acceptance of sun or shade, serves as a stage. Flanking the borders, white picket fences and rows of Yoshino cherries direct the eye to a dramatic focal point—a hexagonal gazebo directly in line with that same third-floor window. It's a perspective that only friends, family, and birds get to see.

Above: Liz Tedder divides flowers in her garden.
Left: A gazebo beckons guests to sit and enjoy the garden.

Above: Like a doorman waiting to greet you, pink wood sorrel pokes its head through the gate, while a red climbing rose clambers along the fence.
Right: Planted in groups of three, Liz's peonies came by mail as an unnamed assortment of three different colors. This double pink one is probably 'Sarah Bernhardt.'

Liz credits an elderly friend named Agnes Newton with the idea. At Agnes's house, the formal rooms had a formal garden planted outside their windows for the purpose of capturing the beautiful view. Agnes has since passed away, but her spirit lives on in Liz's design. It survives, too, in the iris, naked ladies, and other heirloom perennials she happily shared with Liz.

Except on winter's coldest days, this garden blooms. Highlights include blossoming cherries, flowering almonds, pansies, tulips, daffodils, candytuft, money plant, irises, peonies, and roses in spring; daylilies, salvias, phlox, coneflowers, roses, balloon flower, veronica, and obedient plant in summer; salvias and asters in fall; and pansies during the winter. Reseeding annuals, such as sweet rocket (*Hesperis matronalis*) and love-in-a-mist (*Nigella damascena*), fill gaps

"Fortunately, it didn't damage the house. Oh well, I'd been meaning to take that tree down anyway. I guess God did it for me."

—*Liz Tedder*

Above: This lavender-pink sweet rocket reseeds year after year, and combines nicely with 'Pink Meidiland' roses, pansies, and other plants.

between plants and carry on the show long after the supernova of peonies, irises, and other brief bloomers burns itself out.

Great gardens spring from good soil. Yet the clay soil Liz started out with was redder than the face of a swimmer who's lost his trunks. By constantly working in copious amounts of organic matter, such as leaves, bark, and wood ashes, together with topsoil, she gradually improved it. She never has used fertilizers. Instead, twice a year, she top-dresses the beds with several inches of chopped leaves. "The leaves don't last long," she notes. "The earthworms take 'em."

Healthy perennials eventually become crowded and stop blooming. So every four to five years, Liz reworks her borders. "I just lay a tarp on the grass and take out everything but the peonies and roses," she says. She divides the plants that need it, replants everything, and then sells the divisions to pay for someone to help her with periodic maintenance. Some of Liz's helpers take their pay in plants.

Liz shares some of her best gardening advice in the box at right.

Above: The reverse view from the gazebo demonstrates Liz's eye for rhythm and scale. The gazebo and fences echo the color of the house, while the brick landing and edging repeat the color of the chimneys.

Left: Liz designed her garden to be enjoyed from both indoors and out. A bird's-eye view from a third-floor window is of a formal lawn and flower borders with a gazebo as the focal point.

Below: One advantage of such sumptuous borders is plentiful cut flowers.

LESSONS FROM LIZ

Sage advice to beginning gardeners from a master

- **Don't let red clay scare you.** You can turn it into pretty good soil by adding organic matter.
- **Go with the flow.** If you have wet soil, it's a lot cheaper to choose plants that like it than regrade the area to improve drainage.
- **For the most color,** concentrate on perennials that bloom a long time, such as salvias.
- **Choose a size area you can easily maintain;** then buy a few choice plants and see how they do. Get a feel for how much time it takes to maintain; then you can decide what size garden works for you.
- **If funds are limited,** ask gardening friends for starts, and patiently wait for yours to multiply.
- **The way to have a successful garden** without a lot of effort or money is to let the soil dictate what you grow.
- **You can't spend your money any better** than on pansies. We get to enjoy them from October to May.

flowers
from the farm

Waist-high rows of multicolored zinnias shine in the hot summer sun. The Peaden family sweats in the field, harvesting the vibrant blooms. They clip the long-stemmed flowers and drop them into galvanized buckets filled with water. Riding in a red wagon, the buckets slosh their way to a small roadside flower shop. Here, the family grooms and divides the zinnias. After the blooms are tucked into tin cans or mason jars, the arrangements are ready for display in the Peadens' small store, Southern Petals.

About five years ago, Gary and Sherry Peaden started growing flowers on their 16-acre farm to harvest and sell. They thought the colorful crop might help generate a little added income for their large family. Sherry was surprised by the immediate success. At first they sold to a local florist, and then they began selling to the public. Gary quickly built a small shed in which the flowers could be stored and sold. Nowadays, the shed's window-unit air conditioner hums constantly in the summer, keeping the small space chilled and the flowers fresh.

MOVING TO THE COUNTRY

Sherry and Gary used to live in Pensacola, Florida, but they saw that their kids were growing up too fast in the city. Looking for a simpler life, they bought an old farm and moved their family to the country. Now, you would be tempted to call the Peadens' six children John Boy, Mary Ellen, Ben, Erin, Jim Bob, and Elizabeth. They are like a modern-day version of The Waltons. Hardworking, good-natured, and polite, they help with the many tasks around the farm.

The shop is open throughout the year, but fresh flowers are available only during the warm months. At the height of the season, the family picks about 3,000 flowers a week. In addition to zinnias, the Peadens grow watermelons, cantaloupes, tomatoes, peas, beans, and okra. Much of the produce is canned or frozen for the family, but they sell some of it fresh from an old farm wagon set up next to the flower shop. They also keep bees and sell honey. In his spare time, Gary even builds rustic birdhouses and feeders that are popular with shoppers when flowers aren't available. In the winter months, they make wreaths of grapevine gathered from around the property. Sherry decorates them with dried flowers and displays them in the shop.

All this keeps the Peadens busy, so there is no one to mind the store. An honor box is the only cashier, and customers just drop their cash or checks into a slot when they make a purchase. So far everyone has been honest, and nothing has been stolen. It surely doesn't hurt that Gary works for the local sheriff's department.

MAKING ARRANGEMENTS

While the whole family helps with

Below: Working on the farm is a family affair. (Back row, from left to right) Robert, Sherry, Gary, and Laura; (front row, from left to right) Chris, Sarah, Matt, and Anna Claire.

Above: Their shop is small but full of lovely zinnias. **Left:** The family grows and harvests thousands of zinnias for the shop each year.

chores, Sherry is the heart and soul of the operation. She loves being surrounded by flowers and enjoys wading through the blooms in the early morning. Each year, she purchases all the seeds and plans the garden. Sherry likes flowers that are easy to direct seed into the field, but they must hold up after they've been cut.

The Peadens set up shop each spring with bachelor's buttons, larkspurs, daisies, and daffodils, which they plant in the fall. As the spring bloomers play out from the heat, they are replaced by summer crops. The warm-season flowers include celosias, cosmos, globe amaranths, sunflowers, strawflowers, and zinnias. Customers love them all, but zinnias are the Peadens' biggest draw. People love the vibrant colors and how well they hold up in arrangements. The California Giants Strain grows tall, making it perfect for big arrangements.

The Lilliput Series has smaller blooms, about the size of a half-dollar, which look nice in a can or jar.

Some customers leave their containers to be filled at the flower shop. The Peadens paint the silver cans bright colors. Once the cans or jars are filled with flowers, the Peadens tie raffia around the containers and attach a small card displaying the shop's name. These rustic arrangements go for $5 to $25.

Those who don't want a can or jar with their flowers can purchase a large bunch of blooms in a florist sleeve for $5. Sherry also takes special orders from people who call saying they need 300 or 400 flowers for a wedding or a party.

WORKING THE FIELDS

Sherry may be the heart of the flower farm, but Gary is the workhorse. Driving

an old 1953 Ford Jubilee tractor, he plows across the dusty fields. To put out the sacks of flower seed, he uses an Earthway seeder, bought at the co-op, to evenly distribute the tiny flower seeds. Weeds and grasses are typically the biggest problems. They grow fast and spread quickly in the warm soil, competing with small seedlings. Gary carefully sprays Round-up around the rows with a handheld sprayer until all the flowers are tall enough to fend for themselves. The drip irrigation system works so well that he wouldn't mind if it didn't rain all summer long. The zinnias mature quickly and can be harvested within about six weeks of planting.

Each morning as the sun rises, Sherry and the girls move down the long, straight rows, clipping the flowers like mechanical harvesters. Their hands move in high gear as they stoop over the rainbow of blooms. Occasionally, they stand upright to wipe their foreheads or fan away bothersome gnats. They want to get the flowers out of the sun and into the shop quickly to keep them fresh.

Tending the farm is hard work, but it's also very rewarding. On this piece of land, the Peadens have witnessed the miracle of seeing tiny seeds transform lifeless rows of dirt into sweeps of beautiful flowers.

a growing dream

At first, all Ram Giberson could grow was patience. When she finally started her garden after more than a decade of dreaming, she dug in with fearless determination.

Ram Sorat Giberson tended the garden growing in her soul for 16 years. The seeds of it were sown even earlier, far away in Thailand. Ram remembers peeking through estate gates as a young girl to admire garlands of roses, but her family worked the land for food crops, not flowers.

When she met American serviceman Tom Giberson on a blind date, Ram was a grown woman with a child of her own. She spoke little English, but love knows no language. Their decision to marry was thwarted by bureaucracy. Though it took a year for Ram to obtain visas for herself and her son, Tom stayed in Thailand until his new family could leave for America with him. Ram packed her hopes for a garden.

The 16-year wait that followed was the price she paid for the American dream. Tom went to college, then medical school.

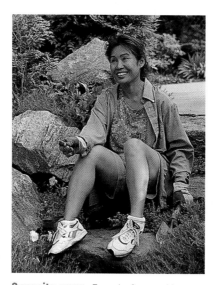

Opposite page: Every leaf, every blossom, and every stone are the result of Ram's resolution to have a garden. This peaceful sitting area was once a thick grove of scrubby pines. **Below and following pages:** Fish enjoy the lush water garden that Ram created.

Money was tight. "You take what all you got and put it in medical school," remembers Ram, "so I was obligated to Tom's career, too. All that time, I wanted a garden."

The Gibersons moved many times for Tom's education and residency. Finally, they were ready to choose a home. "We looked at a lot of things, but the main thing was that Ram needed to be in growing Zone 7 or 8," says Tom. "Before, we had a $3 coffee table covered with plants—that was her garden," He laughs. "How do you, after 16 years, say 'no, let's not do that'? This garden is a personal diary of what we traded off together."

Athens, Georgia—nestled in the top of growing Zone 8—became home. Tom became an emergency room physician at a nearby hospital. The time finally came to start Ram's garden. But she was hampered by an acre of scrub pine and a total lack of experience.

"I visualize the garden as a huge canvas....
I'm going out to paint the land."

—Ram Giberson

"During that time, I know only marigold and begonia. No more," explains Ram with a giggle. But after leaving her culture, language, and homeland behind, these factors hardly seemed formidable. She got out the chain saw, and they went to work, felling some 200 pines. Though she felt guilty cutting down trees, Ram saw the future garden opening up before her. If Tom had any doubts, it was too late. "I wasn't real interested in going out there," he confesses with a grin. "But you can't argue with Ram when she's got a chain saw."

After clearing her backyard, Ram met with a landscape architect to discuss her visions of beauty. "I told him, 'If you are up in an airplane and look down, I like it to look like an island. I want to have everything that moves, like water, no hard things.' "

A drawing was sketched to guide the garden's development. Next came the mud. A red sea of Georgia clay stretched across the property, transforming it into a mess every time the heavens spilled over. One hundred fifty tons of boulders were brought in to build outcroppings. Truckloads of soil built up a berm for privacy plantings along the property line. Walkways were poured. "Starting the garden was very bold. Once you've started, you can't go back. Once you've got a half-acre of mud, you've got to keep going," Tom says.

Ram plunged on. She mastered every piece of equipment used in her garden, working to dig out her dream. "Bobcat is very fun to drive," says Ram. "I move some boulders around. I like that."

At long last, it was time to plant. She tagged along with the landscape architect on nursery trips and listened carefully to explanations of design principles. Then Ram, with help from Tom and her son, Mao, dug the holes and planted her treasures herself.

As her knowledge grew, she began making her own decisions about composition. "I visualize the garden as a huge canvas. I tell Tom, 'I'm going out to paint the land.' "

Today, the garden is a living masterpiece. A stream flows down a rocky bank, splashing into a fishpond. Layers of texture dress the garden like tapestry: Fine-leaved Japanese maples are interwoven with fluffy little ferns, smooth canes of bamboo, and tightly knit mosses. The composition carefully balances color and form. Trees the Gibersons planted to replace the pines—river birch, Leyland cypress, and lots of Japanese maples—define the garden's spaces. And there are flowers, flowers, flowers.

Ram's beloved roses spread through the garden, mixing with every perennial imaginable. "I did all this just so I could have flowers," Ram says with contagious delight. "I come from not speaking any English to being comfortable in this society. We've accomplished a lot. This garden is giving back. In the price of paying for something you earn—this is my earn."

Opposite page: A pair of Meidiland roses was a valentine's gift from Tom. Ram prunes the landscape roses once a year to keep them trained. **Right:** Annuals and perennials thrive in the garden.

a cutting garden for all seasons

When most people want a cutting garden, they exile it to an out-of-the-way place in the yard. But Jane Hagan's garden in Birmingham was designed to provide cut flowers for the better part of three seasons and play a significant role in the landscape.

The design is simple. A central walkway leads you in: the middle of the path widens into a circle where a sundial acts as a focal point. Boxwoods give formal structure by lining the path at the entrance and at several key points. Stately old shrubs also serve to divide the garden into six planting beds.

Each section of Jane's garden is planted with a specific season in mind. As with any garden, planning is the key to success. Almost all flowers suitable for cutting are sun lovers. Sunlight changes as the seasons progress. Paying attention to the available light in each season is essential. In Jane's garden, the earliest spring flowers are planted in the area that receives the most sun in early spring before the leaves emerge on the surrounding large oak trees.

As you move down the garden, the sunlight increases and the floral offerings progress. One of Jane's requirements for her cutting garden is roses, which occupy the sunniest part of the garden. Tiny forget-me-nots *(Myosotis scorpioides)* carpet the ground under the roses. These small flowers provide for miniature arrangements.

When choosing which flowers to use in a cutting garden, consider the blooming habits of each plant. Many annuals, such as zinnias, are well suited for cutting and will repeat bloom. By cutting blooms, you're actually encouraging new flowers to emerge. The same is true of many perennials. By choosing carefully, you ensure plenty of flowers to cut while keeping your garden an attractive part of your landscape.

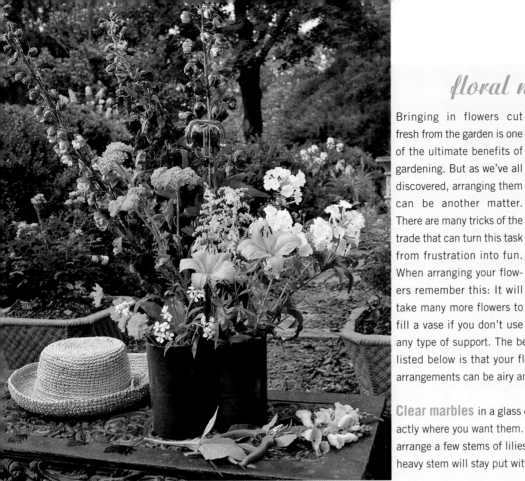

Above: Cut flowers early in the morning, and take a container of water with you into the garden. This will keep your flowers fresher once they are cut.

Opposite page: Boxwoods anchor this late-spring section of the garden and give the flowers a frame for their riotous color.

a *garden* map

This diagram helps the Hagans plan their garden from year to year.

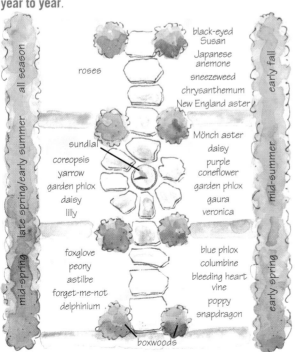

black-eyed Susan
Japanese anemone
sneezeweed
chrysanthemum
New England aster

all season

roses

early fall

mid-summer

late spring/early summer

mid-spring

sundial
coreopsis
yarrow
garden phlox
daisy
lilly

Mönch aster
daisy
purple coneflower
garden phlox
gaura
veronica

foxglove
peony
astilbe
forget-me-not
delphinium

blue phlox
columbine
bleeding heart vine
poppy
snapdragon

early spring

boxwoods

floral mechanics

Bringing in flowers cut fresh from the garden is one of the ultimate benefits of gardening. But as we've all discovered, arranging them can be another matter. There are many tricks of the trade that can turn this task from frustration into fun. When arranging your flowers remember this: It will take many more flowers to fill a vase if you don't use any type of support. The beauty of using one of the devices listed below is that your flowers will stay in place and the arrangements can be airy and delicate.

Clear marbles in a glass cylinder will hold heavy stems exactly where you want them. This is one of the easiest ways to arrange a few stems of lilies or roses. Any flower with a fairly heavy stem will stay put with marbles.

Chicken wire is another simple but effective way to hold flowers upright in a container. Bend the wire so it fits down into the container out of sight. The flower stems will rest between the holes in the wire instead of leaning against the container.

Needleholders have heavy metal bases that will anchor them in containers. Sharp metal prongs sticking straight up from the base hold the stems upright. Needleholders come in a wonderful assortment of sizes ranging from the size of a quarter to 6 inches wide. This enables you to use them in an enormous variety of containers. A needleholder with a heavy metal grid over it will hold heavier stems in place with a bit of extra support.

Florist foam is great when you want to use a container with very low sides or if you want to arrange your flowers at strong angles. Its size may be altered by slicing it with a knife to fit the container. Be sure to soak the porous foam in water prior to using. It retains water, but you must add water to the arrangement daily to keep it moist.

There are numerous other items the well-equipped arranger must have. Florist tape and clay will help hold the above devices in place. A water-filled rose cutter with thorn stripper comes in handy for the rose fancier. A water container with a handle and sharp, scissorlike pruners are musts to take into the garden to cut flowers.

personal paradise

On a quiet street in Coconut Grove, Florida, modest homes reside comfortably on groomed lawns, with an occasional palm punctuating the landscape. In one lovely spot, however, a tropical oasis oozes over the curb, with effusive greenery supporting outbursts of shrieking pink bougainvillea and flamboyant firecracker plant.

By day, Deborah Balter teaches aviation language skills. After hours of highly skilled work, she shifts gears, becoming an artist, designer, and adventurer. This equatorial Eden is her canvas, drawing board, and urban rain forest. It is an enigmatic garden—tranquil and spirited, serious and animated, intimate and sociable.

The appearance of grand scale and large proportions is an illusion, a part of Deborah's mystical approach to design. Her garden, which feels so big, is squeezed into a petite 67 x 140 feet. Every inch of that space is deliberately planned and planted to instigate curiosity and wonder. "The garden is my palette—it fulfills my need to create. The colors, textures, plants, and placement are all part of my creative process," she says.

An unyielding spirit of adventure feeds Deborah's artistic appetite, while her travels from the Tropics to the Orient fuel her garden's design. "A tropical climate signifies easy living, beauty, and lushness," she says. The framework of the garden is established with palms—some native

and some exotic. "I've always been enchanted with palms. They hold an enormous amount of romance," she says. In addition, the towering trees are used to generate depth by going up—a design trick for small spaces.

The garden is a study in shades of green. "It is a refuge from my business," Deborah says. The verdant palette gives her the freedom to add color in carefully chosen places, to focus attention, and to draw an unexpected smile.

Elevated walkways connect one garden vista to the next, with a surprise always just around the corner. "The decks take you on a journey through the garden. I designed them so you can view this controlled tropical jungle without disturbing it or any hidden animals. They're also low maintenance," she says.

From the deck outside the back door, you take the walkway around the garden. The lap pool spans the narrow lot from one side to the other. A cool, serene lagoon appears to stretch lazily for miles, another vision of Deborah's artful eye.

Above: Deborah Balter fills her garden with plants that are carefully chosen to bring color and texture to the landscape. **Left:** The lap pool reflects Deborah's principles of artistic design—the palms' magnificent trunks draw the eye upward for depth, the ferns convey serenity and softness, and the pool's hand-painted finish produces the illusion of a lagoon.

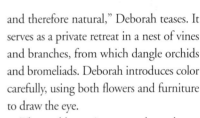

Above and right: Deborah fills her garden with plants that are carefully chosen to bring color and texture to the landscape. **Opposite page:** The garden is tropical in nature, spiced with reminders of Deborah's travels to the Orient. **Below:** The pool house is focused on relaxation. A hot tub on the lower level allows visitors to look out over the landscape while relaxing, and the sleeping porch above holds the promise of an excellent nap. The color of the facade blends seamlessly with trees.

The effect is not difficult to create—a textured paint finish and massive ferns in poolside beds combine for the idyllic illusion. The palm-frond canopy overhead diffuses the hot Florida sun and creates a dancing shimmer on the water.

Next stop is a hike to the top of a mountain. While the garden was under construction, Deborah had a plan for the coral-based soil being dug to make a spot for the pool. "While I was at work one day, the construction crew took away all the soil they had excavated for the pool's foundation. I had plans for all of that—I made them bring it back for my mountain," she recalls. Allegedly one of the highest natural points in Dade County, her "mountain" is an elevated patio tucked craftily into the lot's corner. "The mountain was made from the fill when the pool was dug, so it is earth and therefore natural," Deborah teases. It serves as a private retreat in a nest of vines and branches, from which dangle orchids and bromeliads. Deborah introduces color carefully, using both flowers and furniture to draw the eye.

The pool house is next on the pathway, with a hot tub occupying the lower space and a screened sleeping porch above. Its dual-level design reflects her passion for flight. "The Jacuzzi house is for relaxation, indulgence, and thought," she says. "I designed the second level so I could be among the palm fronds but not have to scale the trunks to get there. It gets me above ground level."

After winding around the opposite end of the pool, the tour is complete. Within this small space, every inch is accounted for—with perfect plant choices, extraordinary design principles, and a large dose of magic.

If gardening has a measure of attitude, Deborah's endeavors are a marvelous model. She refers to her screened porch as a rain room—a place to sit and enjoy the soul-soothing sounds of a tropical shower. Perhaps the sign painted over the porch door says it all: "An hour in the garden puts life's problems in perspective." Grounded in tranquility, this garden is Deborah's paradise.

an enchanting hideaway

This small garden, carved from the rich pastureland of a Tennessee farm, is as inviting as an open gate.

Residents near Murphreesboro, Tennessee, had a real treat when Hilda Bolin's landscape was selected for a garden tour. When you reach the Bolins' property and drive through the gates, all you can see are cows and pastureland. As you continue down the drive, you'll notice a thick cluster of trees on, truly, the back 40. A cabin surrounded by ferns and flowers materializes in a grove of hardwoods. Dappled light filters through a canopy of branches, making the setting look cool on the hot summer day. The rays of light that weave through the numerous limbs are like spotlights shining on the garden floor.

If you're lucky, Hilda will step out of the rustic home and into the yard. Her wide smile is definitely that of an accomplished gardener who's getting ready to show off her handiwork.

Flower arrangements are strategically placed on the gates and tabletops. Hilda says she always puts flowers out when guests are coming—and many guests flock to the garden in the spring and summer. Garden clubs tour the yard, and two of Hilda's children were married in this delightful setting.

When asked if she's had any formal training in flower arranging, Hilda replies, "I don't arrange flowers. I just cut them,

Above: Farm manager Paul Young and owner Hilda Bolin wear the smiles of proud gardeners. Here they stand next to the flowering butterfly garden. **Right:** A basket of hydrangeas on the gate greets guests as they enter the garden.

> *"Plants are a lot like people. Some are real fussy, while others are easy and just kind of take care of themselves."*
> —Hilda Bolin

set them in a basket or container, and they arrange themselves." She refuses to let anything become complicated.

Rocks, gathered from around the farm, edge the bark chip paths that weave through the garden. There are also huge boulders set around the front yard. One of her favorites is a massive gray boulder shaped like a whale. She tells me that her husband, Wendell, maneuvered the giant rock into place with a bulldozer. Farm manager Paul Young works on the Bolin farm during the day and occasionally helps Hilda with some of the heavy gardening work in the afternoons. Together they have selected interesting-looking logs from the woods behind the house and tucked them along the pathways. Many of these moss-covered pieces of wood are crooked and twisted, creating naturally sculpted forms. Ferns unfurl around the wood and rock, making areas in the front look like a woodsy fern glade.

Hilda likes to plant impatiens around the front yard to add color. Big sweeps of these shade lovers make quite an impact in their dark confines. Various selections of large-leaved hostas look great mixed with ferns. Shrubs such as hydrangea, mahonia, and nandina create a nice backdrop for annuals and perennials.

Hilda's excitement grows when she tells stories about plants and the garden. Many of the plants were dug from her childhood home.

The garden that sweeps around the front of the house is now brimming with plants of all shapes and sizes. It's constantly maintained during the growing season, but Hilda is now putting her efforts into a butterfly garden located on the back side of her house.

The back garden is very sunny and quite different from the shady garden in front. The sunny site allows Hilda to grow sun lovers, such as butterfly bush, lantana, blue salvia, and loosestrife, that attract butterflies.

Hilda is a natural when it comes to gardening. She doesn't consider it work; it's more of a love. "Plants are a lot like people," she says. "Some are real fussy, while others are easy and just kind of take care of themselves." She says at this stage of her life she is more likely to set out plants that take care of themselves so she has more time for being a grandmother to Taylor and Caitlyn.

Above: Hilda and Wendell Bolin have a great cabin on the back side of their farm. Over the past 13 years, Hilda has worked to surround the cabin with beauty. Sweeps of impatiens add bright color to the shade.

Opposite page: A galvanized watering pail comes to life with Queen Anne's lace, daylilies, hydrangeas, as well as the veiny foliage of hardy begonias.

Left: Moss-covered logs, carefully placed along the paths, lend a sculptural look to the garden.

beauty in the Bluegrass

Imagine Kentucky in May—gentle hills of bluegrass, long undulating fences, and high-strung horses, restless in their paddocks. The season brings warm breezes carrying the fragrance of flowers, a reminder that spring's visit is brief. But for now, white hydrangeas, purple spiderworts, and orange daylilies brighten gardens, saluting the skies in unison before the hot days of summer arrive to quell their displays. Such is the scene at Kay Bullitt's garden, Oxmoor Farm, in Louisville.

This thoughtfully designed garden of simple flowers stages engaging displays of color throughout the year. But none can match the vibrant beauty that blooms here in spring. Whether you are a beginning gardener or an experienced one, consider this Kentucky treasure a gracious guide for the garden of your dreams.

BEGINNINGS

Designed by pioneer landscape architect Marian Coffin in the early 1900s, this garden had a significant beginning. A native New Yorker, Coffin was one of the first female landscape architects in the country. When no established firms would hire her, she formed her own company, eventually attracting commissions from such prominent clients as Henry Francis du Pont. She is perhaps best known for her design of Winterthur, du Pont's Delaware garden.

Her work is still very evident at Oxmoor Farm, where her plan remains virtually intact, along with many of the original plantings. Coffin created a series of gardens and views that related to the entries of the house and the fields beyond. Structures and paths were softened by both formal and informal plantings of trees, shrubs, and perennials. Crabapples, hemlocks,

Above: Kay Bullitt and Patrick Snider discuss the garden.
Opposite: With their bold foliage, hostas define the border garden.

and cornelian cherries defined the views, outlined the various gardens, and were accented by shrubs such as pearl bush, lilac, and Rose of Sharon. Perennials such as daylilies, iris, peonies, and yuccas provided dependable color and texture.

THE GARDENERS

Over the years, several gardeners have nurtured Oxmoor Farm, including Kay Bullitt who has held the reins for more than 25 years. Kay, who grew up in England, was a two-time Wimbledon doubles champion. After marrying and moving to Kentucky, she focused her energy on champions of another kind: Thoroughbred horses that she raised on Oxmoor Farm. More recently, with the help of gardener Patrick Snider, she has restored the gardens to the full glory that Marian Coffin intended for them to have. They cut back and rejuvenated shrubs, amended the soil, and divided overgrown perennials and replanted them throughout the garden. They also added masses of annuals to complement the perennials. Although they have focused on the border garden and the terrace garden, they have also created a new rock garden. Join us for a tour of two beautiful gardens.

Opposite page: Bird sculptures serve as a focal point of the garden.

Above: The gazebo is reflected in the dark, still pool of the terrace garden.

Left: Yellow and pink yarrow *(Achillea)* line the paths in the rock garden.

Below: Yellow, blue, and chartreuse conifers form the backbone of the rock garden.

Above, left: Daylillies brighten the garden. **Above, center:** Pin oaks form an allée on the entry drive to Oxmoor Farm. **Above, right:** Delicate pink petals of yarrow add color to the rock garden. **Below:** A majestic green ash graces the opposite end of the border garden.

Whether you are a beginning gardener or an experienced one, consider this Kentucky treasure a gracious guide for the garden of your dreams.

THE BORDER GARDEN

A majestic green ash anchors one end of the long path through the border garden. A simple arbor, graced with a climbing 'New Dawn' rose, serves as the entry. Easy-to-grow shrubs such as pearl bush, butterfly bush, and large groups of 'Annabelle' hydrangeas form the backdrop here. Perennials planted en masse scatter dependable color and texture throughout this garden. Daylilies, iris, spiderworts, and yuccas enjoy the area with full sun. Peonies, hardy begonias, and hostas thrive in partial sun.

Annuals bring the final touches to the garden, and Kay and Patrick are careful to select hardy ones that can take the heat of a Kentucky summer. Their favorites include 'Derby' melampodium, 'Purple Wave' and 'Pink Wave' petunias, 'Limelight' and 'Copper Queen' coleus, and several selections of impatiens. "The one thing I have learned from Kay," volunteers Patrick, "is to have lots of variety."

THE TERRACE GARDEN

Designed as a series of circles from the house, the terrace garden, too, is very simple. Brick paths form a figure eight crowned with the white gazebo at one end. A black reflecting pool in the center lawn reflects its crisp image. Kay likes to plant this area with annuals accented with a few perennials. Her choices of perennials include orange daylilies, blue-leaved hostas, and white astilbe.

For annuals Kay prefers 'Climax' marigolds, Grape Cooler and Rose Cooler Series vincas, and white Madness Series petunias, which perfume spring evenings with their fragrances. Kay also includes Johnny-jump-ups, one of her old favorites.

Above: In the shade of a dogwood tree, white rocking chairs provide a cool spot to watch a sunset.
Left: Looking down the path in the border garden, you see 'Annabelle' hydrangeas and multicolored annuals leading to a rose-covered arbor.
Below: Beloved horses and hounds have a final resting place amid orange daylilies.

close to heaven

On a wooded hilltop in Arkansas, Nancy Porter has gardened for 27 years, creating a breathtaking garden that surrounds her New England–style home.

There's a little bit of New England in Arkansas. Right outside Little Rock, Nancy Gunn Porter built her dream home. The house is a 1730s-style New England saltbox with simple design and classic detailing around the front door. After the house was complete, it was time to create a garden to soften the wooden structure.

Nancy's showy garden connects the house to the land and is encircled by a tidy picket fence. But, the first hole she dug—some 27 years ago—made her wonder if she would need a jackhammer. There was only a thin layer of soil covering the rocky hillside. She had to remove all the rocks

from the flowerbeds and replace them with loads of compost, working the soil to make it loose, fertile, and inviting to plants. Pine straw makes cushiony soft pathways leading to the front door and through the garden.

Nancy researched the first plants selected to make sure they were being grown in the 1730s. She tried to match the plants, including old roses, foxglove, larkspur, and hollyhock, with the colonial era. After a few years she found this too limiting so she began to try other plants.

With all the experimenting Nancy has learned what works for her, but each year the garden changes a little because there are always new plants to try. She has a great

Above: Nancy tends to her flowers, while her husband, Duncan, finds the vegetable garden more to his liking. Their dog, Sidney, helps keep the squirrels out of both areas.

Left: Poppies reseed each year. They pop up anywhere they please and are a welcome addition to the garden.

Right: French hollyhocks stand out against the dark weathered wood.

Opposite page: Peek over the picket fence, and you immediately feel the need to walk into this flower-filled garden.

Left: These peonies and iris were dug from Nancy's mother's yard. They fill the garden with both flowers and memories.

Right: Heavenly Glow Louisiana iris sports radiant orange-red petals with green-and-yellow centers.

Below: Roses in full bloom peer over the side of the fence

Preceeding pages: Nancy and Duncan's garden has bloomed nicely over the past 27 years.

sense of design, but she also lets Mother Nature assist. Sprinkles of poppies come up here and there and reseed each year. Seedlings sprout wherever seeds fall, making the garden look loose and natural.

The garden has matured nicely over the quarter century. Roses climb and spill over fences and arbors. Peonies have formed thick clumps and produce pink golf ball-size buds that unfurl and transform into bowl-size blooms. Nancy carefully stakes each clump with round metal plant supports to help hold the hefty flowers up during spring rains.

The peonies were dug from her mother's yard and are more than 50 years old. Siberian iris have colonized and their blue blooms are surrounded by masses of sword-like foliage. Dianthus and verbena grow close to the ground and make a floral carpet by the front door.

The spring garden is a welcome sight after a cold winter, but each season is special. In the summer, towering hollyhocks frame the front door. Butterflies flock to buddleia, white phlox, cosmos, and *Verbena bonariensis*. In the fall, sugar maples Nancy planted years ago rain golden leaves on the garden. Purple asters and Mexican bush sage supply late-season flowers. The winter garden isn't showy, but it allows you to see its framework. Winter is also a great time for Nancy to regroup and select new plants for the upcoming year. Fallen leaves are collected, ground up, and used to mulch the beds.

On top of this rocky ridge in Arkansas, a dream home was built and around it a dream garden was created. Not many people fulfill their dreams, but Nancy is living hers. This garden is very much a part of her—and part of her mother, for plants that her mother grew have been passed down and enhance the garden with beauty and memories. Nancy regrets that her mother isn't alive to see the garden. But she's probably seen it, because anything this beautiful is close to heaven.

contained gardens

plant a garden where you can

how to pack pots with impact

Try these techniques for knockout containers. "A perfectly planted container should be a seamless mix of foliage and flowers," says Jeremy Smearman, owner of Planters Nursery in Atlanta.

A colorful display in containers placed close to your house, deck, or patio adds warmth and charm. If you have minimal time or space, potting up a few planters is the perfect way to garden.

When planting multiple pots on your porch, remember repetition. Try repeating a color or plant in each pot to tie them together. Don't put 10 different colors on one porch. Too many shades or shapes will appear chaotic and cluttered.

Take a look at the planting in the photo at right and how all four pots work together. Five caladiums, a spider plant, and a 'Little Gem' magnolia dress up the steps and porch. Red caladiums on the steps complement the large pot in the corner.

Low-growing plants work well on the steps, and a 5-foot-tall 'Little Gem' magnolia fills the corner, while helping to hide a downspout. Not only are the plants cohesive, but the containers also have a similar look.

Your porch doesn't have to be covered in plants to be inviting. A few pots placed and planted strategically can be visually appealing and give you more bang for your buck.

Containers are available in every size, shape, and color. Select a planter that complements your house. For instance, an orange terra-cotta pot might clash with a redbrick house, whereas a gray concrete container may be better suited. Also make sure your pot is the right scale for where you intend to use it. A 6-inch pot on a large front porch will go unnoticed and won't make an impact.

Once you find the right container, keep the same principles in mind when choosing plants. White blooms in front of a white house won't show up. Use dark foliage and bright flowers against a light-colored house, and use light foliage and pastel flowers against a dark house for maximum impact.

Before you plant, make sure your containers have unobstructed drainage holes in the bottom. If they don't, use a drill to make new holes or expand existing or clogged ones. If the potting soil you are using is light and likely to sift through the drain holes, place a coffee filter, pot shards, or window screen over them. This will keep the soil in the pot, yet allow the water to drain.

There are many potting soils available, so select a premium mix. Some contain lime to balance the pH, controlled-release

Above: The containers on this porch are simple yet bold. No flowers grace these pots, but the foliage provides plenty of impact.
Opposite: In a sunny location, this plant combo can't be beat. Pentas, lantana, and 'Provence' lavender provide color, while sedum, sage, and ivy add texture.

BEFORE PLANT SHOPPING

Make a list of what you'll need. Here are some things to consider.

- Check to see if you have sun or shade. (See page 231 for suggestions.)
- Which size plants will you need?
- How many plants will you need?
- Do you want short, mounding plants or tall ones?
- Which colors will complement your house, not clash with it?
- How much time are you willing to spend watering?
- Do you need potting soil?
- Consider small trees and shrubs. They work beautifully in large containers.

Below: Small shrubs such as this standard peegee hydrangea, underplanted with blue browallia, petunias, and ivy, look handsome in large containers.

fertilizer, and water-retaining polymers. Read the labels and ask for recommendations at the garden center. Avoid buying cheap soils that don't list their contents. You may have to try a few brands to find the one that's right for your plants.

Finally, choose the correct-size plant for your pot. There should be enough room for plants to continue to grow and fill out. Small trees and shrubs add height and nice lines to a large container. Ornamental grasses can also provide bright color with interesting form. Don't forget to use foliage plants. They might not have showy flowers, but they can supply lots of color.

Think about where to place your planters for the most impact. Use plants in pots as design elements. Next to steps, they may signal a grade change or mark entryways. Or use them as focal points to draw you into a garden or onto a deck. A cluster of pots can create a small garden that is manageable with minimum time and expense.

Put out a few pots for a splash of color. They help unify your house with the landscape. Containers are also a good way to introduce yourself to plants if you're not a seasoned gardener. They will decorate your home's exterior and add your own special signature style.

STEP-BY-STEP TECHNIQUES

A container should be the crowning touch of the garden. It's the very last thing you do to complete your landscape. Choose a simple container that will hold large annuals and tropical material. You want your planter to look like it has been growing at least two months the day you plant it.

Also, plan your container's contents to complement the garden, not compete with it. If the flowerbed bordering the patio is a riot of color, plant containers using only one color. In a landscape of green trees and shrubs, your container plantings can run wild with color.

Whether you're planting in sun or shade, another key is compatibility. It is important to use plants that have similar light and water requirements. But it goes further than that. Colors must be compatible, as well as textures. Pair large, coarse leaves with smaller, more delicate leaves for pleasing texture. Avoid planting flowers that all have the same shape or have foliage with the same texture. Visual depth is achieved by varying the size and shape of both flowers and foliage.

CONTAINER TIPS

Make sure your containers are located no farther than the length of a hose for convenient watering.

Shredded bark, pine straw, gravel, or small pinecones make attractive mulches for topping planters. They also help reduce moisture loss.

Change soil every couple of plantings. Reach down in the pot, and loosen soil with your hands between each planting.

When selecting several different types of plants for one pot, make sure they all share the same sun and water requirements.

HOW TO START

First, the container must have a large drainage hole in the bottom. If the pot has a tiny hole, carefully enlarge it using an electric drill and masonry bit.

Next, put a layer of gravel or broken pottery in the bottom to help keep the drainage hole open. Fill the container with lightweight potting soil. Trickle water into the container to settle the soil prior to planting. Layer soils in containers that will be placed in full sun. Use lightweight soil in most of the pot, and top it off with a layer of heavier potting soil. Try to use a soil that contains expanded shale as the top layer. This heavier soil forms a crust on top of the pot, helping retain moisture.

PLANT IT BIG

Scale is the relationship between the size of the planting and the size of the container. Put another way, it's how to keep your container from being skimpy. Jeremy has simplified this idea and developed a rule to ensure the scale of plants to container is correct. The volume of plants should be equal to or greater than the volume of the pot.

Choose mature plants that are already blooming or are close to it. Many garden centers sell annuals and tropical plants in 1-gallon pots. This is the perfect size to give your newly planted container an instant finished look.

Begin planting in the center of the pot with the dominant plant. This is the focal point, or where your eye goes first. Then plant toward the sides, knitting the plants together with color and texture. Remember to loosen the roots of each plant before placing in the container.

KEEP IT FRESH

A pot that is filled to the brim with vigorous plants requires vigilant care. Be sure to keep in mind that a container in full sun needs more water than a shady pot. Expect to water a sunny container once a day during the hottest summer months. Add water-retaining polymers at planting time to help hold moisture.

To keep your container in peak bloom from spring through first frost, feeding is essential. At planting time add a well-balanced (14-14-14) time-release granular fertilizer to the soil. In addition, feed with a liquid fertilizer high in potassium (15-30-15) on a monthly basis. Remove old flowers, and trim any plant that becomes greedy for space. View your container as a tapestry of flowers and foliage.

Below: Geraniums, cape plumbago, and 'Blue Wonder' fan flower thrive in sun or part sun. Variegated Swedish ivy falls gracefully over the sides of its container.

GREAT CONTAINER PLANTS

sun

rose color pentas
(*Pentas lanceolata*)

purple sage
(*Salvia officinalis Purpurascens*)

'Lemon Drop' lantana
(*Lantana camara* 'Lemon Drop')

'Provence' lavender
(*Lavandula intermedia* 'Provence')

'Gold Baby' English ivy
(*Hedera helix* 'Gold Baby')

'October Daphne' sedum
(*Sedum sieboldii* 'October Daphne')

shade

'Pink Cane' begonia
(*Begonia* x 'Pink Cane')

Japanese painted fern
(*Athyrium goeringianum* 'Pictum')

'Pixie Dixie' English ivy
(*Hedera helix* 'Pixie Dixie')

sun/partial shade

'Pink Camellia' geranium
(*Pelargonium* 'Pink Camellia')

cape plumbago
(*Plumbago auriculata*)

'Blue Wonder' fan flower
(*Scaevola aemula* 'Blue Wonder')

variegated Swedish ivy
(*Plectranthus coleoides* 'Variegatus')

pots of gold

A pot of flowers is like a pot of gold. It might not make you wealthy, but it sure will make you smile.

I f there's a plant growing in that pot at the end of the rainbow, surely goldmoss is it. This unbelievably easy-to-grow perennial sets the gold standard for the garden each spring when clusters of feathery flowers shine brightly.

Even when goldmoss *(Sedum acre)* is not blooming, you'll treasure the lemon-lime colored leaves, which show off especially well when paired with dark-green plants. Creeping stems form a dense mat, which lasts through the winter.

Goldmoss is a priceless choice for guilt-free gardening. This tough little succulent likes hot weather, full sun, and poor, dry soil. Too much shade, water, and rich soil disagree with it, making plants leggy with sparse blooms. Goldmoss may be a little too easy to grow; plant it in your garden and be prepared for an abundance of the stuff. You're better off planting it in rock garden pockets or putting it in pots.

When it is properly contained, goldmoss is quite a gold mine. It grows about 4 inches high, making this plant the perfect companion plant for anything spiky or tall. Flowers and foliage creep downward, spilling over the edges of window boxes and pots. Plant goldmoss

Above: Tree forms of Spanish lavender underplanted with goldmoss in pots are a striking addition to this herb garden.

alone or combine it with annuals for a wealth of color.

Extremely cold hardy and tolerant of intense heat, goldmoss can take just about anything. But if you walk on it, you'll kill it, which is another good reason to grow it in a pot.

When you're planting containers this year, do a little gold digging of your own. You're sure to strike it rich with goldmoss.

GOLDMOSS

at a glance

Category: herbaceous evergreen perennial

Light: full sun

Soil: any well drained

Flowers: yellow in spring for about 3 weeks

Rate of growth: rapid (will spread if not contained)

plenty of pansies

Selecting a great-looking container for pansies takes careful planning. First, choose the best pot for your home. Take a good look at its future location, and consider the surroundings—house and trim paint, stone, brickwork, existing landscape, and outdoor furniture all play a part in developing the proper combination of color and texture. The planter's tone and material should relate to these things. Choose a pot that looks comfortable in the location, and the plants will enhance its appearance.

Next, determine your pansy color scheme using the same principles. Choose one color flower for a dressy appearance and several shades for a more casual look. When adding other plants, as we have, make sure they all belong to the same color family.

TERRA-COTTA THREESOME

The clay trio builds a collection around a central color theme. Yellow, orange, and red—all color cousins—establish a range of shades that includes the pots. (In parts of the South where clay may suffer freeze damage, use terra-cotta-colored plastic.) In the yellow pansy pot, an aucuba with golden variegation mirrors the flowers, as well as a leather-leaf mahonia with lemon-colored blooms.

The pot to its left, filled with orange and red pansies, has a redtwig dogwood for height and color. The container below repeats the same flower combination with 'Bright Lights' chard, adding vibrant texture. In this arrangement, the plants and containers work together to create a fun and cohesive mix.

VIOLAS AND COMPANY

An old square planter with aged, peeling paint is a good choice for this landing where the brick meets the stone. The pot and the mortar share the same color, forming a common bond between the location and the container.

Above: Colors in the same family make a good choice for this brick landing. **Below:** Older pots have a less formal side that adds a nice touch.

Purple violas billow over the front of the pot, their color tying together the red brick and bluestone. In back, shades of violet are continued with leafy purple sage, while dusty miller adds a silver surprise and gently relates to the shade of the door frame and bluestone.

Containers are the finishing touch to any landscape, and pansies warm the winter with colorful blooms. Make them work in harmony, and you'll have perfect pansy planters.

SUCCESSFUL CONTAINERS

Follow these suggestions and your pansy pots will flourish.

- A large drainage hole is essential.
- Use good-quality potting soil.
- Thoroughly moisten the soil before planting.
- Mix a granular timed-release fertilizer, such as 14-14-14, into the soil when planting.
- Place the container in sufficient light for the plants you have selected.
- Continually monitor the soil, keeping it slightly moist at all times.

hanging gardens

Suspending plants from porches and porticos is a part of the gardening ritual. Fabulous ferns and masses of brilliant impatiens, dripping over the edges of hanging baskets, have long been favorites to place color in difficult spaces.

This year, look at the hanging container as a potential garden—just as you would a flowerbed. A variety of colors, textures, and shapes will become a focal point, sure to enhance your landscape.

SELECTING BASKETS

Have fun shopping for your hanging container. Only one of these planters (opposite page) was designed for that purpose. The others—a small miner's basket (right) and a cone-shaped fire bucket (below)—were found at a flea market and antiques shop, and then put to garden use. Choose a container that can be suspended easily and is strong enough to hold the weight of soil and plants.

When deciding on the basket, think about the plants to go in it. If it does not hold much soil, like the miner's basket, the plants need to be shallow-rooted to flourish. Consider this when choosing the basket, and purchase the appropriate one for the plant requirements.

PLANTING AND PLACEMENT

Plan color and texture carefully for your hanging garden. If you prefer a single flower color, vary the shades for interest. Instead of planting all pink impatiens in a shady basket (opposite page), add a few light blush and a few deeper rose-hued plants for depth.

Variegated spider plants contribute a long, lance-shaped leaf to the mix. Angel-wing begonias have large leaves with colorful markings, as well as cascading blooms. Ferns and ivy, which thrive outdoors, also bring texture.

The miner's basket (top, right), designed for full sun, is planted with sculptural succulents. Their water needs aren't demanding, and they adapt easily to the shallow container. Hens and chicks provide a round flowerlike shape, and creeping sedums offer several different leaf shapes. This tiny garden, without a flower, illustrates how effective green can be.

The conical fire bucket (below) is planted for dappled light—a little sun and a little shade. A cascading red ivy-leaf geranium highlights the bucket's lettering, and white petunias add lush blossoms for contrast and brightness.

Place your hanging garden where you would love color, but can't find a way to get it there. Loop chain or rope around a sturdy tree limb, placing an old piece of hose between them to prevent damage. Hang the garden, ensuring the branch can support the weight.

Turn your hanging baskets into something special with a creative container and a garden approach to planting. You will enjoy hanging them around.

Above: A miner's basket filled with succulents thrives in full sun.

Left: A red ivy-leaf geranium and white petunias cascade from a cone-shaped fire bucket. Flea markets and antique stores are great places to shop for containers such as this one.

Opposite: Varying shades of pink impatiens add a bit of depth to a hanging basket.

234

make a trough garden

If you've got a free afternoon and don't mind making a mess, here's a project for you. Catherine Webster of Savannah, Georgia, shared her instructions for making the garden that is the centerpiece of her patio.

The planter's rough texture resembles English stone troughs, once used for feeding livestock and now in great demand for container gardening. Making your own trough is considerably less expensive and more fun.

Note: The size of your plastic foam cooler determines the finished size of your planter. It also determines the amount of cement mixture you will need (see Step 6).

Step 1: Lay plywood down to protect your deck or patio. You can work directly on the wood.

Step 2: Cut the sides of the cooler down, leaving it approximately 4 to 6 inches deep.

Step 3: Wrap the cooler with chicken wire, folding the edges under so a couple of inches are inside the cooler. Poke the sharp ends into the plastic foam to secure.

Step 4: Invert cooler and poke holes in bottom with screwdriver. Press dowels through holes so they are half in and half out. (You will remove the dowels in Step 9, forming drainage holes for your planter.)

Step 5: Form a thick mound of wet sand slightly larger than the mouth of your cooler. Invert cooler and press into sand to leave imprint. Dig a moat in sand slightly wider than the imprint. Cover sand with plastic sheeting.

Step 6: Combine 1 part Portland cement; 2 parts sand; and 2 parts peat moss, with large chunks removed. Add enough water to make mixture thick and wet, like cottage cheese. Mixture will look dark.

Step 7: Fill plastic-covered moat with cement mixture. Invert cooler and press it into cement mixture.

Step 8: Press remaining mixture onto sides and bottom of cooler until no chicken wire is visible. Cover entire project with plastic.

Step 9: Remove plastic after a day or so, and check your trough for hardening. When cement mixture is firm but can be dented with your fingernail, your planter is prime for texturizing. Remove dowels.

Step 10: Use a wire brush and screwdriver to roughen the surface of your trough, giving it an aged appearance. Round off sharp corners.

Step 11: Let planter continue to harden without plastic sheeting. Leave plastic foam inside planter, and fill with potting soil as soon as cement mixture is fully hardened.

Above: This handsome planter was made by covering a plastic foam cooler with a mixture of Portland cement, peat moss, sand, and water.

TOOLS & MATERIALS

- small sheet of inexpensive plywood
- plastic foam cooler
- sharp knife
- chicken wire and wire cutters
- screwdriver
- 1-inch wooden dowel, cut into 4 equal lengths
- sand or vermiculite
- plastic sheeting
- Portland cement (not a sand mixture)
- peat moss
- water
- wire brush

planted in a pool

Sometimes there's just no room to garden. If a balcony or terrace is the majority of your outdoor space, or if you want to introduce a little green to any unplanted area, consider a using a cast-concrete pool for a miniature garden.

Because these pools are made to accommodate plumbing, there are holes in the bottom that allow for drainage. If the holes are so large that soil will wash out, partially cover them with a piece of broken terra-cotta pot. Fill the pool with a good quality potting soil, one that is fairly coarse so it will last several years.

Then consider the area where your pool garden will be placed. Will it have sun or shade? Do you want a spring, summer, fall, or all-season garden? Will you see it up close or in passing? Answers to these questions will determine what you choose to plant.

The pool garden shown here relies on shade-loving plants, giving it a foundation of foliage that is attractive all season long. Flowers come and go. The planting is highly detailed so it is interesting to look down upon at close range.

Like furnishing a dollhouse with miniature tables and chairs, planting a pool garden requires scaled-down thinking. The ground cover is a combination of moss and the dainty, diminutive *Lysimachia japonica* 'Minutissima'. Shade-loving and growing all of a half-inch tall, it is an ideal choice. It even sports tiny yellow flowers in late spring.

Pushing through the blanket of green are miniature hostas (that flower in their season), dwarf crested iris (*Iris cristata*), violas, 'Itsy-Bitsy' English ivy, blue phlox (*Phlox divaricata*), and foamflower (*Tiarella wherryi*).

If space allows, repeat the showiest plants in the surrounding beds to tie it all together.

Below: A cast-concrete pool can be pressed into service as a planter. This shade-loving combination includes blue phlox, miniature hostas with golden and variegated foliage, and dwarf crested iris. In the pool, the iris are safe from hungry voles that may devour them in garden beds. A deep bird's bath also makes a nice container.

Above: This three-tiered planting is tall and colorful. Each level has a totally different look. **Opposite, near right:** These two pots filled with herbs offer a tasty treat. **Opposite, top:** Stacked terra-cotta pots create a minigarden. **Opposite, far right:** Three upside-down orchid pots elevate a container of strawberry geraniums and Japanese painted fern.

piggyback pots

How do you get different looks from ordinary pots? It's simple; you stack them. Terra-cotta pots of all shapes and sizes combine to make one interesting container.

The pots are inexpensive, and they look great once they are filled with soil, stacked, and planted. Annuals, herbs, and plants with attractive foliage fill these piggyback pots.

Bagged topsoil works better than potting soil as container filler. Potting soil tends to be spongy and won't pack firmly. Topsoil provides a stable base for the pots. In some of the large containers, two bricks set inside create a level surface. The deeper you sink the upper pot into the lower pot the greater the stability.

Make sure that your containers are secure by using both hands to work the upper pot into the lower one. Then fill around the upper pot with soil, and pack it firmly. When filled, the pots will be heavy. Make sure that they are stable and not located in high traffic areas or close to children's play areas.

For the arrangement shown above, a small strawberry jar is placed in the center of a large bowl-shaped container, the jar is topped with asparagus fern, and the side holes are filled with petunias. Dwarf mondo grass and creeping Jenny are planted in the bowl-shaped container.

For the planting shown at left, a large 5-gallon strawberry jar is placed in a bigger container and filled with herbs such as rosemary, thyme, parsley, and oregano. (Herbs and other plants that require well-drained soil perform wonderfully in strawberry jars.) The pots fill out nicely, and the plants are a tasty addition to the garden. This miniature herb garden can even be harvested in winter months.

The three-tiered planter (shown on opposite page) is created with different-size rolled-rim containers. Pink petunias spill over the edge of the base pot. Begonias and asparagus fern fill the middle, while Mexican heather and a 'Blue Pyramid' cypress point skyward in the top pot.

The shade-lovers combination (below) produces a neat display. Creeping fig and dwarf mondo grass fill the base container, and three upside-down orchid pots form feet to support a pot of strawberry geraniums and Japanese painted fern.

Potting all these combinations takes less than a half-day. Because containers come in so many shapes and sizes, it's like putting a puzzle together. It's fun to stack a few and see if the pieces fit.

playful potted garden

Summertime should be casual and fun. Containers overflowing with color fit right in with that laid-back attitude. These potted gardens add that ambience to places where digging is not an option.

This collection was started with galvanized buckets—two round and one oval. When choosing your own containers, remember it's easy to arrange odd numbers and different sizes. The pails were painted strong colors to complement the flower choices. That way, the brightly hued containers became part of the overall scheme instead of invisible vessels.

UP ON FEET

Elevating the pots serves both functional and decorative purposes. A container sitting directly on a flat surface may have drainage problems. Lifting it slightly allows water to escape easily. This also helps air to circulate underneath, keeping the temperature of the container cooler. And metal—even galvanized—can leave behind a rusty ring when set directly on a deck or patio.

From a decorative aspect, pot feet are an opportunity for amusement. Wooden drapery finials and copper plumbing floats were used here. The finials were painted to match the containers. The round pots each have three feet placed in a triangle pattern; the oval container requires four supports.

To attach the finials, use a nail and hammer to punch holes in the bucket bottom, and insert the finials' screws through the openings. Inside, thread a small piece of wood onto each screw to keep the finial firmly attached. The copper floats are fastened in a similar way; punch holes in the container, and insert washers and screws

Above: You can bring containers to their feet using drapery finials and copper floats. **Opposite:** Hardware stores offer all sorts of materials to create easy and amusing containers.

from inside the pot to the outside. The floats easily thread onto the screws.

Make additional holes in the container bottoms for adequate drainage. Fill containers with good-quality, moist potting soil before planting.

FRIENDLY FLOWERS

These bloom choices work extremely well in areas of both sun and light shade. Red 'New Guinea' impatiens, purple petunias, 'Marine' heliotrope *(Heliotropium arborescens* 'Marine'), and wishbone flower *(Torenia fournieri)* all provide rich color. To add a little sparkle to these vibrant shades, lime-green licorice plant *(Helichrysum petiolare* 'Limelight'), grass-like variegated Japanese sweet flag *(Acorus gramineus* 'Ogon'), green-and-gold Swedish ivy *(Plectranthus coleoides* 'Marginatus'), and chartreuse creeping jenny *(Lysimachia nummularia* 'Aurea'), were added to the arrangement. In the yellow container, asparagus fern and petunias were a good mix.

The planters require water on a daily basis if placed in full sun. In light shade, watering every other day should be sufficient. To keep flowers abundant, feed with a water-soluble liquid such as 15-30-15 once a week. Always water the pots with clear water prior to fertilizer application. As blossoms fade, remove the old, so new ones can form. With a little grooming, you'll have fabulous flowers in fun containers throughout the summer.

window dressings

"Window boxes make an entrance welcoming, dress up the facade of a home, and give you the chance to show off a little," says Janie Singletary. She should know. In Greenville, South Carolina, her business, Gardenhaven, flourishes with good ideas. And from Louisville, Kentucky, landscape designer Barbie Thomas shares her secrets for winter boxes.

"A window box should reflect the owner's personality," she says. "I try to choose plants with that in mind." Besides having personality, the planter should also suit the home. But within that framework, your imagination can grow. "It's a chance to do the unexpected," she says.

PARTY LIGHTS

The collection of white flowers and foliage (right) is simple and elegant. It brightens the shady entrance to Marsha Twiford's brick home.

The base of the window box is a metal frame called a hayrack. It's lined with sheet moss and filled with soil. Impatiens and caladiums fill the top, while variegated vinca and asparagus fern trail over the side. The result is a window box so fat and full that the metal form is invisible.

"Impatiens are great plants to use as water indicators," Janie says. "If you're not sure it's time to water, take a look at the impatiens. They will wilt before anything else and let you know the box is dry," she says. "In a sunny box, add water-retaining polymers to the soil to hold moisture longer," she says.

With company coming, Marsha spruced up using a Gardenhaven idea: Wire glass votive candle holders to plant stakes. Cut the stakes different lengths and carefully push them into the window box. The candles should sit above the flowers and foliage. Light the candles as company arrives. "This is also a great look on a patio near an outdoor dining area. But don't leave the candles unattended," Janie says.

ARCHITECTURAL ADDITION

Peter Allsopp wanted a project. His wife, Jean, wanted to dress up the front of their house. So Peter built a box that matched the trim on their home (opposite page, top). Then he had a tin insert made to slip inside the planter for moisture protection. Peter used Janie's idea of planting small shrubs in the box to give it a formal look. "Manicured shrubs are terrific in window boxes," she says. "They will last for several years and then can be moved into the garden."

An ivy garland softens the edge of the box without hiding the trim. "Purchase ivy hanging baskets with long runners," Janie says. Her instructions: Gently break each plant into two or three pieces. Place them along the front edge of the box at each loop's anchor point. Tie a piece of twine to a short stick. Push the stick into the soil at one corner of the box. Make a loop and

Below: Votive candles perch like fireflies above this window box dressed for a party.

Left: Complement the architecture with your window box.

Center: Clarke the cat peers over the silvery foliage and cool-colored flowers of this vine window box. Artemisia, blue and white tropical plumbago, rex begonia, variegated vinca, and creeping jenny fill the planter with soft colors and texture.

Below: Painted sap buckets filled with basil, petunias, and 'Blackie' sweet potato vine add character to a garage window.

fasten it into the soil with another stick. Repeat this process for all loops, ending at the opposite corner of the planter. Wind the ivy tendrils around the twine. Within a week or so, the leaves will turn in the same direction.

"With a year's growth, the garland will become 5 to 6 inches thick. Keep winding and trimming runners to keep the garland neat," says Janie.

WOODSY AND COOL

Window boxes are not restricted to the front of a home. Catherine and Jon Thompson use their backyard patio regularly during warm months. Their window box adds warmth to this well-used area (right, center). We began with a metal hayrack and turned it into a woodland planter.

Jon dismantled and soaked a grapevine wreath, and while the vine was wet and pliable, he wired it to the metal form. A purchased liner and soil readied the box for planting.

The Thompsons really wanted their window box to have a finished look from the day they planted it. "Don't be afraid to begin with large plant material," says Janie. "Because your planter is a focal point of your yard, plant it to look wonderful from the beginning."

FUN AND FUNCTION

Ellen Riley wanted some herbs in a convenient place, and the garage window, which is close to the kitchen, needed sprucing up. Ellen was looking for a window box that would exemplify Janie's rule of personality and the unexpected (right, below).

Sap buckets are available in rainbow colors. Ellen chose a pastel palette, then mounted buckets to a board that matched the garage, and put drainage holes in the bottom of each.

Choosing plants was easy. Sweet basil, lemon basil, and 'Purple Ruffles' were a must. For color, Ellen turned to petunias. A scented lemon geranium added a different leaf texture and the 'Blackie' sweet potato vine gave her a plant to trail and drape over the iron bars. The combination is colorful and compatible. "Water and light compatibility are as essential as color and texture," Janie reminds us.

Whether your window box enhances the landscape or happens to be your only place to garden, be bold. Allow your creative personality to shine, and don't forget to add the unexpected.

Continued on page 247

Above, left: A container of shrubs takes on new personality with the addition of a small stone bunny and an interesting pot filled with birdseed. **Above, right:** Cut greenery in hard-to-reach boxes is a carefree solution. **Opposite** Cotoneaster and magnolia complement the dark shutters; dried hydrangeas pick up the stone color. **Below:** Conifers make a miniature forest while nandina berries add sparkle.

WINDOW BOXES FOR WINTER

In January, icy winds flex frigid fingers around the garden, where flowerbeds slumber, dreaming of spring. Window boxes, void of summer's hot colors, hug the house, seeming to search for warmth.

"Winter is a real opportunity to do something fun, when things are really drab," says Barbie Tafel Thomas, a landscape designer with Webb-Thomas in Louisville, Kentucky. "You can also use things that would never work any other time of year." Whether you incorporate fresh fruit, small bushes and flowers, cut greenery, or dried material, your planters will take on a full, abundant look reminiscent of summer's substance.

"When you're having a party, pull out all the stops, and do up your window boxes with fresh produce," Barbie suggests. The containers pictured at left show how festive this can look. Barbie first filled the boxes with cut pine boughs to provide a soft-textured base. She added cypress and holly for diversity and then arranged the fruit. As always in good design, one element should be the focal point. Barbie chose a pineapple to center attention in each box and then built the arrangement around it. Clustered on each side of the main attraction, Chinese cabbage and artichokes add volume as well as additional green textures.

Winter fruit provides glorious color. Sunshine shades dominate citrus, and apples bring a drop of ruby red. For maximum impact, Barbie used citrus as the dominant color family and clustered each type of fruit. "The thing about lemons and oranges is that they're not terribly expensive in winter. They will stay fresh for several weeks, and retain color as they dry," she says. She placed apples sparingly throughout the collection for pizzazz. Drawbacks to using apples are their susceptibility to freeze damage and their tendency to show up on a squirrel's radar.

Many garden shops and nurseries stock 1-gallon pots of hardy evergreens such as juniper, cotoneaster, Japanese boxwood, nandina, and ivy. Choose plants with good color, and avoid those with brown tips.

Purchase ivy only if it has been outdoors. Greenhouse plants are not ready to face winter winds and will succumb to the first few cold nights.

Barbie designed the stone box (shown on page 245) with a combination of cotoneaster and brilliant pansies for the plant base. "The box required more impact than just the shrubs and flowers. By using cut magnolia, I added a large leaf, which was needed, and gave the box a focal point," she says. Dried hydrangeas contribute additional texture and color, bringing unexpected lightness to the arrangement. "Using hydrangeas, and even cut magnolia, is a temporary thing. It will last for about three weeks and then most likely need to be replaced. But that's a simple thing to do."

Another application is to use small conifers. A formal look is achieved by repeating one plant type across the back of the box and pansies of one color in front. A more casual look results from mixing the evergreens and using a combination of pansy colors. Ivy is a good choice to cascade over the front. Add texture with clusters of nandina berries or pinecones.

Maintenance can be an acrobat's hobby when a window box is placed in an upper-story location. In such a situation, Barbie employs a combination of cut greenery to fill this vacant space. While it requires occasional replacing through the winter, the issue of watering is nonexistent. Greenery such as magnolia and holly hold up for long periods before browning, so the box always looks well tended.

An easy-care, whimsical technique is to add a single piece of garden statuary to the window box. Moderation is the secret here. Be sure to focus on one element, and center everything else in the box around it.

"When homeowners place window boxes on the front of their home, they are committed to doing something special and unique with that part of their landscape," Barbie says. Winter is a time when imagination and personality can take over. "Use the boxes to have some fun, and make the winter planting something special."

Left: Cut pines, cypress, and holly serve as the base for this vibrant box of fruit.

pipe dreams

Last spring, Charlie Thigpen had a dream—a dream that turned into his wife's worst nightmare. When trying to figure out how he could make a garden path a little more interesting, he came up with the idea of placing pipes along its sides. Charlie thought this might look neat, but his wife thought differently.

He began collecting old terra-cotta, cast-iron, and even metal pipes. Then he set them upright in the garden, burying one end of the pipe in the ground just deep enough for it to be firm and secure. Some Charlie filled with soil and topped with annuals, succulents, and herbs. Others he used as pedestals to hold hanging baskets off the ground. His pipe path was starting to take shape.

One day, a friend gave Charlie a large concrete pipe with a flared end. The pipe looked aged and seemed perfect for his garden. He drove home, proud of his new find. He parked on the side of the house and slowly and carefully began to unload the heavy pipe. Just as he got it off the truck Charlie heard his wife, Cindy, yell "What's that?" in a stern voice. He turned to find her on the front porch with her hands on her hips, and he knew he was in trouble. In a meek voice Charlie told her, "It's a beautiful concrete pipe." "That's it—no more pipes," she said as she turned and walked back in the house. Charlie thinks he was pretty lucky to have set up 14 of them before she stopped him.

Above: Set in a broken pot, this metal pipe holds plants growing from holes punched in its side. An obelisk dresses up the two pieces.

Opposite page: Enhancing this garden path, colorful flowers and foliage pour out of the tops of salvaged pipes that rise from the ground.

The pipes might look a little unusual, but really they are simply tall containers. Plants that require well-drained soil, such as herbs and succulents, work great in them. The pipes also keep invasive plants contained and in bounds. You can use potting soil or any type of soil that the plants require. The pipes are also excellent for holding hanging baskets high above the ground and making them stand out.

By the middle of the summer, the planting began to fill out and Cindy told Charlie that the path looked nice. He asked if he could get some more pipes, but the answer was still no. Oh well, he figures that he should be satisfied with 14. These pipes really did frame the path nicely, and they gave it a unique look. Pipes in the garden aren't for everyone, but they show you how a little imagination can give you a completely different look.

So be open-minded, have fun in your yard, and definitely don't be afraid to try things that are a little out of the ordinary. There are no rules in gardening. Everyone's taste is different. If you think it looks good, that's all that counts.

rooms in bloom

simple arrangements you can do

a long-lasting arrangement

Artfully arranged houseplants in a pretty basket make a thoughtful gift. Add fresh flowers for a vibrant arrangement that's sure to please.

Create a great-looking decoration or gift that will keep your sentiments growing for months.

Find a pretty basket with a handle, and take it with you when you purchase plants. Doing an arrangement is not unlike putting together a new outfit; you will have to try things on to achieve the perfect look. Select a variety of plants in 3- and 4-inch pots, and assemble a mix of different leaf sizes and shapes to make the collection interesting. Include at least one tall plant and several to cascade over the edge of the basket.

Fresh cut flowers add a wonderful touch, but they can be expensive. However, it takes only a few stems to add instant color and freshness to the basket of plants. The large basket pictured on the opposite page includes only three tulips, three iris, and one dendrobium orchid stem. It provides great beauty with a minimal number of expensive flowers.

THE ART OF ARRANGING

Line the inside of the basket with foil to contain moisture. Place the tallest plant next to the handle. Arrange the remaining plants so they decrease gradually in height. Place the trailing plants along the basket edges with foliage tumbling over the sides. To snuggle plants more easily into the basket, remove several from their pots and place them in plastic sandwich bags. Moisture-loving plants, such as maidenhair fern and creeping fig vine, work best in plastic sandwich bags. The bags prevent plant roots from drying out too quickly and reduce plant maintenance. They will now slip in

MATERIALS

- basket with handle
- foil
- houseplants in 3- and 4-inch pots
- plastic sandwich bags
- green sheet moss
- cut flowers
- florist vials
- raffia

among rigid pots. If pots or plastic bags are visible, cover with small pieces of green sheet moss.

Once the plants are settled, add your fresh flowers. Determine the length of each stem, and place the cut end into a water-filled florist vial. Gently push them into the soil surrounding the houseplants so the vials are not visible. Cluster the blooms for big impact.

Choose a flower with a long, graceful stem and small blooms to accent the handle of the basket. Heather and dendrobium orchids are good choices. Push the florist vial into the tall plant's soil, and loosely tie the flower's stem to the handle in several places with a piece of raffia.

CARE AND MAINTENANCE

Check the florist vials every day, and add water as needed. Fresh cut flowers should last from a few days to about a week. As the flowers diminish, remove them from the arrangement—houseplants will still be fresh and attractive.

Learn the water requirements of each plant. A kitchen baster is an easy way to direct water into each pot or plastic bag. Remember that plants in plastic bags don't need to be watered as frequently as plants in containers.

Above: A mix of different sizes and shapes of flowers add interest to the greenery. **Opposite page:** Moisture-loving plants flourish in plastic sandwich bags and fit easily among other pots. Cut flowers in florist vials add sparkle to the arrangement.

flowers straight from the garden

You don't need a special occasion to cut a bouquet of flowers. A few blossoms are all it takes to bring a small piece of the garden indoors.

Loosely gathered, summer flowers seem to find their own place in a vase and require little arranging. What they do need is tender loving care from the moment they are cut. Floral industry consultant Libbey Oliver of Williamsburg, Virginia, has some great tips for cutting and conditioning blossoms to give bouquets a long life. She also has a few hints for simple fresh arrangements that can be used any time of year.

"Our days become hot and humid so quickly—early morning is really the only time to cut garden flowers," says Libbey. "Evenings don't cool down enough before darkness moves in."

Bring along sharp clippers and a container of water. A clean cut made with a sharp tool lets water travel up the stem into the flower head, prolonging the life of the bloom. Dull clippers crush the stem. Choose blossoms that are newly opened and buds just beginning to unfurl. Cut flowers one at a time, and immediately place each stem in the water.

CONDITIONING

Before arranging, remove excess foliage. A few leaves give flowers a natural appearance, but too many will detract from your bouquet. Remove all leaves that will be underwater in the container. Left on, they will breed bacteria in the vase and shorten the life of the arrangement.

Cut the stem again, underwater. This enables water instead of air to travel up the stem. "I never realized what a difference this makes until I tried it," Libbey says. "It especially perks up flowers that have wilted slightly between the garden and indoors." If you've only cut a few flowers, recut the stems under a running faucet. For a larger bouquet,

Libbey puts several inches of water in the sink or a wide container. "Cut the stem below the water's surface, watching out for your fingers," she says. Place freshly cut flowers in water, and place in a cool, dark spot for several hours before arranging.

FOOD FOR THOUGHT

Garden flowers make the freshest bouquets. Taken from yard to vase in a short length of time, few precious nutrients are lost. "There are many old wives' tale recipes for flower food," Libbey says. "Flowers fresh from the garden really don't need extra nutrients. Instead, every few days recut the stems and change the water in the vase. This will prolong their life more than anything added to the water," she says.

If you're giving the bouquet as a gift and feel the need to add a nutrient to the vase, manufactured flower food is available through florists. It has been developed to provide both nutrients and antibacterial agents to keep water clean. It can be purchased in sachet-size packets or large containers. Libbey says, "A small packet is usually sufficient for only 1 quart of water. If you use a flower food, be certain you have enough for the amount of water in the container."

ARRANGING TIPS

Choose a vase that complements the bouquet in size and style. Browse through cabinets and closets for an out-of-the-ordinary container. If it will not hold water or is very large, place a jar or cup inside to hold the flowers.

Simple bouquets can be the most appealing. Interest comes from varying flower shapes and colors. Bouquets need not be

large, but cut flowers should be of similar size.

Before placing flowers in the vase, gather them in your hand. Start with a few stems, and add more, one at a time. Hold the bouquet at arm's length and see how they fit together. If a flower is out of place, gently pull it out from the top. Once you have a pleasing bouquet, use your free hand to cut the stems the same length. Then place them into the vase. Loosen the cluster to fill the container; place more flowers as needed.

Opposite page: The Black-eyed Susan family is well represented in this sunny arrangement. Stems are placed in a pint mason jar inside the tin.

Top: Built around pink and purple, this arrangement is plentiful with only a few stems of each type of flower from your garden.

Above: Calla lilies and yarrow nestle together for a pretty-in-pink bouquet

Left: Zinnias, crocosmias, and dill flower heads stand tall in a rusted container. 'Strawberry Fields' gomphrena carries the color down to the glass vase below.

topiary of roses

Add your frilly best to the table with this great-looking arrangement.

ROSE PETAL CONTAINER

Purchase roses to dry, or dry garden roses during summer months. Dried rose petals also may be used as an ingredient in potpourri. Air-dry roses by hanging from the stem upside-down in a dry place, or try this faster method.

Step 1: Cut the stems of roses 1 inch below blooms. Place through slots on top shelf of food dehydrator. If you're drying large blooms, use only the top shelf. Lower shelves can be used when the flowers are small. Carefully stack shelves without crushing any blooms. Place the top on the dehydrator, and turn on. Roses will be dried completely in about 24 hours. Flowers may be left whole or pulled apart into rose petals. Store in a zip-top plastic bag.

Step 2: Glue dried petals to the 5-inch clay pot, starting at the bottom and working up to the top. Overlap petals slightly. Once complete, place the vinyl saucer inside the pot.

TOPIARY

Step 1: To give the finished topiary extra support, push a green garden stake into the pot along the "stem" and up into the ball at top. Gently tie the stake to the topiary with raffia or twine. Add birch branches around the stem for additional support and to fatten the appearance of the stem. Secure with raffia or twine.

Step 2: Place the topiary in the covered pot, and secure with Spanish moss around edges. Fill water picks with water, and secure tops. Cut rose stems to appropriate length to fit in picks and stay in water. Push the water picks into the top of the topiary. The wire form and ivy will hold the roses and picks in place. Roses of different sizes and colors may be used. Spanish moss can be tucked between flowers to soften the appearance. Add a rose or two at the bottom of the topiary, and crisscross coordinating ribbon around the birch stems.

Roses will stay fresh in the water picks for several days. To keep the ivy topiary healthy, remove the flowers after several days. However, the rose-covered pot can be used as an accent year-round.

Above: An ivy topiary is transformed into a festive centerpiece with a few simple supplies.

TOOLS AND MATERIALS

- roses for drying
- food dehydrator
- zip-top plastic bag
- hot-glue gun
- 1 (5-inch) clay pot
- 1 (4-inch) vinyl saucer
- 1 (12-inch-tall) ivy topiary in 4½-inch pot
- 1 (12-inch) green garden stake
- raffia or green garden twine
- birch branches
- Spanish moss
- water picks
- 7 or more large roses, or smaller spray roses
- ribbon

centerpiece for an outdoor room

Dress up your outdoor table with an easy arrangement planted in a terra-cotta saucer.

The candle nestled in the middle adds an inviting touch to cool evenings and keeps the arrangement compact. Experiment with different candle and plant combinations to fit your tablescape.

Center the 4-inch saucer, upside down, in the larger one. Fill around it with potting soil about a half-inch deep. Gently loosen root balls, and arrange impatiens and ferns toward the inside of the saucer. Place low-growing and trailing plants near the edge.

Slide the hurricane globe on top of the small saucer. Add additional potting soil around the outside edge to cover roots, and water gently to settle the plants and soil. Place a pillar candle inside the globe. Tip: The small saucer serves as a base for the candle. If your globe does not fit over it, remove the saucer and position the glass without it. Keep the hurricane globe in place to prevent potting mix from soiling the candle.

CARE AND FEEDING

Use shade-loving ferns and impatiens for our plant assortment. Soil in a shallow saucer dries out quickly, but these plants require less water attention than those that need full sun. A good drink every other day was sufficient for our arrangement.

The terra-cotta saucer does not have a drainage hole, so water carefully. After rain, gently tip the arrangement to pour off excess water. Feed with a flower-boosting, water-soluble fertilizer, such as 15-30-15, every other week.

As the impatiens begin to mature, they will eventually become too large for the centerpiece. When the plants become leggy, pinch them back to half their height. Always cut directly above a set of leaves. New blooms will appear within a week.

Above: With proper care, pink impatiens, maidenhair fern, rabbit's foot fern, and variegated creeping fig vine will last all summer. **Right:** Place the plants directly into the soil in the saucer.

MATERIALS

- 1 (4-inch) terra-cotta saucer
- 1 (12-inch) terra-cotta saucer
- potting soil
- 3 impatiens plants
- 3 (4-inch) ferns, such as maidenhair or rabbit's foot
- 2 (4-inch) trailing plants, such as ivy or creeping fig vine
- 1 hurricane globe
- 1 pillar candle

257

the best flower bargain around

Chrysanthemums are fall's flowers, bringing the season into your home with inexhaustible blooms. Easily dismissed as rigid and out-of-date, they are, in fact, the best cut-flower deal around. Mums offer shades that equal the flaming foliage of maples and oaks or mirror the colors of an autumn sunset. Enjoy them, and use them liberally.

While chrysanthemums are perfectly suited to easy arrangements reflecting Thanksgiving's bountiful hospitality, some of their other endearing qualities are ready availability and economical price. Purchase plentiful bouquets while you're grocery shopping—you'll get an abundance of flowers for a very small investment. Or visit your local flower shop for more novel selections.

GREETINGS

A wreath on the door packed with brilliant blooms greets guests with a spirited welcome. 'Viking,' a brown-eyed daisy type, is placed in rows around the wreath as if it were a ribbon wound around the form. In between, similarly shaded mums fill in, with each flower touching the next.

Try this colorful flower ring in other ways, perhaps as a focal point on the mantel along with branches of fall foliage. Or place it in a large, shallow saucer as a centerpiece . Fill the middle with small pumpkins, gourds, and squash, or add a cluster of pillar candles in deep shades of burgundy, rust, and gold.

ROUNDING IT OUT

Smaller arrangements also have a place in this holiday's decor. Give chrysanthemums a fresh look in an unexpected way. Brilliant green, button-type 'Kermit' mum spheres mimic osage oranges and add an autumnal accent to a window ledge. Placed on a narrow breadboard with candles and red daisy mums, they create a feel of easy elegance. This easy-to-make arrangement also works well on a mantel or long table.

Above: A partitioned box provides an easy way to display some of the harvest's prettiest players.

Fill an old sectioned wooden box with kumquats, cranberries, flowers, pears, and candles in complementary colors. This versatile arrangement could either serve as a centerpiece on a small dining table, or it can be placed on a sideboard or tea caddy in order to complement other arrangements.

Chrysanthemums are the quintessential fall flower. Use them to add easy, fabulous color to your Thanksgiving celebration.

A HARVEST TABLE SETTING

Capture the spirit of your Thanksgiving dinner with an overflowing centerpiece. Our arrangement is contained in an old-fashioned chicken feeder filled with florist foam. You might also use a weathered wooden toolbox, or simply place blocks of the foam in saucers lengthwise down the table.

Again, it's easy to purchase your materials while grocery shopping. Choose large pompon football mums and a bunch or two with smaller blooms in complementary tones.

From the produce section, bring home heads of colorful kale and selections of persimmons, pomegranates, lady apples, and artichokes. To make arranging simple and avoid a structured look, purchase odd numbers of these items.

Beginning with the kale, secure leaves in the florist foam down the length of the container, alternating sides. Fill in between with the large chrysanthemums, and attach the fruit and vegetables with wooden florist picks or skewers. Cluster the smaller flowers, filling in any gaps.

Trickle a few blossoms and other elements onto the table surrounding the centerpiece. Monitor the florist foam, keeping it moist to preserve the flowers' freshness.

Left: A warm welcome awaits with this tapestry of flowers on the front door.

Left, bottom: Long and overflowing, this centerpiece is an inviting part of each guest's place setting.

Below: These tiny 'Kermit' mum spheres round out Thanksgiving decorations.

Who's who among mums

There are several different flower styles to choose from. Here are the names that go with the blooms.

Cushion mums: This type of bloom has no visible disk. It is purely petals, tightly packed from the center to the edges.

Button mums: A smaller version of the cushion mum, this usually grows no larger than the size of a quarter.

Daisy mums: This style blossom has a round, central disk with petals surrounding it. Almost always yellow, newer hybrids may have a different "eye" color, such as 'Viking,' with a brown center.

Football mums: This is the big boy we all remember from high school football games. About the size of a softball, the blooms are held high on thick, sturdy stems.

branch out

In January, winter flirts with spring. Occasional warm days entice quince, forsythia, and pussy willow to emerge from dormant sleep. With the slightest swelling of buds, it's time to cut a few branches and invite spring indoors before winter turns its cold shoulder.

You don't have to prune heavily to have branches for forcing. A few cuttings can provide plenty of flowers for a small arrangement. Remember, any cut you make will alter the plant's appearance, so treat this as an opportunity to gently shape and trim trees and shrubs. A branch cut now will also lessen the show later, so avoid being heavy-handed. You don't want to take away from vibrant spring blooms. Cut branches headed in the wrong direction or crossing other limbs now. Major pruning should wait until after spring bloom. Choose twigs with rounded, fat buds. Leaf buds are usually smaller and pointed.

A LITTLE PUSH

All it takes to coax budded branches into bloom is some fresh water, moderate indoor temperatures, and a little patience. Cut each stem from the shrub at an angle, and put it immediately into a container of water; once indoors, make a fresh cut. Then place branches in a deep vase with tepid water. Keep the vessel in a cool spot out of direct sunlight. Change the water every three to four days, and recut stems once a week.

A bud that has begun to swell should begin to open indoors

Above: Small arrangements can make a big impact. A simple trio of quince tips brings life to this windowsill.
Opposite: Forsythia and quince are a color burst. The tin-lined basket is filled with crumpled chicken wire to hold tall stems upright. Forsythia is one of the most vigorous candidates for cutting, with pruning necessary almost every year.

in one to two weeks. Dormant branches will also bloom, but patience is necessary, as they may take up to four weeks to flower. The more dormant a branch is when cut, the more subtle the blossom's color will be. For vibrant color, it is best to wait to cut until buds are close to blooming outdoors.

When the first flowers open, cut stems once again and loosely arrange them in a decorative vase. In a large container, a needle holder or chicken wire can support larger branches. Avoid using florist foam with woody stemmed branches. It will inhibit fresh water uptake.

While masses of dayglow forsythia may light up a room, a few snips from a spring-flowering specimen can provide colorful blooms for a windowsill or small arrangement. If you would like a large display but don't have the materials in your garden, purchase tall branches from a florist.

This is a good time to have a dalliance with spring. A small vase filled with delicate blooms is not unlike a stolen kiss. There's surely more to follow, but for now, these few flowers will keep us going through winter.

Above: Pale pink quince and Bradford pear twigs are a soft understudy to tall pussy willow branches.

Right: Forsythia branches needn't be cut long and lanky. A small arrangement can highlight color in surrounding accessories and add a splash of sunshine to a room.

Opposite page: Tiny cherry twigs and a star magnolia stem breathe spring's promise in a gentle manner. Cut branches take up large quantities of water, so small vases need fresh water added every day.

flower garden
checklist

a monthly to-do list for beautiful blooms

January

Protect your garden throughout this chilly month, and prepare for the growing season ahead with these helpful hints. It's a great time of year to do some pruning and to prepare beds for beautiful spring flowers.

TIPS

Bed prep: Use this time to turn under fall leaves or compost or add lime and other amendments to your soil. Remember, if your soil is too wet, you could do more harm than good. Wait until it crumbles easily in your hand.

Seeds: If you buy flower seeds through the mail, this is a good time to order. Sometimes you get early-season bonuses, not to mention quick delivery. That way, you'll be ready to plant for spring.

PLANT

Flowers: Even on cold January days in the Lower and Middle South, you can still plant sweet Williams and English daisies. Don't worry too much about freezing temperatures. Work the soil, plant, and water thoroughly as you would with any other annual. Mulch heavily if a hard freeze in the teens or below is predicted in your area.

Glads: In the Lower South, begin planting gladiolus corms now, and stagger plantings every two to three weeks through February. Plant them in groups of at least 8 or 10 placed 6 to 8 inches apart.

Paperwhites: As the holiday round of paperwhites stops blooming, most stores still have a supply of bulbs. You'll probably find them on sale. Select firm bulbs that have not sprouted. Place in a watertight container, and spread gravel around the bulbs to anchor them. Add water up to the bulb bases, and place in a sunny location indoors. In a few weeks, the blooms will perfume the room.

The tiny blooms of snowdrops add a bit of color to the winter landscape.

Peonies: Plant in well-prepared soil where they are protected from afternoon sun. The peonies' eyes or crowns should be set an inch or two above ground level, and then covered with about an inch of prepared soil mix. Early-flowering types such as 'Festiva Maxima' are best for Lower South gardens. Tree peonies are best grown in the Upper South.

Transplants: A simple way to get a lot of new plants is from the old ones. Transplant suckers that pop up around the base of sweet shrubs, forsythia, hydrangea, spirea, viburnum, and weigela.

PRUNE

Annuals: Cool-weather annuals, such as dianthus, snapdragons, petunias, and calendulas, can be renewed by simply deadheading. If the plants have become too leggy, prune the stems back to a desirable size and shape. They will reward you with more flowers within a few weeks.

Perennials: When frost kills the above ground portions of perennials, remove the unsightly dead portions. Also rake around the base of the plants to clean out fallen leaves and replace them with a neat mulch such as pine straw or bark.

Crepe myrtles: Remove twiggy growth and limbs that cross or touch one another to expose the beautiful sculptural quality of crepe myrtle trunks. You can train them for single or multiple trunks. Either way, remove excess suckers from the base of the tree.

FERTILIZE

Bulbs: Spring-flowering bulbs, such as narcissus, hyacinths, snowdrops, and tulips, should be emerging shortly and will really profit from an application of water-soluble 20-20-20 fertilizer. Also, cottonseed meal applied at a rate of 5 pounds per 100 square feet of bed area provides an organic and slow-release form of fertilizer that is excellent for all kinds of plants such as vegetables, bulbs, roses, and other ornamental plants.

Pansies: Pinch off withered and cold-damaged blooms. This will encourage the plant to keep new blooms coming. When night temperatures continue to remain above 40 degrees in your area, feed pansies with a liquid fertilizer, such as 20-20-20, every other week to both encourage growth and promote blooming.

February

This month offers Southern gardeners the first glimmers of hope that bleak winter days will soon give way to spring. It won't be long before the daffodils and other blooms will beckon gardeners outdoors.

TIPS

Azaleas and camellias: Make color choices while plants are in bloom and readily available at garden centers. That time is now for the Coastal South. Camellias and azaleas prefer slightly acid, organic, and well-drained soils. Shade from afternoon sun is recommended.

Daffodils: The best time to cut these bulbs for indoor arranging is when they are still at the bud stage but showing a hint of flower color. By cutting then, you can add several days of life to your arrangement.

Valentine flowers: To keep them fresh as long as possible, add water to the vase when the arrangement arrives, and check it daily. If they're in a box, snip an inch off each stem, remove leaves that will be below the water level of the vase, arrange, and enjoy.

PLANT

Bedding plants: In the Lower and Coastal South, this is your last chance to plant cool-weather annuals. Dianthus, lobelia, pansies, snapdragons, and violas can still be planted before hot weather arrives. You can still plant pansies in the Middle and Upper South. Wait until the worst freezes have passed, and set them in full sun. Incorporate slow-release fertilizer pellets such as 14-14-14 at planting time. Other choices include violas, sweet Williams, calendulas, English daisies, and sweet alyssum.

Perennials: In the Lower South, yarrow, coreopsis, purple coneflower, lantana, 'In-

Violas are a staple of the winter landscape.

digo Spires' salvia, cannas, and blue plumbago may be set out now in sunny areas of the garden for late-spring and summer color.

Pineapple lily: Plant these bulbs now for handsome foliage and intriguing blossoms. Bury the bulbs shallowly, just barely covering them with soil. They like partial shade and moisture. Be sure to water during drought. They'll bloom in four to five months.

Roses: Plant in a spot that has at least five to six hours of direct sun and good drainage. If the soil is clay and compact or dry and sandy, add organic matter to improve the quality. Most shrub roses also grow nicely in containers.

Spring annuals: Plants such as pansies, violas, ornamental kale, cabbage, stock, and snapdragons may still be set out now if they are started from 4-inch or larger pots in gardens in both the Middle and Lower South. Sweet alyssum transplants are available in a variety of colors including traditional white, purple, or blends and are excellent choices for either masses or low borders. Six-inch pots or gallon-size spring-blooming perennials, such as columbines, Shasta or ox-eye daisies, daylilies, purple coneflower, and Louisiana phlox will also perform well if they are planted now.

PRUNE

Climbing roses: Don't prune these roses now; wait until after the first flush of blooms. However, now is a good time to tie main canes to a support before they leaf out. It is okay to remove stray canes that will not cooperate.

Snapdragons: Encourage snapdragons to grow more spikes from the beginning by pinching off the tops of young transplants when you first set them out. Snip the flower stalk off its base, just before the topmost set of leaves.

FERTILIZE

Camellias and azaleas: Fertilize these shrubs this month. If your azaleas and camellias fail to thrive, check the soil. These two shrubs prefer an acid (pH 5 to 6), well-drained soil containing lots of organic matter. Mulch azaleas well, as they have shallow fibrous roots and tend to dry out easily.

March

This is a wonderful time of year in the Southern flower garden. Azaleas are budding, daffodils are blooming, and warmer temperatures make working in the garden a genuine pleasure.

TIPS

Annuals: When it comes to buying transplants, bigger isn't always better. Choose the branched plant that is well-proportioned, not the tall one that has become root-bound. The transplant without flowers will perform better, and a young healthy plant is a better bet than an old stressed one.

Azaleas: Choose your plants while they're in bloom so that colors can be effectively combined. Partially shaded locations are best. Well-drained soils enriched with organic material such as peat, composted pine bark, or compost help retain moisture during the dry months of summer. Indica azaleas, such as 'Formosa,' 'George Lindley Taber,' and 'Mrs. G. G. Gerbing,' may grow 6 to 8 feet tall with a similar spread, while 'Kurume' and 'Glenn Dale' hybrids usually range from 2 to 5 feet at maturity.

PLANT

Bulbs: After the last frost, plant cannas, dahlias, tuberoses, gladioli, and crinums. All like full sun and well-drained soil. While most bloom in summer, dahlias don't start blooming until late summer and fall. Use dahlias to add life to a flowerbed that will look tired by the end of summer.

Butterflies: Four plants that are sure to encourage butterflies to visit your garden are lantana, zinnia, pentas, and butterfly bush. Be sure to plant these flowers in full sun. If they are placed in the same bed, the

White azaleas are a popular spring choice.

mass of color will attract more winged beauties.

Perennials: This month is a great time to set out new perennials and to divide and replant those emerging from your garden beds. The best candidates for division are clump-forming ones such as perennial phlox, hostas, daylilies, Southern shield ferns, Siberian iris, and old-fashioned chrysanthemums.

Roses: The selection of rose plants at your garden center is at its best now. Look for old favorites, as well as new ones, offering fragrance and disease tolerance. Consider

how you can use roses as climbers and shrubs. Soak bare-root roses in a bucket of water overnight before planting them in the garden.

Zinnias: Sow seeds of zinnias as soon as the danger of frost has passed. Tall types for cutting are usually best grown by direct seeding. If you sow a few seeds every month through July, you can have fresh flowers through October.

FERTILIZE

Cool-weather annuals: Fertilize violas, pansies, and other overwintering annuals as the weather warms and growth begins. Use a slow-release fertilizer such as 9-6-6 for the remainder of spring, or give them a quick start with liquid 20-20-20.

Orchids: Give orchids the bright, filtered light that they need by hanging them from the lower branches of oak trees or placing them under another low-branched tree or in a south-facing window. Feed with a diluted liquid orchid fertilizer through spring to encourage growth, especially on plants that have spent the winter indoors.

Perennials: As new growth begins to emerge, feed established beds with 12-6-6 or a similar formula at the rate recommended on the label. Water well to wash granules from leaves and down through the mulch to the soil.

April

Step into the spring season with some new planting ideas, such as a cut-flower garden. Zinnias, marigolds, celosias, and nastutriums are all nice selections. Southern neighborhoods are beginning to awaken with beautiful flower blooms.

TIPS

Daisies: You may want to cut the bloom stalks off when Shasta daisies finish blooming to prevent them from reseeding around the parent plant. Or if you want them to reseed, wait to cut until the seedheads are dry and crisp and the seeds have already scattered naturally.

PLANT

Annuals: Plant zinnias now for summer arrangements. Choose long-stemmed selections such as 'Big Red,' 'Royal Purple,' 'Canary Bird,' 'Envy,' or 'Scarlet Queen.' Pick a sunny spot and sow seeds directly into the soil. You can start planting early this month in the Lower South, late in the month in the Middle South, and next month in the Upper South. After the danger of frost has passed, plant beds of summer annuals such as marigolds. Work the soil first to loosen, and incorporate organic matter and timed-release fertilizer. Rake the bed smooth, and apply mulch before you plant. Water thoroughly. Sunny areas provide ideal exposure for marigolds, zinnias, celosias, cosmos, and petunias. For shady areas consider impatiens, begonias, pentas, coleus, and caladiums. Arrange in drifts (elongated masses) or at least a dozen or more individual plants.

Cut-flower garden: In the Middle, Lower, and Coastal South, select a sunny, well-drained area of the garden, and devote it to flowers suitable for cutting and bringing indoors. Zinnias are the all-time favorite with large and intermediate types preferred. Marigolds, celosias, and nasturtiums are all

Rose and Sweet William add nice spring color.

well adapted to the area and are easily grown. They also tend to produce over a fairly long season if blossoms are harvested every few days.

Easter lily: Take advantage of after-Easter sales to buy additional plants for your garden. One of the few lilies that thrive in frost-free areas, these bulbs need a sunny spot where the soil drains well. For the best effect, plant a cluster of at least six. In future years, they will bloom early in summer.

PRUNE

Azaleas: If your azaleas need pruning, do so immediately after their flowers fade. Make sure you remove stray branches and shape the plants to look good for the summer. Apply 16-4-8 or similar fertilizer at the rate recommended on the label. Sprinkle around the dripline of the plant to avoid letting the fertilizer touch the branches.

Roses: Repeat-blooming roses should be pruned early this month in the Upper and Middle South. Remove dead or weak canes. Shorten healthy canes to 18 to 24 inches. For climbing and once-blooming roses, prune after spring bloom.

Spring shrubs: Prune spring-flowering shrubs soon after they flower. Climbing and once-blooming roses such as 'Lady Banks,' climbing 'Cecile Brunner,' and climbing 'Don Juan,' are also pruned after spring bloom. Keep the natural shape in mind as you trim and avoid excessive cutting except to control size.

FERTILIZE

Annuals: Plants can actually absorb a variety of nutrients through their leaves, so you'll often find liquid fertilizers sold in hose-end sprayers. These are excellent for getting your warm-weather annuals off to a quick start, but for long-term growth, work slow-release granules into the soil when you plant. Rejuvenate pansies, violas, and snapdragons by removing spent flowers and then applying fertilizer at the rate of 2 to 3 pounds of 5-10-10 or similar for every 100 square feet of bed area. Water them well. Also be ready to protect newly planted annuals from an unexpected frost.

May

Spring is a funny season in the South. It enters gently in February with the early bulbs and wildflowers and then departs with a rush by the end of May. As the heat and humidity return from the Gulf, Southern gardens make the sometimes abrupt transition to summer.

TIPS

Daffodils: As the foliage of daffodils begins to die, right now is the perfect time to divide clumps that did not bloom well. An application of bulb booster encourages good root growth.

Support: Tall-growing annuals and perennials that are top-heavy need to be staked before they fall over. These include foxgloves, delphiniums, lilies, and peonies. Use 6-foot stakes driven into the ground about 6 inches from the base of the stalk. Tie stalks to the stakes with strips of soft fabric.

PLANT

Annuals: Prepare beds by working in plenty of organic material such as compost, composted manure, or soil conditioner. Also add timed-release fertilizer such as 10-15-10 or one that will encourage flowering, such as 11-40-6. Apply an insulating mulch over the bed, and then set transplants at the appropriate depth and spacing through the mulch. Sunflowers, French marigolds, salvia, impatiens, purslane, and dusty miller are just a few of the annuals that can be planted now in the Lower and Coastal South. To attract butterflies to the garden, plant porterweed (*Stachytarpheta* sp.), pentas, and bloodflower *(Asclepias curassavica).* If plants are in pots or trays, make sure the roots are not so matted that they can't expand outward into the soil easily. If they are matted, gently pull the roots apart.

Coleus: Plant for quick color and textural contrasts. Most selections prefer shade or partial shade, but certain coleus, such as 'Solar Flair' and 'Alabama Sunset,' thrive in the sun, provided they receive sufficient water.

Plant porterweed to attract butterflies to the garden.

Consider drifts of similar shades of coleus in areas where spring bulbs are past their prime.

Mexican sunflowers: Also called tithonia, these heat-loving annuals attract butterflies and create a tall background (up to 6 feet) for a flower border. The new selection called 'Fiesta Del Sol' features saturated reddish-orange flowers atop 2- to 3-foot plants that are as easy to grow from seeds as old-fashioned ones.

Roses: It's not too late to plant container-grown roses. Remember, if you buy disease-tolerant selections, you don't have to spray at the first sign of black spot or mildew. Allow the plants to grow through the disease.

PRUNE

Annuals: Groom summer annuals to keep them both shapely and in bloom. Petunias, marigolds, verbena, melampodium, and cosmos can all be cut back by about one-third their height if they get leggy. After trimming, fertilize with a liquid food.

Blooming shrubs: Prune azaleas and gardenias when these shrubs finish blooming. Trim the main stem in order to encourage side shoots, a bushier plant, and a shrub that has more possible blooms. Apply a sulfur-coated fertilizer such as 14-14-12, following the directions on the label. Check the undersides of your camellia leaves for scale and red spider mites. Use Safer Insecticidal Soap or horticultural oil if either condition is present.

Bulb foliage: Spring-flowering bulbs need their foliage to mature and yellow before it's removed so that they will bloom again next spring. To help conceal the unattractive foliage, interplant bulbs with long-blooming annuals such as petunias, wax begonias, or marigolds.

Magnolias: Do not remove lower limbs if you can avoid it. Southern magnolia has two sins: Its shallow roots will not allow anything to grow beneath it, and the fallen leaves are notoriously slow to decay. Keep a skirt of branches close to the ground to hide both sins.

FERTILIZE

Bulbs: Fertilize amaryllis, crinum, Easter lilies, and other bulbs now to help them produce big blooms for next year. Apply a product especially formulated for bulbs, such as Holland Bulb Booster (9-9-6), at the rate recommended on the label. Remove foliage if it yellows, but never cut off leaves while they are still green.

June

This is the finest month for most flower gardens, as roses, hydrangeas, and most other plants are at their peak. Soon, however, heat, humidity, and drought will take their toll. To get blooms all summer, choose flowers that can stand up to summer's heat.

TIPS

Container plants: Hot and sunny weather can quickly dry out plants in containers. To reduce the need for frequent watering, move the container to a less exposed location, and keep a saucer under the pot. Add water-retaining gels to newly potted flowering plants.

Vines: Train the new growth of clematis, yellow jessamine, and other twining vines to guide them onto the trellis. The new canes of climbing roses usually need some help, too. Use loose, dark green twist ties to hold the new growth in place.

PLANT

Annuals: Plant heat-tolerant annuals, such as globe amaranth, cockscomb, cleome, cosmos, zinnia, portulaca, periwinkle, sunflowers, and tithonia, from seed or transplants. Work in several inches of organic material such as sphagnum peat moss, composted pine bark, or compost into the soil. Then spade or till to a depth of 6 to 8 inches prior to planting.

Iris: Bearded types can be transplanted now while they are in bloom. Actually, that is the best time to buy them because you can see the color. You can also divide and replant existing clumps after they bloom.

Summer bulbs: Cannas, caladiums, gladioli, dahlias, montbretia, acidanthera, and tuberoses are all in the garden center, offering excellent opportunity for summer flowers. Set them in a sunny, well-drained spot.

Train new growth of Carolina jessamine.

PRUNE

Chrysanthemums: Keep mums from getting too tall by cutting back to about half their height. Continue pinching any new growth through at least June to encourage branching.

Petunias: Pinch back plants several inches to prevent long, stringy stems and to encourage repeated bloom through the summer. You may need to pinch a couple more times during the season. Fertilize with timed-release granules, such as 17-17-17, or water with liquid 20-20-20 every other week.

Flowering shrubs: Continue to prune flowering shrubs, such as gardenias, Indian hawthorne, and azaleas, as they finish blooming. Hand-prune them for a natural look. After trimming, add fertilizer per label directions.

Impatiens: If you grew these annuals last year, watch for familiar seedlings. Although they may not be exactly the color that you had in mind, sometimes volunteers have a spontaneity of placement that a determined gardener can not match. Thin them to 8 to 10 inches, and then let them bloom.

FERTILIZE

Azaleas and camellias: These shrubs develop next year's blooms now, so be sure to water if they go without rain. Renew mulch over their roots. Fertilize with an azalea-camellia food that contains iron and other micronutrients.

Crepe myrtles: An application of fertilizer at bloom time should give you a longer flowering period. A granular 6-6-6 around the dripline works well. Apply according to label directions, and water in thoroughly afterwards. As soon as trees finish blooming, remove the seedpods to encourage a second bloom and possibly a third. If mildew is visible, spray with a fungicide. Black sooty mold may indicate an aphid infestation that can be treated with an insecticidal soap.

Flowers: Annual and perennial beds can use a boost, especially where the soil is sandy or the season has been rainy. Apply slow-release fertilizer for maximum benefit with minimum effort. For a quick but brief effect, water plants with soluble 20-20-20.

July

For many Southern gardeners, July is a defensive month. With the intense heat and humidity, you don't try to make your flower garden more beautiful, you simply try to hold onto whatever beauty you have. This usually means a lot of watering.

TIPS

Cuttings: This is a good time to root cuttings of roses, hydrangeas, viburnums, azaleas, and other woody trees and shrubs. Cut stems that grew this year and that have at least two pairs of leaves. Remove the lower leaves, dip each stem in rooting hormone, and stick 2 or 3 stems into each pot of sterile potting mix recommended for starting seeds. Cover with a glass jar or plastic bag, and wait for signs of new growth to tell you roots have formed.

Daylilies: Divide crowded daylilies now. Dig up clumps, and separate the small plantlets. Replant the pieces with good roots in amended soil. If summer rains aren't frequent, water every couple of days until the divisions sprout new leaves.

Water: Provide extra moisture for large-leaved plants such as hydrangeas, coleus, and caladiums. Even in shade, water is used quickly at this time of year, and usually there are tree roots competing for available moisture. Soak the soil at least 3 to 4 inches deep every five to seven days when rains are inadequate.

PLANT

Annuals: For quick impact, plant celosia, globe amaranth, zinnias, melampodium, marigolds, and coleus. Select 4-inch pots or larger to ensure easy transplanting and continuous summer color. Sow seeds of cosmos, sunflowers, and cleome into prepared beds. After seedlings are about 2 inches tall, thin them out in areas where they are too crowded. You can transplant extra seedlings to other parts of the garden.

Make a dynamic impact with cosmos.

Flower seeds: To raise your own transplants of biennials, such as hollyhocks, or perennials, such as purple coneflowers, sow seeds in a pot of seed-starting mix, and then transplant into individual containers when the second set of leaves develops. They'll be ready to place in the garden in October. Replenish tired flowerbeds by pulling out the old and putting in the new. Annuals such as cosmos, zinnias, marigolds, and dwarf sunflowers will make a spectacular late-summer show in five to six weeks for the price of a few seeds.

Fragrance: Plant petunias, flowering tobacco, four o'clocks, and sweet autumn clematis to add scent as well as color to late-summer gardens. Vitex, a small tree or large shrub, blooms several times in summer, is carefree, and has purple spikes of fragrant flowers.

PRUNE

Annuals: If your impatiens are getting leggy (too tall with foliage only at the tips of the stems) cut them back by half, and fertilize with a timed-release product such as annual booster 17-17-17. They'll be back in shape in a few weeks, about the time the weather cools down enough to enjoy being in the garden again.

Crepe myrtle: After your crepe myrtles bloom, clip the old flowers from as many branches as you can reach with hand pruners or a pole pruner. Fertilize with a granular blossom booster such as 11-40-6. New blooms will appear in about a month.

Perennials: Continue to cut back the top few inches of fall-blooming perennials such as mums, autumn asters, Mexican mint marigold, obedient plant, and Mexican bush sage. Prune every three to four weeks until the first of September to encourage compact plants.

Salvia: Snip back the blossom stems of long-blooming salvias such as scarlet sage, autumn sage, and mealy-cup sage to encourage a continual show through fall.

FERTILIZE

Chrysanthemums: Give mums a last trimming at the tips to promote a dense bloom before they start to set buds at month's end in the Coastal South. Feed them early in the month with a balanced fertilizer, and keep them well-watered.

August

No Southern gardener, no matter how dedicated, can honestly profess to enjoy working outside during the dog days of August. Fortunately, most of the tasks to keep flowers in bloom don't take much time at all.

TIPS

Bulbs: Take time now to mail-order spring-flowering bulbs to plant this fall. Order plenty to make a good show; don't stop with a dozen of this and that unless you are growing them in pots.

Seeds: This is a good time to mail-order flower seeds for fall planting. If you have seed packets that are more than two years old or that have been exposed to heat or moisture, throw them away and order fresh ones. Also take advantage of end of the season sales on seed packets. For transplants ready to set out this fall, sow one type of seed per container of seed starting mix. Label and keep them moist until large enough to transplant into individual pots. Fertilize weekly with half-strength liquid 20-20-20 until planting time.

PLANT

Annuals: Continue to set out transplants of warm-weather annuals to fill the gaps of color this fall. Marigolds, zinnias, celosias, begonias, and geraniums can provide blooms until frost. Water well the first few days after transplanting, and then weekly as needed.

Bulbs: In case you think bulbs are only for spring, check your garden center. Fall-blooming crocus, colchicum, and spider lilies are available now and offer immediate results. They will bloom almost as soon as you put them in the ground.

Fall crocus: Colchicums or fall crocus are available at garden centers. Plant now, and you will be rewarded with a multitude of beautiful fall blooms for years.

Sunflowers produce a beautiful late summer show.

Fall flowers: Start seeds of favorite biennials and other fall-planted flowers in 4-inch pots. Seedlings will be ready to transplant in the fall. Those that are easy to start from seed include foxgloves, poppies, hollyhocks, larkspurs, wallflowers, and Canterbury-bells.

Mums: When you see mums for sale this month, buy them while the buds are still tight. Plant them in your garden or in containers where they will have maximum impact. Getting mums started early will mean a more natural appearance and longer-lasting color when they bloom.

Sunflowers: Plant sunflower seeds for an Indian summer display. Choose selections with fast bloom times—the number of days it takes a seed to germinate, grow, and

flower. This time of year, sunflowers that would normally mature in 60 days may take 70 due to shorter day length. A few favorites are 'Sunbright,' 'Moonbright,' and 'Sunbeam.'

PRUNE

Annuals: Renew summer annuals a final time before fall. Pinch leggy marigolds, cut back or replant zinnias, and remove browned blooms from scarlet sage. Also feed your flowering plants with a liquid fertilizer such as 20-20-20 to encourage growth for fall.

Perennials: Lightly trim fall-blooming perennials such as Mexican mint marigold, Mexican bush sage, autumn sage *(Salvia greggii)*, and chrysanthemums so that they will be more compact and less likely to need staking when they bloom.

Roses: A light pruning in the middle of August helps stimulate an abundance of fall flowers on everblooming, modern, and old garden roses. Remove dead wood; then cut back current season's growth by about one-third. Apply either 5-10-10 or rose fertilizer as instructed on the label or ½ cup cottonseed meal per plant; water thoroughly.

FERTILIZE

Impatiens: These popular and versatile annuals tend to get leggy by late summer, so trim them back to half their height now. Then feed them with a general-purpose, water-soluble fertilizer, such as 20-20-20. They'll quickly start to leaf out and get bushier and covered with vibrant blooms.

September

This month in the South has two different climates. The first two weeks are hot and sticky, but then a sudden cool front shows us mercy, and we begin to envision autumn leaves and trips to the countryside.

TIPS

Garden cleanup: Wake up a tired garden by pulling out the dead and dying, cutting back and staking the leggy and leaning, and filling in the gaps. Marigolds and chrysanthemums make excellent fillers now when it's still too early to set out winter annuals. Otherwise, use mulch to groom bare areas.

Garden planning: Take a moment to write down your horticultural successes and failures over the past summer. These notes will come in handy next year when planning your garden.

Perennials: Spring-blooming perennials such as existing clumps of ox-eye daisies, penstemon, violets, Louisiana and prairie phlox, columbine, and purple coneflower may be lifted with a garden spade and separated into individual plants. Reset the plants into prepared beds.

Seeds: Dry the flower heads of zinnias, cosmos, and tithonias (Mexican sunflowers), and store the seeds in a cool, dry place. Sow these seeds late next spring for your cutting garden.

PLANT

Annuals: Continue setting out transplants of celosia, globe amaranth, periwinkles, petunias, melampodium, zinnias, marigolds, impatiens, coleus, and sweet alyssum. They will thrive when planted in early fall and bloom until frost.

Purple Coneflower can stand up to September's heat.

Chrysanthemums: Choose budded plants in pots, and arrange them in drifts of at least five to seven plants of a single color. Locations having at least a half-day's direct sunlight work best. Chrysanthemums prefer well-drained soil and fairly moist condition.

Perennials: In the Upper and Middle South, shasta daisies, daylilies, irises, peonies, and purple coneflowers may be set out now for spring bloom. Arrange them in elongated masses of at least 7 to 10 individual plants spaced about 12 to 18 inches apart. In the Middle and Lower South, set out spring-flowering perennials, such as 'Texas Gold' columbine, yarrow, ox-eye daisies, purple coneflowers, Louisiana and prairie phlox, and Louisiana and bearded iris now, so that they will have enough time to become established before next spring. Prepare the soil well before planting by mixing in 3 to 5 inches of organic material, such as sphagnum peat moss, along with 4 to 5 pounds of cottonseed or alfalfa meal.

PRUNE

Crepe myrtles: Continue removing spent flowers from crepe myrtles to encourage one more crop of blooms before frost. Save major pruning jobs for December and January when trees are dormant.

Perennials: It is time to cut back tired stalks and faded flowers of veronica, verbena, artemisia, canna, salvia, and other perennials. Feed with a liquid fertilizer such as 20-20-20 for renewed growth and fall blooms.

FERTILIZE

Azaleas: Apply iron (Ironite or iron sulfate) according to label directions to give the plants a deep green color. Don't prune now or you will remove next year's blossoms.

Chrysanthemums: Fertilize mums with Scotts Blossom Booster or a similar formulation every two weeks until the buds show color. Pinch or clip fading flowers to encourage additional blooms.

October

It's hard to think of any problem in your life that two weeks spent in October can't cure. The air freshens and cools, the days are sunny and dry. Work in the flower garden is no longer a chore.

TIPS

Cleome seeds: Saving seeds of cleome is easy. To harvest, simply open the slender beanlike pods, and brush the seeds into an envelope. Store in a cool, dry location for sowing next spring.

Cuttings: Take cuttings of tender annuals such as coleus, salvias, begonias, New Guinea impatiens, Cuban oregano, and double impatiens. Dip each cutting in rooting hormone, and plant it in a pot of moist soil. Keep watered and out of direct sun. Place in a greenhouse or sunny window through the winter until it is time to plant next spring.

Seasonal plants: Make sure your outdoor lighting doesn't shine on Christmas cactus, kalanchoe, or poinsettia from about 6 p.m. to 8 a.m. Continue to keep them away from night light till late November or early December. This will encourage the plants to set flowerbuds.

PLANT

Annuals: Set out cool-weather annuals this month for flowers this fall, winter, and early spring. Pansies and violas are the hardiest, flowering through winter when the weather is mild. Other good bets in the Lower and Coastal South include calendulas, English daisies, snapdragons, nasturtiums, and sweet alyssum. Sow seeds of larkspur, poppies, sweet peas, and money plant now for flowers next spring and sum-

Calendulas, also known as Mary's gold or pot marigold, add bright fall color to the garden.

mer. Prepare the bed by loosening the soil and adding organic matter such as compost. Rake smooth, and sow the seeds. Be certain not to mulch, or you will smother your seeds along with the weeds.

Perennials: This is the ideal time to plant perennials. They'll have months to develop roots to support new growth that begins again next spring. In the Lower South, ox-eye daisies, daylilies, Louisiana and bearded iris, purple coneflowers, yarrow, and Louisiana and prairie phlox do best when divided every one to three years. Now is a good time to divide them. Set individual

divisions or transplants 8 to 10 inches apart in groupings of five or more. Water them well every three to five days until fall rains thoroughly moisten the soil.

Spring bulbs: Begin planting your spring-flowering bulbs such as hyacinths, narcissus, and tulips. Buy large bulbs that are firm to the touch, choosing as you would when selecting onions or potatoes. A well-drained location and six hours of sunlight are essential. Most tulips and hyacinths are treated as annuals in the South, requiring about six weeks of cold treatment in your refrigerator before planting. Many narcissus will naturalize in Southern gardens, increasing in numbers slowly each year. Good narcissus for naturalizing are those in the tazetta class, such as 'Grand Primo, ' 'Silver Chimes,' and 'Golden Dawn.'

PRUNE:

Roses: Roses will benefit from a light tip-pruning now. Remove no more than one-fourth the height of the bush. This will stimulate a strong fall bloom flush.

FERTILIZE

Hardy annuals: Prepare soil for pansies and violas by working in several inches of organic material along with 2 pounds of slow-release fertilizer such as 9-9-6 per 100 square feet of bed area. Wait until soil and air temperatures have begun to cool before planting; water well if rains are inadequate.

November

Fall color peaks in November. If you plan to plant a tree to add bright autumn color to your yard, visit the nursery now when you'll be able to tell what color the tree will turn. It's also a good time to plant winter annuals and transplants for spring.

TIPS

Slow down: As growth slows and most plants start to go dormant, you can stop fertilizing and cut back on irrigation, watering just enough to prevent wilting.

Winter color: Pansies, violas, and snapdragons, available now in garden centers, will help you welcome winter with bright, warm colors for the cool months ahead. Find a sunny, well-drained location, and set out transplants now so they can become established before the weather gets too cold.

PLANT

Amaryllis: Plant amaryllis in pots and keep outdoors until frost. Plant them in sunny areas of the house or greenhouse to bring them into flower for the holidays.

Camellias: Check local nurseries regularly for your favorite selections. With careful shopping, you can find a camellia to bloom each month from now through March.

Paperwhites: Buy them by the dozen, and stagger plantings every two weeks through February. They'll bloom outside within two to three weeks of planting. New ones will open as the earlier ones fade. To force these bulbs to bloom inside, start in mid-November for fragrant

Plant snapdragons now for vibrant spring blooms.

blossoms throughout the holiday season. It takes about two to three weeks from planting to flowering. Paperwhite kits can make great holiday gifts for your children's teachers.

Peonies: Plant peonies now in the Middle and Upper South. It is important not to plant them too deeply. Set the tubers no more than 2 inches below the surface in rich, well-drained soil in a sunny location. For best results, choose a variety that blooms in early to mid-season.

Spring seasonal flowers: Set out transplants of snapdragons, stock, candytuft, Bells-of-Ireland, sweet alyssum, and sweet peas. Space the transplants 6 to 8 inches apart. Fertilize new plants with a water-soluble fertilizer, such as 20-20-20, or a slow-release fertilizer applied according to label instructions. Also set out spring-flowering bulbs such as daffodils and tulips.

PRUNE

Perennials: Cut back late-summer and fall-blooming plants after frost has killed their tops. Autumn asters, chrysanthemums, perennial salvias, and bachelor's-buttons should all be cut back to just above ground level after the first killing frost.

Spring-flowering shrubs: It is too late to prune shrubs that flower in spring, such as azaleas, spireas, quince, and forsythias. They have already set their flowerbuds, and pruning now would remove next year's blooms.

FERTILIZE

Bulbs: Now is the time of year to feed established beds of daffodils with Holland Bulb Booster (9-9-6) and about a half cup Epsom salts per 10 square feet of bed for magnesium. Bulbs have already sprouted their roots and are ready to take up the nutrients.

December

This month's gardening activities center around the holidays. Poinsettias, narcissus, and amaryllis all provide beautiful blooms indoors. Fortunately, few outdoor garden tasks are required during this busy season.

TIPS

Mulch: This is a good time to mulch roses and other flowerbeds. Popular materials include pine bark, pine straw, and oak leaves. A mulch layer 3 to 4 inches thick will discourage weed growth.

Poinsettias, narcissus, and amaryllis: Add color and cheer to indoor holiday decorating. For several weeks of color, select poinsettias that are just beginning to open their small yellow flowers in the center of the colorful bracts. Amaryllis, narcissus, tulips, and other pots of flowering bulbs should be kept cool and moist for much longer life.

PLANT

Annuals: Continue to set out transplants of petunias, snapdragons, pansies, violas, sweet alyssum, and ornamental kale and cabbage now. Be sure to work in several inches of organic material such as composted pine bark, peat, or compost into the soil prior to planting.

Bulbs: Pre-refrigerated tulips and hyacinths are ready to plant during December and early January in the Lower and Coastal South. Choose a sunny site where the soil has been amended by incorporating 3 to 5 inches of organic material—such as sphagnum peat moss, composted pine bark, or compost—into porous, well-drained soil. Incorporate around 3 to 5 pounds of

Pansies planted with cool weather vegetables add interest to the garden.

cottonseed, alfalfa meal, or bulb booster fertilizer into 100 square feet of bed area. For continuous spring blooms, set bulbs amid masses of pansies, violas, sweet alyssum, or dianthus.

Gifts: Plant pots of bulbs for gifts this month. A single amaryllis or a half-dozen paperwhite or leucojum bulbs in a 6- to 8-inch pot make a lovely present. Recipients can set them in the garden later.

Vegetable and flower combos: Don't overlook cool-weather greens for the interest

that they add as winter annuals. Lower and Coastal South gardeners will particularly enjoy the bronze leaves of 'Red Giant' mustard. Others include the blue frills of 'Dwarf Blue Curled Scotch Vates' kale and the chartreuse of 'Black-seeded Simpson' lettuce. Coastal and Tropical South gardeners can plant cabbage, broccoli, carrots, peas, and collards for pot greens. Tomatoes and peppers can also be planted.

Perennials: Cut back mums, purple coneflowers, lantana, and Mexican bush sage to ground level as soon as frost has killed their foliage. Spring-blooming perennials such as phlox, bearded iris, daylilies, ox-eye daisies, and penstemons may still be planted or divided in December. Place in elongated drifts of five to seven plants about a foot apart to achieve a full effect by spring.

PRUNE

Perennials: Cut back chrysanthemums, salvias, Mexican mint marigold, asters, and other perennials after the first hard frost. Remember to leave only 1 to 2 inches of stem growth above ground.

FERTILIZE

Winter annuals: Feed pansies with a soluble plant food such as 15-30-15 to encourage blooms. In the Coastal South, fertilize snapdragons, too. Keep winter flowers watered during dry weather.

answers to frequently asked

Reblooming amaryllis: How do you get potted amaryllis bulbs to bloom year after year? All I ever get from mine are leaves.

Mrs. J.E. Wall   Ridge, Maryland

First, buy a bulb that already has a big, green flowerbud showing at the top. That way, you know it'll bloom at least once. After it finishes blooming, put it in a sunny window. Then take it outside to a sunny spot once the weather warms up in the spring. Water as necessary, and fertilize once a month with bloom-booster fertilizer. About the beginning of October, quit feeding and watering. When the leaves turn yellow, cut them off. Bring the pot inside to a cool, dark, dry place. Let the bulb sit there until it starts growing again. Then repot it into a slightly larger container, add fresh potting soil, and water thoroughly.

garlic chives

Blooms for tight spots: What kinds of perennials can I plant that have bright, showy flowers but stay small for the tight space in my garden?

Michael Cleland   Baxley, Georgia

You have numerous plants from which to choose. Those that fit your criteria include many different types of pinks, sedums, creeping phlox, catmint, thyme, coral bells, society garlic, Japanese roof iris, ajuga, chives, and mazus.

Non-blooming camellia: On the north side of my house, I have a camellia growing in a pot on a screened porch. It has never bloomed. Any ideas?

Connie Little   Ackworth, Georgia

Your camellia may not be getting enough sunlight. Camellias bloom better if they get at least a half-day of sun. And try to be patient. It takes some plants a couple of years to really start blooming well.

Daisy dilemma: I have several clumps of Shasta daisies growing in full sun. They get plenty of water and fertilizer but don't produce a single bloom. What could I be doing wrong?

Gloria C. Will   Plant City, Florida

Maybe you're being a little too nice. You may be encouraging a lot of leafy growth at the expense of your flowers. Try holding back on the water and fertilizer a bit. Also make sure the fertilizer you're using is a bloom-booster type such as 12-40-15, which contains more phosphorus than nitrogen.

Lily-of-the-Valley: A few years ago, I bought some lily-of-the-valley bulbs and planted them as directed. They come up each spring, grow to just over an inch tall, and just sit there. They don't bloom. Can you tell me how to get them to grow?

Iris Keirn   Calabash, North Carolina

One of our prettiest ground covers, lily-of-the-valley blooms best in light shade and moist, acid, well-drained soil that contains plenty of organic matter, such as compost, sphagnum peat moss, or chopped leaves. The roots should be planted 1 inch deep and 4 to 6 inches apart. You will want to top-dress the bed each fall with an inch or so of chopped leaves or rotted manure. You might also sprinkle Holland Bulb Booster around the plants in early spring. Be sure to water thoroughly during summer droughts.

flower garden questions

Flowering ground covers: We have a cabin in the woods in Middle Tennessee. The ground is filled with rocks and red clay. What kinds of flowering ground covers can we plant that will thrive in sun or shade?

Sandy Reynolds   Germantown, Tennessee

periwinkle

Poor soil limits your choices, but there are a few ground covers to suggest. For sun, try liriope, creeping phlox (thrift), and carpet bugleweed (ajuga). For shade, you can also try liriope or carpet bugleweed and common periwinkle.

Hydrangea help: Our 5-year-old French hydrangeas haven't bloomed in the past two years. What should I do short of tying artificial blooms on them?

Dorothy B. Wallace   St. Ann, Missouri

Hey, there's an idea! Now anyone can have blooms all year and never have to fertilize, water, or prune again. But for those purists out there who insist on real flowers, there are several reasons why hydrangeas fail to produce them. The first is a late winter cold snap that kills the flowerbuds. The second is pruning heavily in fall, winter, or spring, which removes the flowerbuds. A third reason is too much shade. The more sun your hydrangea gets, the more blooms you'll get.

Impatiens: I loved the impatiens I had this year and want the same ones next year. Do you have any suggestions about how to keep them from dying this winter?

Troy Purvis   Brandon, Mississippi

In the Lower South, where you live, impatiens growing in a very protected spot will sometimes overwinter, if you cover them in fall with leaves or pine straw. But the chances are less than 50-50. You'd do better to overwinter the plants indoors. One way is to pot up your plants this fall, cut them back, then bring them inside to a sunny room. Or you can root cuttings in potting soil or water and grow them indoors this winter.

Jasmine: I've enjoyed the fragrance of night-blooming jasmine in Florida and along the North Carolina coast. Are there any jasmines that will withstand the winters of Winston-Salem?

Page Lowry   Winston-Salem, North Carolina

Most of the fragrant jasmines are semitropical, and so aren't reliably hardy outside the Coastal and Tropical South (in Winston-Salem). Of course, you can grow jasmines indoors. Just make sure you give them plenty of bright sun.

Daylilies: Last year, many of the blooms on my daylilies were very deformed. And the foliage had ugly yellow-brown streaks. What could be the problem? I thought daylilies were essentially trouble free.

Caroline Christopher   Durham, North Carolina

Welcome to the hard, cruel world of gardening. Tiny insects called thrips, which suck juice from the flowers, cause the problem. To control them, spray the flowerbuds with Cygon just before they open. Follow label directions carefully. The streaks are the work of a fungus. To get rid of it, spray the foliage this spring with a Bordeaux mixture. Repeat monthly throughout the growing season. Next fall, pull off and destroy any infected leaves.

Mandevilla: I recently acquired a beautiful, pink-flowering mandevilla vine. Can you please tell me how to care for it? Will it bloom indoors?

Libby Watkins   Midlothian, Virginia

Mandevilla is a very popular semi-tropical vine that will bloom all summer long. It does best in full sun, and it likes moist, fertile, well-drained soil. The plant is cold hardy to about 25 degrees; where winters get colder than that, you have to pot it up in late fall and bring it indoors. It probably won't bloom indoors during winter, unless you have a bright sunroom.

Rose woes: I have four 7-year-old rosebushes that produce green foliage, but never any flowers. I have fertilized them regularly for two seasons with no luck. I need some help!

Liz Ruffing   Rowlett, Texas

The first thing that you will want to check is whether or not your roses are getting enough sunlight. Most roses prefer full sun. The next thing to think about is when and how you prune. Hybrid tea roses bloom repeatedly during the growing season, so you can prune them just about anytime. But many climbers and old-fashioned roses bloom just once a year in spring. The best time to prune them is early summer. If you prune them in late summer, fall, or winter, you'll cut off most of the flowerbuds for next year. A third possibility is that the good part of the rose—the top graft union—has died, and the foliage is coming from the rootstock. An indicator of this is if the foliage has changed color or shape in recent years. If this is the case, you'll have to replace your roses.

Vines: Please advise me of a good vine to cover my new pergola and shade my garden swing. What about clematis?

Robert Smith   Columbia, South Carolina

Clematis probably wouldn't do the trick, as it doesn't grow thickly enough to provide much shade. Better choices include Carolina jessamine, Cherokee rose, Lady Banks rose, and trumpet creeper.

Winter care for azaleas and rhododendrons: Last spring I was given two Satsuki azaleas and two yellow hybrid rhododendrons. What sort of protection will they need to survive winter here in the mountains?

John L. Waldroop   Tuckasegee, North Carolina

The methods for protecting azaleas and rhododrons in the mountains aren't much different than those for milder climates. First, shield the shrubs from winter sun and wind to prevent their foliage from drying. You can do this by planting them in shade or by erecting burlap windbreaks. Second, water the plants thoroughly this month before the ground freezes. After it freezes, mulch around each plant with at least 3 inches of shredded bark or pine straw. Finally, brush off snow from brittle rhododendrons to prevent broken branches. But leave the snow on Satsuki azaleas; it provides insulation.

Wisteria: I have a 5-year-old wisteria that has never bloomed. How can I get it to start?

Arlene Peace   Mechanicsville, Virginia

Wisteria may fail to bloom for several reasons. First, it may not be getting enough sun. This vine blooms best in full sun. Second, the plant may be an unnamed seedling, rather than a grafted, named selection, chosen for early flowering. Third, you may be overfeeding it. Never fertilize a wisteria. Finally, you may be pruning incorrectly. Throughout summer, prune the tips out of all new shoots when they reach a foot long. In winter, shorten these shoots again so that approximately six buds remain on each one. Cut away any suckers from below the graft union, as they will produce inferior blooms.

Opposite page: Carolina jessamine thrives above a bay window. Once planted, it takes only a few years for this graceful Southern vine to surround a window or door.

index

T

V

W

Y

Z

plant hardiness zone map

The United States Department of Agriculture has charted low temperatures throughout the country to determine the ranges of average low readings. The map above is based loosely on the USDA Plant Hardiness Zone Map, which was drawn from these findings. It does not take into account heat, soil, or moisture extremes and is intended as a guide, not a guarantee.

The southern regions of the United States that are mentioned in this book refer to the following:

Upper South: -10° to 0°F minimum

Middle South: 0° to 5°F minimum

Lower South: 5° to 15°F minimum

Coastal South: 15° to 25°F minimum

Tropical South: 25° to 40°F minimum

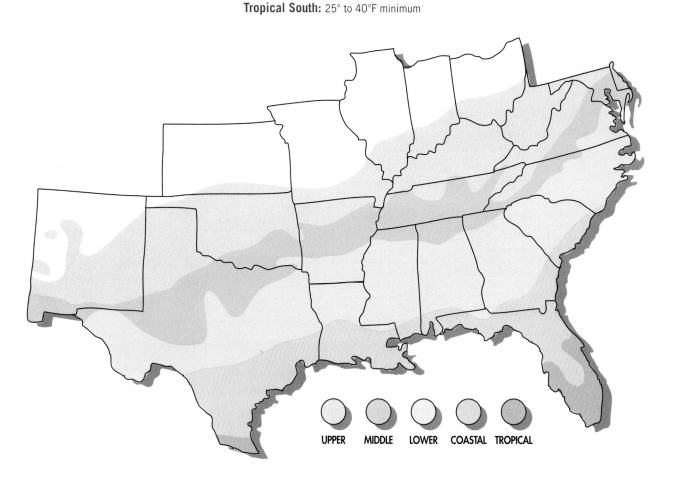

UPPER   MIDDLE   LOWER   COASTAL   TROPICAL